GARDENING WITH A WILD HEART

Gardening

with a Wild Heart

RESTORING
CALIFORNIA'S
NATIVE
LANDSCAPES
AT HOME

JUDITH LARNER LOWRY

UNIVERSITY OF CALIFORNIA PRESS

University of California Press
Berkeley and Los Angeles, California

University of California Press, Ltd.
London, England

Second paperback printing 2007

Botanical drawings © Ane Carla Rovetta. Title page: male flower of blue oak.
Part I: wild grapes. Part II: blue oak. Part III: coyote bush, male and female.
Part IV: native blackberries and grasshopper. Part V: soaproot bulb, with soap-
root brush and mortar.

Chapter 1 epigraph: W. David Shuford is quoted from David Shuford, *The
Marin County Breeding Bird Atlas* (1993); used by permission of Bushtit Books.
Chapter 4 epigraphs: Michael Barbour is quoted from Michael Barbour, Bruce
Pavlik, Frank Drysdale, and Susan Lindstrom, *California's Changing Land-
scapes: Diversity and Conservation of California Vegetation* (1992); used by permis-
sion of the California Native Plant Society, Sacramento. Jack Turner is quoted
from *The Abstract Wild*, © 1996 by John S. Turner; used by permission of the
University of Arizona Press. Chapter 9 epigraph: Maria Copa is quoted from
Mary E. T. Collier and Sylvia Barker Thalman, eds., *Interviews with Tom Smith
and Maria Copa: Isabel Kelly's Ethnographic Notes on the Coast Miwok Indians of
Marin and Southern Sonoma Counties, California*, © 1996 Mapom; used by per-
mission. Chapter 10 epigraph: Henry David Thoreau is quoted from *Faith in a
Seed*, edited by Bradley P. Dean, © 1993 by Island Press; used by permission.
Chapter 11 epigraphs: the quotation from *The Jepson Manual: Higher Plants of
California*, edited by James C. Hickman, © 1993 by the Regents of the Univer-
sity of California, is used by permission of the University of California Press.
Gene Logsden is quoted from *At Nature's Pace: Essays*, © 1994 by Gene
Logsden; used by permission of Pantheon Books. Chapter 12 epigraph: Marge
Piercy is quoted from *Circles on the Water*, © 1982 by Marge Piercy; reprinted
by permission of Alfred A. Knopf, Inc. Chapter 13 epigraphs: Rich Stallcup is
quoted from "Fire in Birdland," *Point Reyes Observatory Quarterly Journal*, Fall
1995; used by permission. Paul Shepard is quoted from *Man in the Landscape: A
Historic View of the Esthetics of Nature*, © 1967 by Paul Shepard; used by permission of Alfred A. Knopf, Inc.

Library of Congress Cataloging-in-Publication Data will be found at the back
of this book.

Printed in the United States of America

13   12   11   10   09   08   07
12   11   10   9   8   7   6   5   4   3   2   1

The paper used in this publication meets the minimum requirements of
ANSI/NISO Z39.48-1992 (R 1997) (*Permanence of Paper*). ♾

with a Wild Heart

RESTORING
CALIFORNIA'S
NATIVE
LANDSCAPES
AT HOME

JUDITH LARNER LOWRY

UNIVERSITY OF CALIFORNIA PRESS

University of California Press
Berkeley and Los Angeles, California

University of California Press, Ltd.
London, England

Second paperback printing 2007

Botanical drawings © Ane Carla Rovetta. Title page: male flower of blue oak.
Part I: wild grapes. Part II: blue oak. Part III: coyote bush, male and female.
Part IV: native blackberries and grasshopper. Part V: soaproot bulb, with soap-
root brush and mortar.

Chapter 1 epigraph: W. David Shuford is quoted from David Shuford, *The
Marin County Breeding Bird Atlas* (1993); used by permission of Bushtit Books.
Chapter 4 epigraphs: Michael Barbour is quoted from Michael Barbour, Bruce
Pavlik, Frank Drysdale, and Susan Lindstrom, *California's Changing Land-
scapes: Diversity and Conservation of California Vegetation* (1992); used by permis-
sion of the California Native Plant Society, Sacramento. Jack Turner is quoted
from *The Abstract Wild*, © 1996 by John S. Turner; used by permission of the
University of Arizona Press. Chapter 9 epigraph: Maria Copa is quoted from
Mary E. T. Collier and Sylvia Barker Thalman, eds., *Interviews with Tom Smith
and Maria Copa: Isabel Kelly's Ethnographic Notes on the Coast Miwok Indians of
Marin and Southern Sonoma Counties, California*, © 1996 Mapom; used by per-
mission. Chapter 10 epigraph: Henry David Thoreau is quoted from *Faith in a
Seed*, edited by Bradley P. Dean, © 1993 by Island Press; used by permission.
Chapter 11 epigraphs: the quotation from *The Jepson Manual: Higher Plants of
California*, edited by James C. Hickman, © 1993 by the Regents of the Univer-
sity of California, is used by permission of the University of California Press.
Gene Logsden is quoted from *At Nature's Pace: Essays*, © 1994 by Gene
Logsden; used by permission of Pantheon Books. Chapter 12 epigraph: Marge
Piercy is quoted from *Circles on the Water*, © 1982 by Marge Piercy; reprinted
by permission of Alfred A. Knopf, Inc. Chapter 13 epigraphs: Rich Stallcup is
quoted from "Fire in Birdland," *Point Reyes Observatory Quarterly Journal,* Fall
1995; used by permission. Paul Shepard is quoted from *Man in the Landscape: A
Historic View of the Esthetics of Nature*, © 1967 by Paul Shepard; used by permission of Alfred A. Knopf, Inc.

Library of Congress Cataloging-in-Publication Data will be found at the back
of this book.

Printed in the United States of America

13 12 11 10 09 08 07
12 11 10 9 8 7 6 5 4 3 2 1

The paper used in this publication meets the minimum requirements of
ANSI/NISO Z39.48-1992 (R 1997) (*Permanence of Paper*). ♾

Earth, be glad to see me.

———————————————————

KARUK TOBACCO PRAYER

TO MY PARENTS

CONTENTS

PREFACE

When I started my mail-order seed business specializing in California native plants, I thought I would spend my days on sunny hillsides and within shadowed canyons, gathering jewel-like seeds of all shapes and colors. I thought I would be largely involved with seed cleaners and drying racks, with packets, scales, and catalogs. Yet it has turned out quite differently. Much of my time for the past twenty years has been spent in conversation.

More or less willingly, I have been a participant in countless conversations about many aspects of native plants. On the way, I have become fascinated by the assumptions, both implicit and stated, that govern gardening choices. I have gotten a sense of what people wanted to know, what I needed to learn, and where it all might lead. The activity of gardening with locally native plants has become a vehicle for ranging freely over the rich territories of land use history, local ecology, and land management.

I've tried to put it all together here, a long, lingering look at many aspects of this kind of gardening, from specifics on techniques of wildflower sowing to musings on the subtle effects of restoration gardening on a town. From a personal essay on wildland seed gathering to information on the linkages between voles and grasslands. While answering frequently asked questions of a practical nature, I seek at the same time to enliven the personal sense of living in a specific place with a complicated human, literary, and natural history.

The more I work with clients, the clearer it becomes that gardening as a restorationist has much to offer in strengthening newly established human roots and in deepening those ties to the land we inhabit that have been a given in human life for centuries. By seeing your particular piece of land as part of a larger plant-animal community and seeking to enhance old and established relationships through your style of gardening, you join that community.

Along the way, we find ourselves living in gardens of pleasure and hope.

ACKNOWLEDGMENTS

Acknowledgments and grateful thanks:

To my sister, Marjorie Larner, for discerning and encouraging manuscript review, and for a lifetime of sweet sisterhood.

To my brother, Bernard Larner, for his unique humor, sound advice, and staunch brothering.

To my father, Irvin Larner, for parenting of a superlative order, who helps me to persist in an inordinate number of ways.

For the texture of my days, thanks to Anna Harrington, Helen Londe, Ann Young, Judy and Phil Buchanan, Nancy MacDonald, Lea Earnheart, John O'Connor, Joanne Kyger, Mary Nisbet, Lynn Murray, Chris Weingarth, Kurtis Alexander, Meghan O'Hare, and Cabin Three, Christine Lisetti, the One P Three J Writing Group, Leslie Creed and Lloyd Kahn of Shelter Publications, Barbara Deutsch, Georgia Carmichael Connon, Meg Simonds and Mark Butler, Kathleen O'Neill, Bob Levitt, and StuArt, for always asking.

To Dave Fross, for the saving grace of a seamless friendship and professional association, both essential. To Freeman House, for the inspiration of his work and his writing. To Jeffrey Creque, for prairie talk of the highest quality. To Craig Dremann, a fortuitous connection, replete with steadying good counsel.

To my helpful agent, Andree Abecassis. To my excellent and painstaking editors at University of California Press, Doris Kretschmer, Dore Brown, and Peter Dreyer.

To Peter G. Smith, for years of all kinds of help, including a saintly patience in electronic matters. But mostly, for all that we have seen together.

To my daughter, Tarin Molly Patterson, cross-country girl, whose blithe and beautiful spirit has lighted and lightened my days these seventeen years.

To the memory of my mother, Sara Larner, who loved words, and of Gerda Isenberg, for the opportunity and the example.

And to my town. Home.

PART I

Beginnings

CHAPTER ONE

Gardening
at the Seam

I wish so to live ever as to derive my satisfactions and inspir-
ations from the commonest events, everyday phenomena,
so that what my senses hourly perceive, my daily walk, the conversation of my neighbors, may inspire me, and I may dream of
no heaven but that which lies about me.   *Henry Thoreau*

Biodiversity has recently become a fashionable concept to promote, but should we try to enhance biodiversity just at the state
and federal level and not at the county level or even in our back
yards? Should we settle for small populations of species in dis-
tant parts of our state and nation, when with protection viable
populations could exist as well in our own neighborhoods?
W. David Shuford, 1993

It's not as if they learned about willows and grasses in order to
make baskets, but as if they learned to make baskets by knowing willows.   *Mary Austin, 1912*

Discovering Home

Moving fifteen years ago to a small town on the north central coast of
California, I was entranced by the miles of protected land that surrounded
us. My first walks into those public preserves revealed to my grateful eyes
the beauty and variety of coastal plant associations.

All shades of green and gray made a rich foliar tapestry, accented in
spring and summer with the rainbow colors of coastal wildflowers.
Rounded forms of shrubs and trees cast beautiful shadows on soft coastal
hills. Where water seeped through cliffs, willows threaded surprising rib-

---

Part-opening illustration: Wild grapes. Drawing by Ane Carla Rovetta.

bons through the seemingly dry slopes. Light dappled the shade-loving ferns and flowers of dim canyons. I couldn't look enough.

Yet when I visited the gardens of my town, these local plants were conspicuous by their absence, as was any conversation about them. I came to see that I lived in a uniquely protected location that reflected little of its surrounding plant communities. My rambles revealed a slow but inexorable lessening of these native plant riches, a blanking out of natural values, beginning in gardens and towns and spreading into adjacent public lands. Observing small losses adding inexorably up, part of what Paul Ehrlich calls "the nickel-and-diming to death of our environment," I began a gardening, walking, and thinking investigation.

Walking and looking, I came to hypothesize that the group of native bluff and coastal scrub plants that hold these cliffs, hills, and valleys have just the right characteristics for the job. Their leaves filter rain to the soil in just the right way, their roots dig into the cliffs in just the right way, and the habitat structure they provide enables the greatest number of fauna of all kinds to thrive. I began to explore the ways, both obvious and subtle, in which we could benefit from the incorporation of the wild into our gardens.

Coyote Bush

I began my own garden, juggling its creation with trips into the nearby wildlands for seed and idea collecting. Without quite knowing what I was doing, I began to try to work myself into my new home through gardening on my one-acre homesite with these plants. I never drew up a plan but depended on visions gained through explorations of the surrounding wildlands. I haven't been tied to these visions but have kept open to surprises; indeed, I have come to see surprises as the highest kind of gardening experience. Gardening with our local flora has allowed me to study and live with plants in such a way that I have discovered qualities of which I was previously unaware.

Take coyote bush ("coyote brush" to some).

On my flat, once heavily grazed, piece of land, the only species representing the northern coastal scrub plant community was coyote bush, *Baccharis pilularis consanguinea,* an undervalued species often removed when a garden is made. When we began the removal of weedy grasses, brambles, and French broom, we left islands of coyote bush, good places for mysterious rustlings in the early morning. I began to think about and appreciate coyote bush, and slowly I found others who had thoughts about this plant. As I talked to people about coyote bush, information began to emerge. What had begun as a solitary conversation expanded to include many talkers, and eventually a loose association formed, dedicated to protecting and restoring habitat in our town. At first jokingly and then as a matter of course, we called ourselves Friends of the Coyote Bush.

SAGE LA PENA *I asked Sage La Pena, an indigenous Californian of the Wintu tribe, how she learned about native plants, and how she began growing them. Sage is the manager of the native plant nursery at Ya-Ka-Ama Indian University in Forestville, California.*

"It started when I was born," said Sage. "I don't know why I know how or when to collect seeds. I just absorbed it growing up."

She told of trips down the Russian River with relatives, where conversation about the plants they were passing was the background of the trip.

"I didn't think I really knew anything until I applied for a job as a naturalist; then I realized how much I had absorbed."

"So," I said, "you learned about native plants from your family."

"That was one way." she said, "But there's a second way. Like my brother wakes up with a new song, I wake up knowing something about plants that I didn't know before. I dream it."

We learned that coyote bush, with its late bloom, is an indispensable source of nectar in the autumn, when hundreds of insects take advantage of its nectar, including *Paradejeania rutillioides,* the Tachina fly, whose larvae are parasitic on numerous insect pests harmful to important agricultural crops. An electrician working on my house opened some buried electrical boxes to find soft deer mouse nests made of the fluffy pappus of coyote bush seeds. A local hiker, caught in a tight spot on a steep cliff, grabbed onto coyote bush, sturdily rooted into the cliff, and pulled himself to safety.

The soil under coyote bush is rich, good for growing vegetables or for sheltering native herbaceous plants like checkerbloom or brodiaea, native bunchgrasses like the blue fescue and coastal hairgrass. Its flowers when gone to seed cover the bush like white snow, gleaming in the winter sun.

Some birds, like wrentits and white-crowned sparrows, live their whole lives in coyote bush, finding there all they need for perching, nesting, breeding, eating, and resting. Creatures like the rare mountain beaver find homes and food where coyote bush is. Coyote bush is enough for them.

We pondered the mysteries of its many forms, from the graceful shrub-sized mounds, like clouds on a hillside, to the low-growing, ground-hugging form, to those individuals that unaccountably shoot up to tree size. As we learned more, one of us said, "It's hard to remember that once I thought coyote bush was just . . . coyote bush."

Some call it "tick bush" and hold it in low regard, considering it a mere interloper where there could be grasses and colorful wildflowers, but here on the coast, bunchgrasses and perennial wildflowers thrive in its gracious company. When the exotic grasses are dry and dormant in late summer, look near the skirts of *Baccharis pilularis* to find soft tufts of native grasses, still partly green, interspersed with late-blooming wildflowers like the tarweeds, both madias and hemizonias.

In the garden, its rich green foliage and neat mounding habit make a satisfying background plant for other, showier species. One gardener discovered that cutting coyote bush seedlings to the ground when they are small will cause them to sprout back shapely and round. In other situations, where competition causes it to grow in a distorted fashion, it can be pruned to enhance its sculptural qualities. After fires, we watch the new green shoots sprout from the crowns, under a burned hoopskirt of blackened branches. Galls form on its leaves; some of us think it is helpful to remove them, but we don't know for sure. It is to coyote bush that I turn when discouraged or in need of a reminder of all that is available to learn in my own back yard.

Visions

I began to see the dim outlines of a vision of my home, nestled into the intricate earth, surrounded by those trees, shrubs, grasses, and wildflowers that at one time graced this land, and surrounded also by those birds, insects, rodents, and mammals that have slept in, eaten off, hidden in, bred in, and otherwise hung out in these plants for the past ten thousand years. Home was becoming more particularly defined, more specific, more tied to the details of smell, color, and form, as we searched out the clues and looked at the pieces. The white-crowned sparrow, famous for its different dialects, has a clear, sweet whistle, called the Palomarin, or clear dialect, heard only in the area reaching from my town to a lake three miles away. Along our coast, the California poppy occurs in a lemon yellow rather than crayon orange variety.

While the land around my house, and in my town in general, can no longer be called pristine, the kind of gardening I have become interested in appears at the place where my plant choices and the general direction of the wild landscape meet, where I can work to locate myself and my garden in the ongoing evolution of life forms as they have become evident in this post-Pleistocene era, on this marine terrace, at the edge of this sea.

I am increasingly eased by my association with these plants. Collecting, cleaning, and sowing their seeds, planting and transplanting them as young plants, and collecting seeds from those in turn, all create a long intimacy somewhat reminiscent of, although not nearly as rich as, the complicated, layered involvement of the native Californians that used and continue to use them. When Mabel McKay, a deceased Pomo basket weaver and doctor, heard somebody say that he had used native medicinal herbs but that they hadn't worked for him, she responded, "You don't know the songs. You have to know the right songs."

With no one to teach us, we don't know the songs either. The native practice of dreaming songs about the nonhuman world seems as valuable and elusive as a piece of pure bunchgrass prairie or the truth about this land.

Our retreat hut in the garden is called the Coyote Bush House, and its door handles are made from the hard, twisted limbs of its namesake. We use this hut for restorative naps, on a cot so situated that what you see out the open door before you fall asleep in April is the intense blue of lupines against the creams, yellows, and golds of tidy-tips, goldfields, and the lemon yellow form of the California poppy. What you see in the winter months is coyote bush regenerating after the long time of no rain, its new leaves the freshest of greens. The structure sits low to the ground, providing a good place for guard quail to perch while watching their flocks feed — their calls spring through the garden. Here, our first plant songs might be dreamed.

The Larger Garden

Twenty years ago, when I first began working in a California native plant nursery, I wasn't sure why I was drawn to work with native plants. In the middle of a major drought, they seemed important elements of the water-conserving garden, although now I no longer focus on the drought-tolerant aspects of native plants. The reasons to garden with locally occurring native plants have more to do with joining in, with setting in motion interrupted processes that are unique to this place. It has to do with recreating a garden that connects the gardener with that larger garden beyond the fence.

In that larger garden, many plant/animal relationships are finely tuned and easily disrupted. Certain butterflies, for example, are called "host-specific," meaning that they will lay their eggs only on one or a few different plant species. When these larvae hatch, they require the kind of food that the leaves of their host plant provide and the kind of shelter that the leaf litter at the base of the plant provides. Without that particular plant, they will not survive. One example is the pipevine swallowtail, whose larvae are found only on the leaves of one of California's most beautiful native vines, Dutchman's pipe, *Aristolochia californica*. Without this plant, you won't be seeing the huge, iridescent, greenish black wings of *Battus philenor*. It all starts with the plants.

Gardening this way has changed me in ways I couldn't have predicted. My previous employer, Gerda Isenberg, the founder of Yerba Buena Nursery, had a demonstration garden of native plants, but around her house were a cutting garden, a formal rock garden, and some of the beloved plants that reflected her European birth. When I set up our demonstration garden, I followed her model, starting at the edge of the property with natives and working my way up to the house, where I half-consciously assumed that I too would grow exotic plants that caught my fancy.

By the time I got to the house, which took years, I was different. What I wanted to be greeted by in the mornings were the rusty green, roughish leaves of the California hazel, its horizontal twigs slanting against the office wall. I did not want to have to go anywhere to experience the sleek gray limbs of the California buckeye or the deep green leaves of the handsome coffeeberry. I wanted my fog gray house to melt into the grays of the coastal sages. These are friends whose seasons and graces go beyond novelty, friends with whom I have become quite comfortable.

I want to be able to walk directly into the coastal scrub and see it jumping with those resident birds, such as the wrentit, the bushtit, and the white-crowned sparrow, that favor it for nesting and feeding. Quiet can make me nervous now, reminding me of what Robert Michael Pyle calls "the extinction of experience — the loss of everyday species within our own radius of reach." He says, "When we lose the common wildlife in our immediate surroundings, we run the risk of becoming inured to nature's absences, blind to delight, and, eventually, alienated from the land."

When I hike into the surrounding wildlands, I have a purpose, a reason to be there. As well as collecting seeds, I am seeking inspiration and information. We think we know what these plants can do, but surprises are the name of the game. Led by my friend John, who has made it the business of his retirement to know and protect this watershed, we once went deep into a coastal canyon, past marshy grasses, to a grove of Pacific wax myrtles so large that their ancient limbs created a sheltered glade. Here we picnicked, reclining on foot-deep, cinnamon-colored leaf litter. Having previously seen these plants only in their shrub form, I could only guess at how old these individuals were.

I brought back a bit of the duff to scatter at the base of my own small wax myrtles, in case some mycorhizzal connection in the soil has enabled the spectacular growth of these plants. These treasured bits of information let us know what was once and what might be again.

In the way that our coastal creeks spread out over the land in a broad floodplain before they empty into the lagoon, so the plants in this garden and in these wild gardens have begun to spread and seep out into our lives. At the end of a performance at our community center, we threw handfuls of coyote bush seed into the audience. The shining fluffy white seeds floated and drifted and landed in people's hair, adding to the layers of memories about coyote bush. Some people grabbed at them and put them in their pockets, as though the seeds were something valuable they had never seen before. For a while afterward, people would stop me on the street to talk about coyote bush.

Food

One part of the garden where the domestic and the wild meet is the food garden for humans. (The rest of the garden is food for something or somebody else.) In this area, I have planted both domestic and wild bush fruits, the domestic raspberry and blueberry alongside the wild huckleberry and thimbleberry. In the greens department, we have two kinds of Indian lettuce, every backpacker's favorite green, *Claytonia sibirica* and *Claytonia perfoliata,* side by side with domestic lettuces. The California woodland strawberry sends runners alongside *Fragaria* 'Sequoia'. Asparagus beds flourish next to a plant of cow parsnip, said to have shoots that taste like asparagus. Native alliums and Bermuda onions sometimes share a bed.

Some farmers are thinking about agriculture based on natural models. Wes Jackson and others at the Land Institute in Kansas look to the prairies for possible perennial grain crop combinations that may give health back to some agricultural lands. We have used native legumes, like sky lupine,

Lupinus nanus, as cover crops, which provide the bonus of a spring crop of beautiful flowers for pollinators and people to enjoy. Some wildflower species, like tansy-leaf phacelia, *Phacelia tanacetifolia,* and meadow foam, *Limnanthes douglasii,* are used to attract beneficial insects to agricultural crops.

In order that the smells and colors particular to this place be joined by the tastes particular to it, once a year I immerse myself in food preparation tasks involving our local plants. At our annual spring open house, the menu may include roasted bay nuts, pinole made from blue wildrye, sugar cookies studded with chia seeds, miner's lettuce on cheese and crackers, manzanita berry tea, and chia seed lemonade. We may not eat like this most of the time, but the ritual acknowledgment and honoring of this aspect of our local plants has come to feel compelling enough that I find myself preparing these foods and adding to the menu every year.

INDIAN LETTUCE   *One rainy year, our lettuce seedlings were all devoured by slugs and snails or drowned in downpours, but all was not lost. Indian lettuce,* Claytonia perfoliata, *and the closely related peppermint candy flower,* Claytonia sibirica, *had self-sown all around the oak trees, so we had succulent, nutritious spring greens for several months. Establishing native clovers, choice spring greens loved by indigenous Californians, would make our spring salads even more diverse and reliable. New shoots of checkerbloom,* Sidalcea malvaeflora, *although a bit furry, are also quite edible, returning every year. One round, perfoliate Indian lettuce leaf on a round cracker with a slice of a round cheese makes a pleasant hors d'oeuvre.*

Once I went to visit a friend on First Mesa on the Hopi Reservation. Inquiring as to her whereabouts, I was told that she was "whitewashing the kiva," the sacred ceremonial space. She emerged from that task with a certain virtuous glow. I remember that glow while roasting the seed of red maids, *Calandrinia ciliata,* shelling bay nut seeds, or cleaning bunchgrass seed to make pinole. These are mundane activities that set the stage for important events. It is a time for honoring continuous ways — in this case, ways having to do with the plants. Like whitewashing the kiva, this food preparation is the background activity for a sacred experience — the incorporation of the molecules of local foods into our bodies. As Thoreau said of native fruits, "They educate us and fit us to live here."

WILD GRAPES *For Mary Austin, the plants, landscape, and indigenous cultures of California were essential components of her writing. In her autobiography,* Earth Horizon, *she tells about the malnutrition she suffered when her family took up homesteading in the Tejon Valley in 1889. Surviving mainly on game, and concomitantly suffering from a deep, almost desperate passion to understand and become rooted in her new home, Mary grew weak and lethargic.*

When the leaves fell off the grapevines in the canyons, Mary discovered wild grapes. "After a week or two of almost exclusive grape diet, Mary began to pick up amazingly." At the same time, she met a local rancher able to make available to her the explicit knowledge of the Tejon region that she craved. Through eating wild foods, she regained her health, beginning an exploration of the people, animals, and landscape that resulted in literary treasures like The Land of Little Rain.

Sagebrush

Where you see coyote bush, you often see its partner in the coastal scrub plant community, California sagebrush, that plant of ineffable, shining silvery gray green. The smell and the color are the essence of California shrub lands, both interior and coastal. A good medicine smell, a heart-easing smell. A smell with some of the sharpness common to chaparral plants, which tells us where we are and seems to cut through grief or ennui.

I walk through the garden with Ann, who has worked here with me for seven years. She hands me a wand of pungent, palest silvered green sagebrush and says, "Smell this." Wandering, we stop at a large soaproot plant and look through the stems and leaves to the shadow they cast on the leaf litter at the base of the plant they come from. We experience a certain lack of ambition. We note a marked lack of plans. Now that we have reinjected the native virus, it is, to a greater and greater degree, out of our hands. Not that there isn't plenty to do; weeds are forever, especially in a Mediterranean climate, but the balance has been tipped in the native direction. Now that the California hazel is established and thriving, we can let the rose from France next to it arch its long canes in the hazel's direction.

As the years go by and the plants develop their character, I begin to accept them at their worst. The California sagebrush, during its long summer and fall dormancy, turns a ghostly pale color and looks, with its empty seed stalks, as though it had just got out of bed. But ours is not a relationship based only on looks. The wrentit uses scrapings from its bark to make its nest, bound together with cobwebs. Dried sagebrush leaves are sold as local incense at our Christmas Fair. If, as you walk through the scrub, your coat brushes the sagebrush, you become redolent of a fine fragrance, at once spicy and sweet.

Music and Baskets

Twice a year, a Pomo Indian named Milton "Bun" Lucas used to visit our garden. We would place a chair for him between two elderberry bushes. From there, he would direct us as we scurried about cutting elderberry shoots for him to turn into carved clapper sticks and flutes, musical instruments used by many Californian tribes. Our cutting goals included fostering those stems that next year would be the right size and shape for a clapper stick or flute.

Gardening can be an anxious pastime, as the demands of weeding, watering, fertilizing, and pruning accrue. I have never experienced such peaceful gardening moments as when we planned for next year's "music bush" harvest. "Cut here," said Bun, "and cut here."

Now that Bun is gone, the bushes don't look the same. Some native peoples say that plants not honored by being used become sad and don't flourish. No one attends this tree anymore to make gambling pieces out of the twigs or to carve parts of the limbs into beautiful clapper sticks and whistles, so that music can be made.

Obtaining suitable basketry materials can be difficult for native California basket weavers. Lack of access and policies involving the spraying of herbicides and the control of fire are all stumbling blocks in the way of the pursuit of this art. Basketgrass, *Muhlenbergia rigens,* used by a number of California tribes, is hard to find and often not of suitable quality. At the same time, however, this grass has become extremely popular in landscaping. A large, fine-textured handsome grass easily grown horticulturally, it is being planted very extensively throughout California and seems to be adaptable to many conditions; there is no reason for indigenous basket makers to go without. One fall, I was able to offer sheaves of its beautiful pale seed stalks to a Yowlumni basket maker.

I have talked with other indigenous Californians about plants they used to see but can no longer find, plants of cultural importance to their tribe. These include a plant gathered for its edible leaves, a variety of wild tobacco that no one has seen for a while, and an elusive grass with seeds as large as wheat. All these might be found and brought into the native garden. Recent anthropological theories about Indian land management indicate that to the indigenous people of California, there was no "wilderness." Human activities have always transformed the landscape. The distinction between the garden and the wild blurs further. The seam shifts, cracks in some places, holds more closely in others.

Illuminations

I am a patron of used book stores, alert for the odd find that may illuminate some hitherto unknown aspect of this kind of landscape and these plants, of previous human interactions with them and reactions to them. Except for the redwoods, our coastal plants go largely unsung. They have no John Muir. Easily removed for development or ranching, of little evident economic value, they are the underdogs of California plant communities. I think of myself as becoming of them, becoming "of the coastal scrub."

For this kind of garden, plant lists are not taken from charts in glossy garden books. Ideas for plantings come from local floras, from hikes with naturalists into nearby undisturbed areas, from visits to botanic gardens, from the recollections of old-timers, and from the oral histories stored in our museums and libraries. They come from the diaries of early Spanish explorers, from the journals of wives of doctors living in gold-mining communities, from the casual asides of English tourists.

My garden is not the wild, but it looks to and is in conversation with the wild. It backs on and is backed up by natural systems. The goal is that the quail living next to us will find in our arranged mosaic of coastal prairie, coastal scrub, and wildflower fields the forbs they need for greens, the seeds they need for protein when nesting, and, in our shrubs, the habitat structure for shelter and protection. Subclover, *Trifolium subterraneum,* a plant widely sown for forage, will not be found in our garden, as it is in nearby lots, since it is now known that this plant contains chemicals that inhibit reproduction in quail. Nor will the naturalizing pyracantha, for although its berries may seem to make birds amusingly inebriated, they actually expose them to predation and interfere with the activities necessary for their survival. Instead, we plant toyon, *Heteromeles arbutifolia*, with its bright hollylike berries at Christmas time, the shrub for which Hollywood was named.

With plantings of toyon, we join the great feeding schedule, whereby food is available at the right time for the right creature. In early summer, the buckeye blooms, sometimes for three months. Its great pendant blossoms attract the insects that nourish the protein-hungry nesting birds. Even birds that are usually herbivorous require animal food while nesting. In midsummer, annual and perennial seed crops ripen, bee plant, poppy, miner's lettuce, clarkia. By early fall, the native honeysuckle drapes succulent red berries on trees and shrubs. Midfall brings acorn and hazel harvests, and late fall sees the ripening of madrone and toyon berries, while the coyote bush pumps out the nectar. In January and February, the flowering of pink flowering currant coincides with the return of the rufous hummingbird.

An editor of a gardening magazine questions whether this kind of gardening, where ethics and aesthetics merge, using local natives and natural models, is truly representative of the fine art of gardening. "Some might consider such simplification the abandonment of gardens as art," he says.

But choices have been made, plants have been arranged, an aesthetic has been developed. It embraces all I know, all I hope to know, and all I wish I knew about this set of ancient processes and associations.

Is it the way of a lazy gardener, as he implies? I find that the horticultural challenges are many. For example, I want to establish a stand of Indian paintbrush here, a hemi-parasitic plant that probably grew here once but has so far not survived in my garden.

Indian paintbrush, appearing in a radiant palette of apricot, scarlet, and yellow, hosts a particular kind of aphid-eating mite. This mite lives in the flower, where it eats nectar, till a hummingbird comes along to share the nectar. At this juncture, the mite runs up the hummingbird's beak and into its nostril, where it sits tight while the hummingbird flies down to Baja California. As the hummingbird approaches a nectar-producing plant, the mite gets ready, rears up, and races from the nostril, down the beak, and into the flower. Since it must move so quickly, this creature is equal in speed to the fastest animal on earth, the cheetah. By establishing this flower in the garden, with its as yet elusive cultural requirements, we may be facilitating this mind-boggling nasal journey.

The Beginning of the Eucalyptus Story

My town is bordered on the north by Jack's Creek, which feeds a rancher's stock pond before wending its diminished way to the ocean. As along many creeks in California, the north bank of this creek was planted with a windbreak of eucalyptus trees. Under these trees, which continually drop large, acidic leaves, little is able to grow except French broom and brambles, shallow-rooted, non-native plants. The bank on this side is continually crumbling and eroding, as the eucalyptus trees, now some eighty feet tall, become increasingly top-heavy.

On the other side of the creek, the bank is covered with native plants from the coastal scrub, including monkeyflower, sagebrush, coyote bush, lizard tail, mule's ear, and cow parsnip. The bank on that side is intact, verdant, complete, even down to the smaller plants, such as the tiny, narrow-leaved native plantain (a larval food plant for the endangered Bay checkerspot butterfly) and the spring-blooming bulb named pussy ears for its pointed, fuzzy white petals.

Where Jack's Creek empties into the ocean, the bank becomes a steep bluff. On the northern, eucalyptus-covered side of the creek mouth, the tree currently nearest the end of the bluff will cling precariously for a while, providing dramatic photo opportunities, and then fall, taking with it a great chunk of cliff. The beach below is already littered with bleached eucalyptus trunks, resembling an elephant's graveyard. One by one, the trees fall, and the end of the cliff moves further back into the land. The other side of the bluff, where the native plants grow, erodes slowly, imperceptibly, at a leisurely Californian pace. Recently, I saw that a eucalyptus sapling has appeared in the previously intact coastal scrub on the south bank. This young tree will, in not too many years, be the progenitor of its own grove of cliff-destroying eucalyptus trees.

In other places, seeking to save their sea-bluff properties, homeowners have planted species reputed to help in erosion control, such as iceplant. Used in many places throughout California, iceplant quickly covers the ground, but it is not deep-rooted and does not lace the soil layers together as will the deep-rooted native bluff species. I have seen its heavy, succulent leaves pull down sections of cliff. When the plant dies, too, the salt stored in its leaves changes the chemical properties of the soil into which it decomposes, impeding the germination and reestablishment of native species.

The native plants have become the exotics, lone voices in a chorus of eucalyptus, passion flower vine, French and Scotch broom, Cape ivy, English ivy, and so on. I speculate that one reason so little respect is given to native plant communities in my town is that they are now so little in evidence. The thrilling sweep to the sea of low-growing prairie, scrub, and bluff plants that must once have been here is hard to visualize, interrupted as it is now by mini-forests of eucalyptus, pine, and cypress. Where coastal scrub still exists, it is usually diminished by the rampant growth of Himalayan blackberry or ivy, which eliminate the beautiful herb layer, one of the elements that distinguishes northern coastal scrub from southern coastal scrub. It is hard, and getting harder, to get a sense of what the land used to be.

I can base my gardening choices on information gleaned from naturalists and scientific papers, on data on habitat for songbirds, butterflies, insects, voles, and lizards, motivated by the hope of providing hospitable surroundings for these creatures. Yet it may be that they will not come, or that only some will.

I shall still want to be surrounded by these plants. Knowledge of their qualities seems to fill some of that cavity of longing for knowledgeable connection with our tribe, both human and other, that some of us carry around like an empty burden basket. I no longer see plants as isolated acquisitions, representing triumphs of my horticultural skills, although I use those skills, from propagating oaks from acorns to pruning California hazels into the elegant, horizontally branched form they can assume.

My goals, perspectives, and visions have so changed through this endeavor that a beautiful flowering plant at the nursery that might once have fired my blood with the longing for ownership is a matter of some indifference to me now. Most noticeably, I can no longer be disappointed in my expectations of what plants might do. "I have these pictures in my mind of how the garden will look. But it never looks that way," one client complained. "I know," I said. "Isn't it great?" It's all information on the characteristics of old friends. Surprise, change, and flow are the stuff of gardening life to me now.

Protecting, enhancing, and bringing close the coastal scrub and other native plant communities has become my business, and my life is punctuated by phone calls and seed orders and scheduling, but behind it all somewhere always are the color of the litter made by wax myrtle leaves and the smell of coyote bush in the rain.

The Seam

Once I spent some time at a hot springs in Mendocino County. The facilities included a "cool pool" for swimming, built by damming the creek on three sides with poured concrete. The fourth side of the pool was formed by the rocky base of the hill, along which flowed the creek. On the hillside, native clarkias cast a pink net through the grasses.

When, after swimming my laps, I pulled myself up and out of the pool,

I found that one hand was on concrete and the other on native rock. Regarding the seam between the two materials, a hardened flow between substances, it occurred to me that this is the place where I have come to garden: at the seam between the wild and the cultivated, where they merge and mingle, the shape of one giving shape to the other.

It is this conversation, the back-yard, over-the-fence conversation between the gardener and the larger garden beyond the fence, that forms the subject of this book. Sometimes I find myself standing motionless in my garden, a plant in either hand. My neighbor laughs at me over the fence, "What are you doing?"

"I'm thinking," I say. I'm remembering a piece of coastal forest where I first saw these plants, called milkmaids, in a sunny opening created by the demise of an old Douglas fir. My mind flickers through a couple of hundred years of land use history, speculating, evaluating. I imagine myself next spring lying down among these white flowers, watching the white butterflies that frequent them, lost in the fog-bound trembling of this gentle, solemn, silvered land.

PART II

Tipping the Balance in a Native Direction

CHAPTER TWO

Planning Back-Yard Restoration Gardens

He who owns a veteran bur oak owns more than a tree. He owns a historical library and a reserved seat in the theatre of evolution.   *Aldo Leopold, 1949*

I cannot think of a more tasteless undertaking than to plant trees in a naturally treeless area, and to impose an interpretation of natural beauty on a great landscape that is charged with beauty and wonder, and the excellence of eternity.
Ansel Adams, 1966

Hints and Clues, Remnants and Relics

I arrive early for my appointment. There is time, before ringing the doorbell, to scout the neighborhood surrounding the home where I shall be doing a landscape consultation. It may be a tract house in a crowded subdivision, a summer home converted to a residence on ten acres of woods, a ranch house on five hundred acres of grasslands, or a mini-mansion built "on spec." Maybe the land was once a beanfield, and before that, riparian forest. It may have been converted from apricot orchards to houses and yards, or directly from oak savannah to houses and yards, but somewhere in the neighborhood, I am going to find some native plant life.

An oak sprouting by the sidewalk, a small patch of miner's lettuce in the grass, toyon thrusting dark red berries through a fence. Coyote bush along a right of way, the seed stalk of an annual lupine. Hints and clues, remnants and relics. The survivors.

I make a list, a neighborhood flora for the client. It will tell the names

Part-opening illustration: Blue oak. Drawing by Ane Carla Rovetta.

of the survivors, those species possibly easiest to bring back, and provide clues to the land's natural history. I may find places for collection of local seeds, to be grown out by me or the client, or plant combinations that seem like good ideas.

Rare is the land that has not experienced some hard history of use. Usually the "herb layer," which includes the native grasses, wildflowers, and perennials, is least in evidence. When there are venerable oaks or madrones, dramatic and beautiful, they are often spending a lonely old age with no young ones coming along. To suggest taking measures to encourage baby, teenage, and young adult oaks is a way to gauge the long-range interests of the client. Is the imagination stirred by the thought of an oak grove that the owner might not live to see mature? The owner's response provides a clue, a necessary hint, about this particular land manager.

The flora is for the clients, to honor their land. I am usually excited by what I have found, and hope that they will be too. As I talk about what I have seen, I begin to assess how much complexity is of interest to them and what their motive is for wanting a garden of native plants. Sometimes they want to include a few native plants for interest's sake; sometimes they want to lower their water bill. They may want to attract hummingbirds or butterflies or quail. A multitude of motivations are possible. I have seen repeatedly that one thing leads to another and that I can never predict from an initial encounter what the outcome will be.

Once I had my kitchen redone, a major improvement. The carpenter kept saying how small it was. I was thrilled with the changes but couldn't enjoy them till the carpenter had left. I want my clients to love their land, to find in it some glimpse of the perfection indigenous peoples attribute to their homelands. The feeling that it is "just right," that everything needed is present on the site. A willingness to accept its winds, slopes, and exposures with all the pleasures and challenges they bring.

In most cases, the general outlines of what used to grow on the land are apparent without my early morning ramble. But it makes a welcome interlude between the drive and the work and provides an opening for the appearance of the unexpected, a rare fritillary or surprising patch of grassland.

And it is a way to clear the mind for this work. A moment to imagine the past, acknowledge the ghosts, and be reassured by the presence of the natives, still coming through. Yes, we are still around, they say. We have survived plowing, logging, mining, ranching, and now, gardening.

In some cases, it is the gardener who delivers the final blow.

What Is Happening to California?

Once I saw a beautiful piece of land for sale not far from where I live. It was adjacent to a national park, offering views of ocean and bay, and was richly clothed with a mosaic of Bishop pine, sword fern, Pacific wax myrtle, and huckleberry. Soon, the fortunate new owners began to build their home.

Shortly afterward, a hedge was planted. Not a hedge of the species already present on the site — coffeeberry, wild lilac, Pacific wax myrtle, coyote bush, Pacific reed grass, coast live oak, and California hazel — but one of a non-native plant with strong associations of the freeway. The newcomers to the neighborhood had chosen to plant oleander.

There is no shortage of oleander in California. Anyone wishing to see it can drive along Interstate 5 and many other freeways. Everywhere, the "oleanderization of California" proceeds apace. There is, on the contrary, a shortage of relatively intact Bishop pine forest and its floral and faunal associates. Multiply this scenario by the thousands, and you will glimpse how the landscape of California has been changed in the name of gardening.

I once saw a back yard entirely planted with iceplant, creating a perfect rectangle of bright pink flowers in the middle of one of those textured, tufted, woven mosaics of grays and greens unique to the California chaparral. Perhaps the owner had been advised to plant iceplant to prevent erosion, although the chamise, sagebrush, ceanothus, and manzanita had been doing that perfectly well for thousands of years.

In these situations, a new homeowner (sometimes from another state, sometimes not) buys a home or lot partly because of its natural beauty and then immediately proclaims ownership by planting a tree or a hedge or a flower garden that bears no relationship to the surrounding flora or land forms. I call this behavior "planting the flag" gardening, often an early stage in the development of gardeners, who may or may not evolve beyond it. I myself left behind in beautiful upstate New York a relatively pristine hillside that did not benefit from my early gardening activities. Following the advice of an enticing catalog, I planted crown vetch, an invasive exotic plant, to cover the banks of our newly excavated pond, and through my gardening practices introduced weeds that were not previously present.

Organic gardening was my first gardening framework, and Ruth Stout's *How to Have a Green Thumb Without an Aching Back* my inspiration. Her secret was mulch. Mulch on top of mulch, lots and lots of mulch. She said that you could never have too much mulch. Spoiled hay was her greatest source of mulch, and it was also mine, with the difference that she was able to use salt hay, relatively free of weed seeds, while my hay bales, the only ones I could find, included seeds of Johnson grass, one of the most noxious of weedy grasses, and burdock, the farmer's bane in that part of the country. Everywhere I mulched, I introduced these invasive species, nevermore to be absent from this piece of land.

Recently, a homeowner newly arrived from the Midwest was given a consultation with me for his birthday. He had transplanted around his property a hedge of French broom, which had reseeded down the hill, moving into coastal scrub and native prairie. When I expressed dismay, he said, "I had no idea you'd be such a fanatic." I guess I was a disappointing birthday present. Now I make it clear in advance that a fanatic is being hired.

I was not born a fanatic. I became this way gradually because of what I have seen and learned doing this work. When I lived in a pink stucco house in the Santa Clara Valley, I looked back with nostalgia to Blossom Valley's agrarian past, planting apricots and pruning almond trees. For five years, I kept cutting back the annoying scratchy plant sprouting from a stump under our hammock. It took me that long to realize that it was a coast live oak, a precious reminder of the dense riparian forest that had probably once covered my neighborhood. Later, by the channelized creek down the block, I found an ancient elderberry, larger and older than any I had ever seen, another survivor.

Although I was working as a propagator at a native plant nursery, collecting acorns and growing native oaks, and although it was dreadfully hot in the summer, and shade from an oak would have been a welcome thing, apricots and plums were on my mind, and I kept cutting back that oak sprout. But it kept coming up again. My pruning only seemed to make it more vigorous.

I was not comfortable in that neighborhood. I wanted to live in a wilder place. What a strong wild impulse that oak demonstrated, repeatedly crown-sprouting, borrowing strength from its ancient root system. The wildness we are buying second homes to experience, eating up the remaining open spaces of California and driving up and down freeways to find, may be in our back yards, knocking at the door.

Restoration Ecology

I ask my clients to write out a list of their questions, concerns, priorities, and dreams. We read through it together, then walk the land. They are the local experts, the ones who see the water stream past the side of the house after a storm and feel the intense heat where the sun beats down in late summer. The work is a collaboration, where I arrive with my experience and perspective, but the gardener is the inhabitant, the one with local knowledge, the one who is continually gathering on-site information.

Restoration ecology teaches us a sense of how much there is to know about every place, guiding the mulching, planting, pruning hand to move with knowledge behind it. Gardeners as land managers, people who make decisions about how land will be used, invest some $23 billion every year in their visions. This amount of money may well be more than is spent on managing all our public lands, national parks, seashores, and forests put together. It matters what gardeners do.

A gardener plants pampas grass in the front yard, and three years later that single plant has spawned a whole field of baby pampas grass down the road. Somebody plants Cape ivy to hide an unsightly shed, from which it spreads into and destroys a whole coastal scrub remnant, a willow grove, or a thicket of native blackberry. A gardener chooses capeweed, *Arctotheca calendula,* as a "ground cover," and it moves relentlessly into a small remnant coastal prairie. In all these cases, it is gardeners, not logging companies, mining companies, or shopping mall developers, who take steps resulting in an unintended but nonetheless devastating loss of scenes and relationships from which we might be learning.

Mike Kelly, president of the Friends of Los Penasquitos Canyon Preserve, consisting of 3,700 acres near San Diego, writes of the inventory of weed problems in the preserve. Of the eight or so invasive species he names, six are present because they have been planted by gardeners and public agencies as ornamentals.

I daydream of a law requiring that no planting be done by a new homeowner during his or her first year of ownership, until the new owner has watched the sun rise and set on the land many times, walked the paths, felt the wind and noted how it changes through the seasons, experienced drainage in the rainy season, and let the land do its work, talked to the neighbors about what weedy problems they contend with and which plants they regret having planted.

Mitigation for the Gardener

In the field of restoration ecology, the term *mitigation* refers to the legal requirement to make reparation for harm done — in other words, for the developer who builds a shopping mall on a wetland or condominiums where vernal pools once went through their seasonal changes to create equivalent wetlands or vernal pools elsewhere.

Although mitigation may be seen as representing a real shift in consciousness, questions of the possibility of such replacement of natural systems inevitably arise. Do we understand enough about natural systems to begin to recreate them, or to evaluate the mitigation effort once it has been made? All those associated with this field recognize that the cost of attempting to replace functioning natural systems with artificial ones is astronomical, that it would be better simply to protect them in the first place. But development proceeds, roads are cut through wildlands, houses sit on vernal pools, video parlors occupy coastal scrub, and the landscape of California is changed for the worse in ways both apparent and hidden.

In an ideal world, the restored wetland would be created first, before the building project was begun. It would be observed for a number of years to see if it could actually meet restoration criteria before the first bulldozer arrives to destroy the original site. Critics point out that restoration in this arena serves to legitimize destruction, but the revolutionary aspect of even this kind of restoration is that it recognizes that the world cannot absorb endless destruction. It legalizes the concept of "payback," or returning the gift, and gives the natural world the status of a player.

Back yards, where fewer economic motives usually prevail, offer direct opportunities to ally ourselves with the forces of restoration. Planting native penstemons instead of petunias won't take food out of your mouth, but it may put it into some other creature's, somebody you didn't know about but will be glad to meet. Grizzlies and wolves will not appear in your urban yard, but there's a lot else that can happily inhabit the place where nature and culture meet. The endangered San Joaquin kit fox may not build a den by your deck (although a gray fox, with cubs, lives comfortably near one of our clients), but if your home at the edge of the wildlands is a rich, chirping, buzzing, yowling island, with no invasive plants leaking out from its edges, possibilities abound.

If the vegetable garden takes up a quarter of an acre, a food garden for birds and turtles might take up an equal amount. If the construction of a new home disrupts a woodland, let the builder plant another. If the commute to work requires roads that bring weedy species to wildlands, vow that your yard, and then your neighborhood, will be pest-plant free.

A sense of atonement is not inappropriate for the back-yard restorationist. Neither craven nor guilt-ridden, but almost practical, it points a new way. To look at what has been done to the land and begin its redress at the back door brings concrete relief, soothing like hands patting the dirt around the roots of a young oak. With the premise that all land is sacred land, the gardener finds herself doing important work. While corporations are forced to mitigate, homeowners can do so voluntarily, joyfully.

I know a woman who planted capeweed in the yard of her rented home. Eleven years later, when she moved, the capeweed had spread throughout her yard and into adjoining farmlands, beyond her physical means to remove it. Where it will stop is anybody's guess, but that land adjoins a national park where volunteers spend weekends removing this very species.

She might make reparation by tackling some restoration project in her next yard, something within her capabilities. She might "mitigate" for damage done by joining a volunteer group working to restore public lands. She might pressure her local nursery owner not to sell capeweed and talk to her friends about the significance of their gardening choices. Such actions would reflect a change in consciousness, assuming responsibility for our gardening choices.

MY KIND OF CLIENT *I am at the beginning of a consultation. I am not sure yet what I can do for this client — the gardening problems he wants to solve seem to require plants not found in the native palette, such as evergreen vines that form thick privacy screens and are fragrant through the summer.*

Then he shows me three oak saplings on his property, two valley oaks and one coast live oak. One of the valley oaks has been jay-seeded right next to a recently built gardening shed. We admire its shapely promise. "Of course, we'll have to remove the shed," he says matter-of-factly. Now I know I can work with this client.

I don't expect clients to tear down their buildings for native plants, but it's nice when one offers.

Tipping the Balance

After walking the land with a client, I walk it alone, then sit in the best place I can find to ponder on plant associations to be recreated and how they can be combined with what already exists. Important information to elicit is which plants the client wants to keep.

I seek to avoid the tearing out of well-loved plants. Ripping out roses and fruit trees, a fragrant daphne, or a time-honored wisteria is not the way I like to begin. The kind of gardening described in this book simply sets in slow motion the process of tipping the balance in a native direction. Returning the natives, seeing how they work, making thoughtful choices, the gardener can move slowly to a vision of commitment arising, not from a sense of loss or deprivation, but rather from a sense of enrichment.

Roses and fruit trees can be protected from deer by encircling them with coyote bush or Oregon grape, *Mahonia aquifolium.* In coastal gardens, coyote bush can visually tie a garden together; its rich green foliage makes a good background for roses, particularly the climbing roses that don't require spraying and coddling. The back-yard orchardist may find that the only nut trees that do well on the coast are the native hazels. When the raspberries are done, the berry lover can head for the native huckleberries.

Fruit trees can be underplanted with native bunchgrasses, whose slow and steady intake of water and deep fibrous root systems make them good cover crops for orchards and vineyards. The native grape, *Vitis californica,* tangy and sweet after the first frost, is well worth growing. Food growers, including permaculturists, who focus on perennial crops, and organic truck farmers might profitably begin serious conversation with native plant people.

The back-yard gardener, with no deadlines to meet, no committees to please, has the opportunity to change slowly. No massive replantings or clear-cuts need be scheduled in the back yard. We remove one or two Monterey pines a year around my house, replanting oak trees, buckeyes, and red elderberries as we go. If any creatures have adapted to existing garden plants, we aim to provide them with alternatives before eliminating their habitat.

Appropriate Expectations

In working out the sequence of events for the homeowner, I hope to establish that less than total certainty is the essence of this kind of gardening. Surprise, both good and bad, provides opportunities to learn more about a particular site. Accumulating information about what works where, sometimes developing site-specific techniques, and using that information to rework the project as it proceeds are part of the evolving native garden.

In order that expectations and reality mesh, I make it clear that some native plants have a longer adjustment period after planting than nonnative plants commonly used in the trade. They may not begin to thrive till the fall after planting, or till two or even three years down the line. I want to avoid the situation where the homeowner, used to the "quick off the mark" growth rate of standard landscaping plants, gives up just as the plants are about to come into their own.

Where slow-growing plants are used, I include quick-growing annuals and perennial wildflowers and native bunchgrasses to give the homeowner immediate satisfaction and pleasure. The early garden is often quite different from the mature garden, which expresses the realized forms of trees and shrubs. I often plant willows, elderberries, or alders with slower-growing oaks. These riparian plants are quick to take off and provide good screening fast. It usually takes about five years for the oak to overtake them.

I am alerted to potential problems when a client indicates particular flower color dislikes or preferences. The client who dislikes pink, all pinks, from lavender-tinged to nearly red, from opaque to translucent, or all yellow flowers, may be applying "interior design" principles that indicate a critical difference in our perspectives. I recall an experience I had on one of my first bird walks. Pausing in an opening near a creek, we were asked to count the number of bird calls we heard. Trying to decipher which one was under discussion, I asked, "Do you mean the musical one?"

"Musical is in the ear of the beholder," said one participant.

That little comment revealed to me that in the bird world as in the plant world, personal tastes differ. I have often been confused by a customer's request for "something pretty" in the way of wildflowers, since "beauty is in the eye of the beholder." Many times I have fielded requests for a wildflower mix that includes nothing yellow, or nothing pink, or nothing red.

I have never been asked for a mix that excludes blue flowers. People almost universally like blue flowers. To most bees and day-flying butterflies, however, blue is not attractive. Which perhaps accounts for its relative rarity in the world of flowers, and, therefore, its appeal for novelty-seeking humans.

The other relatively rare flower color, red, attracts birds rather than insects. Because most insect pollinators do not see pure red as a color, such flowers are to a certain extent an unoccupied ecological niche, available to the birds that do "see red." "Bird red" is a particularly valuable color for long-range attraction. It stands out starkly from all colors in the background and is clearly visible even early in the morning and late in the afternoon — times when many birds prefer to fly.

Bird nectar seekers not being as common as bird berry eaters, there are correspondingly fewer red flowers and more red berries, including, here in California, toyon, hairy honeysuckle, red elderberry, wild rose, and chokecherry.

Discussing this kind of plant/bird interaction may produce either startled attention or stifled yawns. I try to establish whether or not the client wants to see plants in this full way, and whether considerations of providing food for a wide variety of creatures can influence preferences.

I also assess the degree of seasonality, including dormancy or semi-dormancy, the client can tolerate. Some native plants may demonstrate change through the seasons more dramatically than the kinds of non-natives chosen for freeway, shopping mall, and bank parking lot. The gardener's pruning hand helps keep dormant plants tidy, but attention through the year is required. To the best of my ability, I attempt to make all this clear to the clients.

A tricky juggle is being performed here. I weigh the preconceptions of my clients concerning a desirable landscape, the vision that has formed in my investigations, and an assessment of the difference between the two. A moment may later arrive, which I try to imagine now. It comes after we have done the planting, watering, and final mulching. It is a time before the inevitable problems of watering, weeding, and the unexpected. Sitting in my car in a crowded neighborhood that I believe was once solid oak woodland, I salute the small oaks we have planted, the bunchgrasses, brodiaeas, calochortus, and toyon. I regard the huge old valley oak down the block that validated my assumptions about this piece of land. It is a moment of cloudy triumph, acknowledging the unknown ahead, while resting for the moment in the hope of having done something for that which is thought valuable.

In anticipation of that moment, I go through the private, final phase of the initial consultation, before discussing my ideas with the client. I ask, "Help me know what it is that the land wants." Whom am I asking? I'm not sure, and I know there will be no one answer, but rather a series of them. Still, I ask.

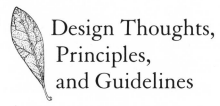 # Design Thoughts, Principles, and Guidelines

These things it must be, to be Californian. One gets a hint of it in the flower-decked glades in our mountain forests, in our canyons, many-colored with spring flowers, on our seashore slopes, carpets with purple and gold; but when it comes to making a garden, we all, like sheep, have gone within the lines, the old, old lines of other lands, and in so doing have gone astray.   *Alfred Robinson, 1913*

Ways to Garden with Native Plants

The growing and nurturing of California native plants in California gardens takes place in several distinct contexts. Let us distinguish among them as a way to begin exploring their role in the back-yard restoration garden.

TRADITIONAL GARDENS USING NATIVE PLANTS INCIDENTALLY

In this type of garden, native plants are mixed with exotic plants following the principles traditionally espoused by landscape architects. Focal points, axes, specimen plants, perennial borders, bedding plants, foundation plantings, ground covers, and screens are ways in which native plants are used in this kind of garden.

Xeriscaping, in which drought-tolerant native plants are mixed with drought-tolerant plants from places with Mediterranean climates similar to California's, is one example of this kind of gardening. The aesthetic is traditional, the goal low water use. Some native plants lend themselves admirably to this kind of gardening and will therefore be more readily available in "the trade" — that is, at non-specialty nurseries. Examples are many species and cultivars of manzanitas and ceanothus and perennials like penstemons, yarrows, monkeyflowers, heucheras, the coast strawberry, and dwarf coyote bush.

THE COLLECTOR'S GARDEN

Collectors may focus on one genus, such as salvias or penstemons, growing as many different species within that genus as possible. Or they may want to see how many different species from different parts of California they can grow. Design considerations are secondary to the interest inherent in each plant.

The gardener may be motivated to include plants that she has enjoyed on forays into the wild. Challenged by the difficulties inherent in bringing montane species to the lowlands, or desert species to the coast, she is triumphant when they succeed. Miniature back-yard botanic gardens satisfy the love of variety and provide horticultural challenges.

THE RESTORATIONIST

Restoration indicates the process whereby an attempt is made to return land that has been disturbed in a negative way by human activity to an earlier condition. Choosing a moment in time or a stage in natural succession is required. Natural models are selected and analyzed to provide information for the restorationist. Historical materials may be reviewed. Seeds and cuttings from nearby plants are gathered in order to preserve the integrity of local gene pools. Techniques have been developed to allow for large-scale plantings where plant survival must be relatively non-labor-intensive.

The field involves state and federal agencies, private citizens working in volunteer groups, academic research, nonprofit organizations like the Nature Conservancy, and professional environmental consulting firms. Some endeavors, such as the huge project restoring the Kissimee River in Florida, are intended to redress problems that already exist. Other projects are intended to mitigate for destruction consequent upon future development.

In the back-yard restoration garden, the homeowner looks for inspiration to the landscape he or she inhabits. He wants to make California look more like California and to fit his house snugly into that picture. Like the artist Gottardo Piazzoni, when asked if he has a religion, he might reply, "I think it is California."

If he lives in an oak grove, he does not set out to create a redwood grove. He learns about the grasses, wildflowers, and shrubs that grow with oaks. If he lives in Riverside County or in San Diego, he may plant the endangered Engelman oak, *Quercus engelmanii*. If he lives in the foothills overlooking hot valleys, like the San Joaquin, he may plant a grove of blue oaks, *Quercus douglasii*. In mountainous areas away from the coast, he may plant black oaks, *Quercus kelloggii*, with their showy fall colors and sweet acorns. In the Santa Clara Valley, he may plant the largest oak of all, the valley oak, *Quercus lobata*, or the canyon oak, *Quercus chrysolepis*, or the coast live oak, *Quercus agrifolia*.

He finds lists of the hundreds of insects, birds, and mammals that are associated with oak trees and looks to their appearance as markers of his success with the project. He learns about the factors that are impeding the reproduction of oaks and seeks to eliminate those factors from his grove, striving for a mixed stand of babies, teenagers, young adults, the middle-aged, and the venerable.

He lives with his oaks, creating ways to be among them on oak benches. He carefully harvests firewood from them. He considers different understory plants, from *Ceanothus nipomensis* on the Nipomo Mesa in San Luis Obispo County to hazels on the north coast. He experiments with acorns, both growing trees from them and eating them. Perhaps he joins the California Oak Foundation and attends the symposia that focus on the ecology and preservation of native oaks. *Oaks of California* is a frequently consulted reference work.

The oaks enrich his life. They are a presence, leaned against, noticed, attended to, climbed, viewed from many angles. Nourishment is exchanged.

The family photo album may include snapshots of germinating acorns, young saplings, and thriving adults.

Or a southern California gardener might attempt to restore a "walnut woodland." Southern California black walnut, *Juglans californica* var. *californica*, is classified as "very threatened" by the Nature Conservancy Heritage Program. These tall and graceful deciduous trees are fast-growing from seed, and a grove of them is a lovely place to be. They are often found near old California Indian village sites. The nuts, though small, are tasty and nutritious.

Design Principles

Let us explore some of the "principles" or notions behind this vision of the naturally designed garden.

USE NATURAL MODELS

Plant associations and combinations from nearby pristine areas are recreated in the back yard. The gardener seeks to gain as great an understanding as possible of the land both within and beyond the fence, an understanding that is continually applied to the planning and planting of the garden.

How does this notion apply to the urban gardener with a small fenced yard in the middle of a densely populated city? She searches out relatively pristine sections, perhaps a nearby nature preserve, the unused parts of a cemetery, or an old estate to use as models and as textbooks. In many cases, the native presence has been thoroughly erased from the fertile and buildable valley lands; in that case, she looks beyond the city streets to the encircling hills, Mount Shasta, the Santa Cruz Mountains, San Jacinto Mountain, or Mount Diablo.

REMOVE OR CONTROL NON-NATIVE PLANTS

This endeavor (thoroughly addressed in chapter 8) accounts for at least 50 percent of most garden projects we undertake. The particular weeds removed depend on the plant communities involved, and the methods employed depend on the weeds. Persistence is almost always required.

Once we climbed to an alpine meadow. Masses of lupine and paintbrush lay before us, but little else. After a slight initial botanical disappointment (it had been a killing climb), I began to notice the multiplicity of effects possible with just these two species. There were random and equal scatterings of both species, there were pools of lupines set off by a few scarlet paintbrushes, there were glowing masses of deep scarlet paintbrush dotted with sky blue lupines. Paintbrush was set off by a gray-white granite boulder. Lupine fields drew you on toward the lake. Mixed in different proportions, growing in different situations, these two species produced a satisfying variety of results.

I began to realize that effective design statements can be made by a limited plant palette. Groves, forests, prairies, chaparral, all imply repetition of appropriate species, where arrangement and disposition create interest, where the particular situation of each plant gives that specimen its unique aspect, balanced with the sense of harmony that results from repetition.

Limiting the number of species can deepen appreciation of the plants already in place, their seasonal changes, their aspects from different viewpoints, their fragrances and textures. Robert Michael Pyle, butterfly expert and nature writer, talks in his book *Wintergreen: Rambles in a Ravaged Land* about his decision to move to the Willapa Hills in Washington State, a place where the number of butterfly species is mysteriously few. Colleagues and friends, puzzled by his choice, wondered why a butterfly lover would choose a place not known for its variety of butterfly species. Pyle replied that he is thus forced to know one species deeply, rather than being distracted by variety. The time and focus it takes to understand the flutterings and movements, the larval necessities, or the inexplicable arrivals and departures of any single species absorb a significant chunk of a lifetime. Depth of understanding is the goal and the reward of the back-yard restoration gardener.

Choosing a keynote plant, to be repeated throughout the garden, can give a garden "bones," a structure that the eye can follow throughout. *Ceanothus nipomensis,* in San Luis Obispo County; black sage, *Salvia mellifera,* along the south coast; bigberry manzanita, *Arctostaphylos glauca,* in the

Sierra foothills; toyon, *Heteromeles arbutifolia,* in Santa Clara County; and western rhododendron, *Rhododendron macrophyllum,* in a woodland garden in Mendocino, are evergreen plants that can hold the garden together through seasonal changes.

ARRANGE PLANTS WITH A LIGHT HAND

Natural models of spatial distribution and vegetation architecture can give us a sense of how we want to arrange plants in our garden. For example, the plant association known as "Douglas fir–mixed evergreen old growth forest" is two-tiered, the tall Douglas firs overtopping the lower-growing tan oaks and bays. The gardener working with that plant community can recreate and work with that spatial arrangement.

In some stands of coastal scrub, the coyote bushes are spaced far enough apart so that each expresses its own mounding shape. In other stands, plants are exuberantly crowded. In my coastal garden, I have used both schemes, providing an opportunity to draw tentative conclusions about the consequences of plant placement. To avoid some weed problems, "plant cramming," leaving no openings for weedy species to fill, can be effective. Spaced according to their ultimate mature widths, plants can display the full beauty of their form, but more time will be spent weeding until they reach adult size.

The "mosaic" is a way of describing patches that visually knit together. Chaparral and scrub communities on faraway hillsides, with their close weavings of shrubs, can inspire the designer in the use of these species.

For an Ojai garden, take the sacred plant of the Chumash, white sage, *Salvia apiana,* as your keynote and form a grouping of its associates, ascertained from a local flora or from John Sawyer and Todd Keeler-Wolf's *A Manual of California Vegetation,* to make a cluster of plants that can be repeated, with variations, throughout the garden. This cluster might include California buckwheat, chamise, chaparral yucca, chaparral whitethorn, deer weed, and, of course, white sage, whose flowers are a powerful lure for bees and whose pungent leaves make a prized incense.

California fescue is a large grass that expresses its nature on many an oak-studded hillside, coastal bluff, or partly shaded road cut. On one striking bank, each plant is spaced so that a perfect staggered design is formed, and the eye takes pleasure in the arrangement in the wild, where it contrasts with less-ordered plant arrangements. The eye seeks repetition, while variation maintains interest. Give the eye a strong message through repetition, as nature does.

Interesting garden designs come from the play between symmetry and asymmetry. Take, for example, a neat threesome of wax myrtles at one end of the fence, one wax myrtle at the other end of the fence, and one wax myrtle somewhere off-center in between. Large garden spaces give opportunity for mass plantings — fifty California fescues rather than eight. The eye strongly registers the growth pattern of this grass, the fountainlike leaf blades, the upright flowering stalks, the silvery skirt of old leaves at the base. Plants that are subtle in shape and color can be given impact by numbers.

The ways plant communities intergrade, the ancient oaks giving way to the silvery shrub lupines, giving way to the tufted bunchgrasses, can be reproduced in the garden in such a fashion as to enhance different kinds of movement through the garden. Openings planted with low-growing forbs, grasses, and wildflowers are places for garden furniture and activities that require free movement. Close plantings of shrubs along pathways that require the garden walker to squeeze through or brush past create a moment of actual physical contact with the plants, feeling and smelling the soft leaf of the hazel or the stiff twigs of coffeeberry. It is pleasurable to be forced to brush past fragrant plants like ceanothus in bloom. Such moments enhance the dimension of immersion in local sensuality.

LET THE PLANTS DICTATE HOW THE DESIGN GROWS

In many landscaping situations, success is based on the notion of a complete plan, precisely and absolutely implemented. The designer's vision is enacted upon the land, and the plants are considered static design elements, whose ultimate heights, widths, textures, and colors can be previsioned and planned around. The operating assumption is that the designer knows his plant "materials" so well that they can be spaced precisely to the distance required. The designer will have failed if the plants do not perform as planned. Such implicit expectations lead to the use and reuse of the same tired but reliable non-native plant species.

Many gardeners expect plants to be predictable. Garden books that use charts perpetuate the notion that height, width, and growth rate are fixed quantities. A close examination of such charts often uncovers unhelpful information, such as height ranges defined as "two to six feet tall." The chart format implies predictability. Horticulturists sometimes laugh among themselves about the unpredictability of plants, but there seems to be an unspoken pact to keep this aspect of horticultural reality from the gardening public at large.

I have seen oaks shoot up two feet a year in some situations, while in others they eke out a bare eight inches of new growth yearly. Many coastal shrubs, like Pacific wax myrtles and coffeeberries, initially grow slowly in our sandy soil, then take off after two to four years. Other gardeners see quicker growth, possibly because they have more clay in their soil. A chart that reflected such complications would be an unwieldy vehicle for making planting choices.

Some plants are more predictable than others; it is a horticultural goal to breed plants that provide uniform results. Natives have a reputation for being unpredictable. Some are and some are not, but this reputation is a major factor preventing more frequent use of natives. It provides part of the impetus to the search for garden selections of native plants that will behave reliably in different situations.

I have a friend, a sculptor, who said she both admired and felt sorry for landscape designers. "It's like making sculpture, only with unpredictable elements that change through time." Although appreciative of her compassion, I feel, however, that the gardener's dynamic relationship with soil, insects, sun, and rain is to be rejoiced in, rather than regretted.

Seedlings may appear of their own accord. We look for signs of reproduction as an indication that processes have been set back in motion that may previously have been interrupted. Combinations of plants not hitherto thought of may then occur. To take advantage of this aspect of natural gardening, plant in sections, using a plant grouping that, if it thrives, can be repeated, with variations, throughout the garden. The back-yard gardener has the advantage of being able to take time, gathering information as it comes in, without meeting imposed schedules. Information from the first planting can be used in succeeding plantings, as may seedlings that have been generated by the first planting. When plants move around, we formulate questions. Why did you prefer it here to there? Pet theories are enjoyed and lightly held.

LUPINUS PROPINQUUS IN THE GARDEN   *One species that distinguishes the particular series of coastal scrub plants in my area is* Lupinus propinquus, *purple bush lupine. Leaves of a fine blue gray and showy, often fragrant flowers make this plant attractive, although short-lived, in the garden. I have seen stunningly beautiful stands of* Lupinus propinquus, *with flowers varying from pale purple to pink to white to deep blue to dark purple. Sometimes the fragrance knocks you out; sometimes it is absent. It appears in disturbed areas, where it looks great for two to four years, then may succumb to root maggots. Often nearby seedlings will replace the defunct parent, hardly missing a beat.*

I wanted to include this plant in my garden but wasn't sure how, as its unpredictability could create large gaps in the garden. I decided to make a bed where this lupine could freely grow, reseed, and decline, where it was not required as a long-term structural element. Treated as a long-lived (and very tall) annual, we can enjoy the surprising colors and youthful vigor of this species.

Quail eat the seeds, which are often laden with seed weevils, also bird food. Purple bush lupine is worth growing in the garden, once its temporal nature is accepted, as a kind of "quadrennial shrub."

At our open houses, I describe plantings that have not worked, and tell what was learned. I describe changes that took place without my consent but have formed the basis for future garden plans, as well as tentative conclusions about this place. Sometimes I am surprised at how many times I hear myself saying that something appeared somewhere, rather than that I intended it to be there. "People might think I have no garden ideas of my own," I worry. But I sense that there is a place where the seam between my ideas and the ideas of the land gets blurry, a place where I choose to spend my gardening time.

With its tools, herbicides, and air-brushed photographs of perfect gardens, the mainstream thrust of gardening suggests the desirability of total control. I read that a famous garden is being restored to the design of a well-known landscape architect of the early part of the century. The stated goal is strict adherence to this famous person's design. No random seedings will be allowed. This resolute stance implies that our ideas are better than nature's ideas. To maintain the sense that it is acceptable to be responsive to input from the land, it is helpful to be in conversation with others working in a similar way.

INCLUDE A RANGE OF PLANT-CARE STRATEGIES

One way that the restoration garden is distinguishable from the wild is by the amount of attention individual plants receive. Tricky-to-grow plants may do best closest to the back door, where the attention of the gardener rests on them regularly. A range of "attended-to-ness" can begin with those closest to the house, which are groomed, dead-headed, pruned, mulched, and weeded. Plants at the further reaches may be left more to their own devices. The hazel by the house is pruned to emphasize its horizontal branching structure; long vertical suckers sprouting from the base are removed and handed over to a basket maker. The hazels in the hedge are allowed to sucker and spread.

A continuum of regimens and maintenance strategies, from close attention to benign neglect, will allow the busy gardener to avoid the undesirable state of "overwhelmedness." This state would deny the condition of pleasurable acceptance of natural occurrences desirable for the garden based on natural relationships. Where a more "gardened" look is desired, many native plants can thrive with garden conditions of watering and pruning. Remember that all newly transplanted plants need care till they are established. Many gardening failures with natives have resulted from the notion that native plants, because they grow in nature, can be planted out and ignored.

The area surrounding my house has developed into what I think of as a native plant cottage garden. Some effort is expended on achieving that well-known horticultural goal of "continuous bloom." Plants here are more closely attended to than in the further reaches of the garden. A fence creates a private enclave here, the gray-water system spreads water throughout, and flowery species like Douglas iris, tansy-leaf phacelia, hummingbird sage, the white form of the California poppy, coast plantain, tufted poppy, Bolander's phacelia, columbine, coast wallflower, grindelia, and miner's lettuce run rampant. I have been surprised by their vigorous reseeding. This part of the garden demonstrates an intense floriferousness useful for impressing those who look only for bloom. Photographers tend to congregate here.

Surprising combinations appear, for which I am happy to take unjustified credit. In early spring, dark purple Douglas irises bloom, along with deep lemon yellow coastal poppies. After two months of splendid bloom, when the dark purple irises are forming fat green seed capsules, the pale lilac form of the Douglas iris begins its flowering time. Concurrently, deep yellow poppies form long narrow seed capsules just as the cream-colored form we call "Moonglow" makes its welcome appearance. I had no idea that these iris forms were on a different blooming schedule, and maybe next year they won't be.

I make one of those gardening decisions that call for a consistency of which I may not be capable. Early in the spring, I decree, intense colors will break the gloom of the rains; deep yellows, of meadow foam, goldfields, creek monkeyflowers, and coastal poppies, will stunningly contrast with the dark blues of desert bluebells and blue bedder penstemon, rich reds from paintbrush, columbine, and hummingbird sage. When summer comes, pastels, pale, fairy-book colors, will soften the sun's glare.

A pink penstemon intertwines with the pale lilac of Bolander's phacelia by a large ceramic water jar. Orange and yellow columbines are set off by the dark gray fence. Where a tree fell last year, bare soil is filling in with seedlings of yellow-eyed grass, always an opportunist in my garden. Red fescue, luxuriant and green for months, begins slowly to fade. After it goes to seed, we'll cut it to four inches above the ground. Or maybe not. Here and there it is flattened in the shape of a lying-down dog.

In September, the reddish orange form of the California poppy we call "Mahogany Red" contrasts with the dormant fescues, mirrors the fall colors of vine maple and creek dogwood. Seed was sown in four-inch pots in February; plants were put in the ground in August and bloomed to the end of October.

No plant community has been particularly thought of here, and forbs from moist creek and semi-arid grassland and oak savannah demonstrate their adaptability by thriving together. Blue bedder penstemon from dry hillsides is stunning with bleeding heart from the redwoods; I never would have thought that they would "go" together, and they certainly are from different ecosystems, but this particular year, with consistent and extended amounts of rain, the fluidity of plant requirements is amply demonstrated.

As late as August, I shall continue planting annuals and perennials from four-inch pots. There is a chaotic, flowery, surprising aspect to this part of the garden, a jumble from which patterns can be discerned, information gained, interesting surprises enjoyed.

An arching trellis separates this part of the garden from the wilder part. This trellis is planted with a French rose and a native clematis. Once I saw ten quail perched on the top of the arch, and another morning, an antlered buck paused under it, as though to savor its philosophical implications.

INCORPORATE NATIVE PLANTS THAT ALREADY EXIST ON THE SITE

Coyote bush was almost the only native species to be found on our Scotch broom–infested field. I have learned the garden utility of coyote bush, its versatility, quirkiness, and unpredictability. One elegant specimen, pruned and mulched, is such a perfect rounded mound that many visitors don't recognize it. Other coyote bushes, responding to factors both known and unknown, are uneven in shape, idiosyncratic, as various as oaks. I enjoy working with coyote bush. As I prune, weed, and mulch around it, I ponder its ways.

RESPECT PLANTS AS A CONNECTION
TO THE EARLIER INHABITANTS OF THE LAND

Once the French broom had been removed from our garden, a plant called soaproot, *Chlorogalum pomeridianum,* showed itself. Mounds of large, straplike leaves with wavy edges and spidery white, moth-pollinated flowers that open toward the end of the day in airy sprays, this species is found in many parts of California, in many types of soil. Here they are so large and old that possibly they were present when the Coast Miwok paused here for lunch.

For the Miwok, soaproot served several purposes. The bulbs were roasted for food, boiled for glue to make baskets watertight and for other uses, and thrown into dammed-up creeks to stupefy fish. Neat brown brushes for whisking acorn meal out of grinding rocks are still made from the fibers surrounding the bulb, the brush handles glued together with glue from the bulb itself.

This plant tested our desire to let the garden have a say in designing itself. It appeared in a planting of local eriogonums, and its long straplike leaves did not "go" with the rounded felty leaves of the buckwheats. We decided to play with the design by repeating this unplanned plant combination in the border. It turned out to "work" in an entirely unanticipated fashion. By using the design technique of repetition, we were able to satisfy our gardening aesthetics as well as to preserve this reminder of an earlier human-plant relationship.

At the annual gathering of the California Indian Basketweavers Association, some kids were making traditional soaproot brushes from soaproot bulbs. One of the adults, in order not to waste the bulbs from which the fibers were gathered, offered to demonstrate how the bulbs are used as shampoo. We gathered around to watch as he brought up a lather in a bowl of water, then rubbed it through his hair. Besides the unusual experience of watching somebody wash their hair at a conference, this act contained a sense of an old relationship being maintained, and the respect that avoidance of waste implies.

MAKE A KINDER, GENTLER FENCE

In my town, the vistas were once unimpeded, and everyone could see the ocean from their house. Now redwood plank fences dot this marine terrace like mini-stockades. The dullness of the view and the thought of the redwood forests such fences devour make walking down a country lane flanked by solid wooden walls a grim experience.

See-through fencing, including various kinds of wire stock fencing, helps to maintain the visual connection to the larger garden beyond the fence. It is cheaper than wooden fences and easier on the environment. Fences with spaces between the boards use less wood and are both more visually appealing than solid fences and more resistant to wind damage. Wind encountering a solid barrier is forced up and then over it. Wind filtering through an airy fence or multi-layered hedge is diffused.

Our property is a medley of fences, some part of the original property, solid redwood fences and old-fashioned pickets, and some recreated with components of original fencing mixed with wire and other materials. One stormy year, a Monterey cypress came crashing down on a section of old fence. A local tree surgeon with a small mill took the tree away and brought it back in beautiful planks, for yet another kind of fence.

One section of fence was designed by a carpenter who also does beadwork. The combination of wire fencing strongly reinforced top and bottom by recycled redwood boards, sections of old fence moved from old boundary lines, and eucalyptus poles is strung like a beautiful necklace along the property line. It is varied and pleasing, a part of the play between randomness and order.

Somewhere between "Good fences make good neighbors" and "Something there is that doesn't love a wall" exists a kind of fence that reflects a desire to be part of the larger picture, with flexible and friendly boundaries. I want to see my neighbors, but not too much and not all the time. I want privacy but a friendly wind blowing through, a barrier that is permeable to quail, seeds of California oatgrass from the field across the street, and my sense of connection to my neighborhood.

STUDY THE NATURAL LANDSCAPE

When garden problems reach a dead end, ideas can come through personal exploration and reading. A red elderberry in a coastal garden became huge, thriving beyond what we had expected. Nothing seemed to do well near it. Reading that elderberry and sword fern hold the nests of Swainson's thrushes and Wilson's warblers near coastal creeks, we decided to use sword fern as the nearby underplanting, hoping to draw these lovely singers. On a hike, I saw that creek dogwood, a deciduous shrub comely at all times of the year, but particularly in the fall when its leaves turn shades of purple and orange, was thriving near elderberry. We planted that too.

PLAYING FAVORITES: DESIGN FOR THE WHOLE PICTURE

In an otherwise excellent book about butterfly gardening, one author advises against planting berry-bearing shrubs or trees. Such plantings will attract birds, he says, which might prey upon the caterpillars that turn into butterflies. Since his focus is on butterflies, he wants to enhance the environment for butterflies only, advising readers, "Avoid cultivating plants which have fruits or seeds that birds eat and which do not attract butterflies."

Once I watched an enraptured mammalogist rush toward a badger hole, crushing a lone specimen of a rare *Dichelostemma* at which I was gazing. I know butterfly fanciers who welcome the devastating advance of certain invasive non-native plants because a favored butterfly may be able to use this plant. Favoring a particular species over others seems to be a human propensity.

I have a new neighbor next door. At the edge of her property is an extremely tall Monterey pine. Not long after she bought the place, we noticed a blue milk bottle crate high up in the tree. We gazed at it in wonderment, speculating as to how and why it was there. Turned out my neighbor had placed it there, hoping to attract owls.

Some of us "old-timers" laughed at this hopeful act. Owl requirements are more complicated than a box in a tree, and there didn't seem to be any owls in this coastal scrub habitat. But I was slightly worried. If it worked, which wasn't likely, how would it affect my beloved back-yard quail? Moving to a new neighborhood and introducing a predator right away seemed a thoughtless idea. For a number of reasons, I garden for quail: historical (they used to be here in flocks of thousands), aesthetic (is there a prettier bird than the California quail?), and emotional (such sweet, home-loving creatures). Counting back-yard quail is a way I have of reassuring myself, like counting rosary beads, that things are still somewhat okay.

It is hard for humans to avoid playing favorites. The vole specialist must have some innate fondness for the vole, the lily fancier for the lily. On the positive side, our natural tendency to divide and specialize, from which much knowledge has been gained, is a form of love. It may be that tribal divisions into clans, each of which had its own totem, was an example of this human proclivity for alliance.

Specialists studying family dynamics advise noninterference in most sibling quarrels. By planting in such a way as to replicate natural plant associations you can, like a good parent, avoid playing favorites. Provide habitat for basic needs, and let the kids fight it out.

WHAT BIRDS REALLY WANT

Much has been written about gardening to attract birds or butterflies. In seeking to draw birds to the garden, note that, in general, birds (unlike butterflies and some insects) require a certain habitat structure rather than a particular plant. Habitat structure supplies shelter, roosting, nesting, and food-finding opportunities. Some birds want open plains, some prefer deep woods, some want access to both. Some require proximity to a number of different plant communities, one for each life function. Some stay close to home all their lives; others travel great distances. What birds visit your garden depends on many factors, only some of which are under your control.

The Point Reyes Bird Observatory studies birds of the coastal scrub. I learn from them what birds I might expect with my plantings of coastal scrub plants. Since that particular plant association is being removed or overcome by non-native species in my neighborhood, my decision to use this plant community as a backbone for my garden includes the hope that wrentits, bushtits, and white-crowned sparrows, all denizens of the coastal scrub, will find what they need in my garden.

Birds need to eat all the time. Although $80 million or so is spent annually on bird feeders and birdseed in the United States, some experts recommend instead the careful planting of the right native plants to feed birds throughout the year. For instance, nesting birds, even ones that are usually seed-eaters, require the extra protein provided by insects. Spring flowers draw those insects. Long-flowering native plants, like the California buckeye with its two to three months of bloom, come at just the right time for the spring-nesting local and migratory birds. As usual, timing is critical.

Bird feeders and birdseed are big business, providing pleasure for many, and yet there are questions about their role in the health of our bird populations. Ray Peterson recommends being an inconsistent feeder, so that bird populations do not become totally dependent on being artificially fed. Others recommend consistency, so that birds can count on the food you provide. This controversy provides another opportunity to recognize uncertainty and honor complexity.

The composition of seed mixes sold as bird feed is one problem described by non-feeders. Birdseed that includes millet attracts the notorious cowbird, a dangerous pest in the West. The cowbird lays its eggs in the nests of other species, which find themselves raising aggressive nestlings that outcompete their own offspring. Some birdseed mixes include weedy species that can compound the California gardener's weeding tasks, although sterile seed is also often sold. The back-yard restoration garden, if large enough, might ideally include enough food-producing plants to make birdseed unnecessary. And foster the butterflies. As Barbara Deutsch, a Bay Area butterfly savant, says, "Without caterpillars, birds can neither form eggshells nor feed their young."

LEARN TO LOVE WHERE YOU LIVE

A visitor described my garden setting as "having no natural features." It is flat, there are no rocks, no ocean view, no valley view. Although less dramatic than steep or sloping land, and not my inborn concept of the most beautiful gardening situation, I have become increasingly appreciative of something very "comfortable" about gardens on flat land, where so many of our houses are built.

It's always a good idea to check out the preferences of the original inhabitants of a place. Many tribes chose village sites on flat land. With no erosion concerns, we can plant with impunity whenever we feel like it. And the soil is good. With no rocks, the digging is easy. Kids can learn to walk here; elders perambulate without the difficulties added by dramatic slopes.

I value the easy flow from prairie to perennial border to woodland, from volleyball court to woodpile to our plot of oak-shaded Indian lettuce. I have come to think of it as an encampment, where many activities, from badminton to campfires to food growing, can be encompassed.

DESIGN TIP *While washing the dishes, I see quail fighting from my kitchen window. For some weeks, they seemed to be tranquilly double-dating; now the males are taking each other on. I can look this behavior up in A. Starker Leopold's book* The California Quail, *or I can try to figure it out myself while I wash the dishes. Or I can take a field trip with an ornithologist and hear what an expert has to say.*

The kitchen window can be an important design component in the back-yard restoration garden. When possible, I recommend that clients carefully plan the view from this vantage point. It provides a regular observation post, where the mind, not otherwise occupied, can play the game of drawing conclusions about nature, as it carries on in the garden.

The back-yard restoration garden should be a comfortable place, providing many opportunities to be on the ground. Decks and patios, ways of staying off the ground, are minimized. We are interested in all ways to interact with our garden that bring us out into it. Hiding places, hammocks, shady places for hot days, places to soak up the sun on mild winter days, places for games, places for seed cleaning, even a small, body-sized section of perfect lawn, might all be accommodated by the back-yard restoration garden.

And places for sitting around the fire. A client wanted a fire pit to be the center of her garden, so we designed a circular garden with the pit at the center. Native grasses were planted around the pit, then a ring of coastal scrub plants, then at the perimeters a mix of willows, hazels, elderberries, and oaks, for privacy and enclosure. If you came upon such a place in the wild, you might think you'd died and gone to heaven, restored to an earlier California paradise.

LEARNING TO LOVE BROWN

Bart O'Brien of Rancho Santa Ana Botanic Garden says that the most important reason native plants are not accepted by the general public is the summer dormancy that many (although not all) require. The glowing green of spring, with its bright blossoms, is considered to be the desired state for a garden at all times.

There comes a time in the landscape of California, even along the coast, when nothing much is growing. Summer dormancy, in those plants that employ this drought-evading tactic, holds sway in the native garden. Wildflowers have gone to seed, grasses are semi-dormant, and some perennials have died down to their roots.

Slanting shadows of late summer and autumn afternoons, golden grasses, ripening acorns. A meditative, not lively, time. Newly arrived from the East Coast, I used to be impatient for the quickening of the rains. By November, I might have had enough sunny days in the sometimes worrisome "waiting for rain" times. Depending on the year, this time might last into January. I often found myself apologizing to visitors for the unspectacular state of my garden.

A century ago, Clarence King called summer dormancy "a fascinating repose . . . wealthy in yellows and russets and browns." I measure my true life as a Californian from the time that I stopped apologizing for a garden exquisite in its light and shadow, its still endurance. Reveling in shades of gold, blonde, palomino, gray, and muted greens, it seldom occurs to me to do so now.

A deepening into the season was required, a renewed acceptance of the solemn stillness of golden days, when grasses, perennials, and wildflowers have gone to seed, and shrub and tree seeds are still not ripe. I slide at this time into a kind of suspension, held in that same sensation of stored quiescent power I used to get in a wintry woods back east and I now get from handling seeds. One may fall so entirely into this state of somnolent stillness that the onset of rain brings a sense of disruption rather than of relief. For just a moment, though, before the rains sweep it all away. Pounding or light, cold or warm, the sweet rains of California. How could anybody say there are no seasons here?

Listening to rain — the winter hobby of Californians.

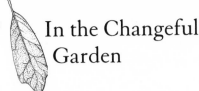 # In the Changeful Garden

Does anything ever stay the same? Seen from the perspective of geologic time, we do indeed live on a restless earth. Land masses shift, plants and animals evolve and migrate, and climates undergo enormous variation.   *Michael Barbour, Bruce Pavlik, Frank Drysdale, and Susan Lindstrom, 1993*

The next time you howl in delight like a wolf, howl for unstable aperiodic behavior in deterministic non-linear dynamical systems.   *Jack Turner, 1996*

Over the years, I have turned from frustration at garden events that thwart my plans to some degree of acceptance and a greater degree of interest. With increasing insouciance, I watch the garden take its own direction. The back-yard restoration gardener learns the benefits of accepting gardening as an evolving situation, appreciative of each opportunity to factor in more complexity. In the privacy of your back yard, it has less to do with success or failure, more to do with lessons to be learned from the uncertainty that accompanies a growing garden.

In my garden on the north central coast, we occupy the shifting interface between northern and southern coastal plant communities. A wet year favors the plants of the north coast forests, including ferns, Pacific wax myrtles, Pacific reed grass, flowering currants, California hazels, redwoods, and red elderberries. A dry year favors plants of the coastal scrub and grassland communities.

Coyote bush, monkeyflower, lizardtail, and California sagebrush are the main coastal scrub plants in our area. For ten years, repeated groupings of these species have been the visual and philosophical heart of my garden. It is the place where quail hide and huge spider webs are newly hung each summer morning. Many people at our open houses pause with me to sniff the fragrance of the silvery gray foliage of *Artemisia californica,* California sagebrush.

One year, severe storms battered the coast. Parts of the garden were flooded for months, and California sagebrush, an essential silver element, rotted and died. This event caused me to note that California sagebrush in our area is usually found on slopes and banks. In drought years, it was able to thrive in my flat garden, but that year of almost constant rain into early summer exceeded the tolerance of its roots for continual moisture. Until garden events brought it to my attention, I had not made this obvious observation about sagebrush. The extremes of temperature, moisture, and exposure ultimately determine what grows in a given spot.

A Plant Is Not a Couch

I am aware of the anxiety some beginning gardeners feel and the personal responsibility they take for plant losses. They understandably seek to know why the plant died, so that they can avoid this failure in the future. More experienced gardeners develop a sense of how difficult it is to make inferences about gardening events. Sometimes we "know" why something died, and sometimes we don't. We can make good guesses, or, at the other extreme, we can send samples of dead plants for laboratory analysis, an expensive procedure for the home gardener and one that may still not yield conclusive information.

In the realm of living things, a multitude of factors determine events; where plants are concerned, soil problems, moisture problems, disease problems, temperature problems, weed problems, and different combinations of the above are involved.

Using local native plants, the gardener can always return to the natural model, to compare situations with the home garden. The land surrounding a house has often gone through changes not apparent to the present occupant. The native soil may have been buried under fill or carted far away. Plants provide clues to the status of the soil. Colonizer plants, like lupines and red maids, will change the soil, making conditions favorable for longer-lived tree and shrub species. Plants like coyote bush, adaptable to many soil conditions, make good nurse plants for small oaks and native grasses.

"A plant is not a couch" has been our motto for some years, somewhat cryptically calling attention to the element of uncertainty that is always part of dealing with living things. We hope to encourage our gardening customers to relax, take chances, be of good heart, take the losses lightly, and enjoy themselves.

This motto was inspired by my daughter's riding instructor. During her lesson, one of the pupils was nervous. "What if my horse bucks?" she asked the instructor.

"We can't be sure he won't," she replied. "A horse is not a car. We just hope for the best."

And a plant is not a couch. Plants are not furniture. Working with living things is much better than that.

Perturbation

"Perturbation" — disruption by fire, flood, wind, and earthquake — renews landscapes, creating opportunities for different species to flourish. When bare soil occurs as a result of some form of perturbation, it is always interesting to see the changes that follow. Species that appear first in bare soil are called "colonizers." They are often nitrogen-fixing, sun-loving, and short-lived, including annuals like red maids and sky lupine, biennials like coast plantain and coast wallflower, and shrubs like blue-flowering lupine. One advantage of creating perturbation in the garden is that new food webs will appear. They may be temporary, as other plants take the place of the colonizers, which have created situations more conducive to the growth of the longer-lived plants. The temporary and the short-lived merit a place in the garden too.

Fire, a major agent of perturbation in California, may be a useful tool for landowners with significant acreage. In more urban areas, the gardener can be the agent of change, substituting pruning techniques (see the section on pruning in chapter 10) for natural occurrences. Severe pruning — six inches to a foot above the ground — can function as a "fire-equivalent," creating vigorous new growth in crown-sprouting shrubs like elderberry, California sagebrush, coyote bush, some ceanothus, toyon, holly-leaf cherry, and some manzanitas. Flooding may bring new life to thicket-formers like willows, twinberry, alders, and creek dogwood, and pruning can simulate that form of perturbation too.

In larger gardens, the homeowner may want to borrow a concept from chaparral management techniques, wherein different portions experience perturbation at different times, so that a mix of different-aged stands exists at the same time. Opportunities for different populations of mammalian, insect, and avian species will be created.

Pruning regimes can reflect this goal. Species that follow disturbance can be given their opportunity in the garden by use of a sequential pruning schedule. Prune a section of the chaparral garden one year, let it regrow, and prune a different section the next year. Perturbation, creator of diverse habitat opportunities, becomes a valuable technique in your gardening repertoire.

"I have this bank behind my house": Erosion Control

One kind of change with a bad reputation is the kind called "erosion," the downward movement of soil on slopes. The Soil Conservation Service, formed as a response to the Dust Bowl (and now called the Natural Resources Conservation Service), has done an admirable job of alerting the public to the loss of topsoil through soil disturbance of various kinds. When homeowners see a bare bank created by road or house building, alarm bells go off. An irresistible desire to scatter seed of or plant fast-growing species is unleashed. In the name of erosion control, we have loosed on our wildlands many destructive plants, including iceplant, capeweed, European beach grass, all kinds of ivy, and the perennial and annual Italian rye grasses.

Erosion control is a complicated topic, but entrenched in the homeowner's and builder's mind is the notion that generic solutions are possible. There are different kinds of erosion, some natural and inevitable, some created by disturbance, either direct or indirect. Erosion isn't just erosion. There are surface erosion, soil splash, and the deep movement of large soil masses that cannot be controlled by any planting. Some naturally occurring erosion gives a whole different set of plants an opportunity to grow. Every situation is different, requiring different treatment.

When building is done, soil is laid bare, and rain is expected, we get many anxious calls from homeowners hoping to seed fast-growing species to hold their banks. Seeds, no matter how fast-growing, cannot hold soil; it is the roots of established fibrous-rooted perennial plants that hold soil. If possible, plant six months before the winter rains, so that tops and roots will be in place, able to protect the soil, when the rains come.

When that is not possible, my favored strategy involves the use of jute netting, of which there are several kinds. Easily stapled into the hillside, this material takes the panic out of planting, biodegrades after two years, and can be planted into or seeded under. I prefer to put grass plugs into the holes in the weave of the jute netting and mulch over the netting and around the plants. Netting allows the homeowner to use slower-growing plants that will often do a better job of controlling banks. Such plants include native grasses, like California fescue, dwarf coyote bush, beach aster by the coast, sword ferns in shady areas, salvias in the south counties.

The California Native Plant Society recommends that seeding of annual and perennial Italian rye grasses, two grasses widely used in erosion control, be avoided. Research has shown that allelopathic substances secreted by their roots will impede the establishment of native plants. These species do not have the deep fibrous roots that will tie soil layers together. Although the quick cover they provide may give the illusion of erosion control, it is just that, an illusion.

Look around you. See how nature holds the hills where you live. Chaparral holds hillsides, forests hold hillsides, bunchgrasses hold hillsides. Erosion control doesn't need to mean the introduction of invasive exotic species but can be an opportunity to learn more about the place in which you garden.

If I owned a house right on a cliff edge overlooking the Pacific Ocean, I would look to nearby intact sea-bluff plant associations for my erosion control palette. I would be careful about watering, as saturated soil can slide. I would be aware of the implications of having a septic system and a driveway in this unstable situation. Enjoying my daily view, I would hope to be philosophical about the perhaps limited duration of my tenancy on the always crumbling, eroding California shoreline.

Gardeners as Students of Process

Every ecosystem has its own lessons to teach. The native grasses taught me the power of weeds; coastal scrub helped me see beauty in the humble; mixed evergreen forests taught me to relish the sight, smell, and feel of leaf litter; and the redwood forests taught me connections. Some of the best descriptions of the latter that I have found are written by Chris Maser, a former Forest Service employee. In *The Redesigned Forest,* Maser describes the nutrient cycles of old-growth Douglas fir forest, reaching conclusions that are exquisitely relevant for those seeking to restore and conserve natural systems, in national forests or back yards.

Maser's account of the fecal pellets of northern flying squirrels is practically a poem. Living in the treetops, coming down to dig and eat fungi, which they excrete as "pills of symbiosis" that cycle nutrients throughout the forest, the northern flying squirrels require old growth, as old growth requires them.

Maser recommends that we be "students of processes, rather than advocates of positions." Comparing a human life span (70 to 80 years) to the life span of a Douglas fir (500 to 800 years), he illuminates the difficulties we humans have in comprehending natural events so beyond the scale of our lives. Analyzing how our forests have come to be managed as they are, he reveals how our minds work.

Redwoods and the Law

I went with some friends to the federal courthouse in San Francisco to witness hearings on the logging of old-growth forest in Humboldt County, California. The judge was friendly, concerned, hopeful about ferreting out the legal basis for saving old growth. She admitted to being overwhelmed by the amount of information presented. Although she did not live with or study redwoods, it was her task in this case to decide their fate.

Having redwoods in your back yard does not guarantee a deeper understanding of forest ecology, but it can help. In this case, a logging plan that involved removing only diseased, dead, and dying trees was presented as harmless by the timber company, disregarding the ecological finding that dead and dying trees are essential to the healthy and diverse functioning of old-growth forests of any kind.

Chris Maser eloquently separates out the four structural components of old growth. They make a lovely litany: standing large living trees; standing large dead trees, or snags; downed dead trees on land; and downed dead trees in water.

Trees in all of the above conditions form the center of a complicated swirl of interactions, involving soil fungi, forest rodents, vegetation architecture, and water patterns. Forests in Germany kept "clean" for years — that is, free of decaying plant matter — have been observed to decline drastically in health. So new are we at this great endeavor of trying to understand the connections that only in the past thirty years has the importance of dead and dying trees in forest ecology been understood,

In the context of this logging plan, it is necessary to define "dying" trees. Some trees take four hundred years to die. Dying is a major part of their life span, an important, lengthy, and productive process. Once they are dead, they are still part of the forest ecology for another six hundred years: beetles and bacteria process them, and a succession of plant species make nurseries of them. The logging plan contested in this court case ignored these ecological realities. In this case, the legal language does not recognize reality, as it is diversely and dynamically manifested in old-growth forest in process. The hours we spent in that courtroom were about the complexity of our legal system, not about the complexity of our natural world, the redwoods and all that swirls about them with the fog. Seeing how the judge and the lawyers struggled with ecological concepts, it behooves us to educate ourselves.

Thoughts of succession, the tendency of plant communities to change over time, can become an element of your gardening life. When oak seedlings appear in the coyote bush, one is free to hypothesize that the land is on its way to becoming an oak woodland. When all the grasses die except for Pacific reed grass, an inhabitant of wet places, one may speculate that recent wet years are shifting the area back toward wetlands. The gardener has some advantages over professional ecologists. "Ecologists do not wish to work in managed systems where the results of their research are site-specific and may not readily lead to new ecological theories," James Luken says. Moreover, the gardener does not have to develop new ecological theories. She already has tenure. And she is always "on site."

Measuring Change

Transects and quadrats are two methods used to quantify changes in plant composition. *Transects,* sampling strips extending across stands of vegetation, are areas of study marked off by ecologists seeking to quantify information about plants. Within a transect, plant counts and measurements are taken. Over time, measurements will be retaken and interpretations made of the data. Changes will be noted in such categories as percentages of native and non-native plants and the health, size, and vigor of plants over time. Often used to correlate differences in vegetation with other factors, such as changes in moisture or soil types, a transect can give the gardener a way to chart change.

A *quadrat* is a sample plot of vegetation, often a rectangle delineated by boards or string. It can be used in a variety of ways. The number of individuals of each species may be listed. Weights and basal areas (used for bunchgrasses) may be computed. Quadrats can be used by the back-yard restorationist to verify the results of different ways of sowing wildflowers or different mowing regimes in the bunchgrass prairie. Going beyond anecdotal observation, sampling methods still rely on the point of view of the observer in deciding what should be sampled, and how.

Sometimes, to encourage myself, I take a mental transect from one point to another. In this way I can be gratified by the reseeding of native plantains and the movement of native grasses. A transect taken in spring will show many young coast plantain seedlings; a transect taken in summer will show that where moisture was less available, they have died out or declined in number or biomass. The extent of this diminution can indicate the range of tolerance for different degrees of moisture in the soil of this particular species. Delving into sampling techniques reveals the multitudinous factors that interact in the garden.

Planting California's Beaches

Along the California coast, dunes shift and blow, forming and reforming with the winds and tides. Returning to a particular beach regularly, you may be confused; things look so different.

On beaches sparsely vegetated with beach bluegrass, *Poa douglasii,* and the California beach grass, *Leymus mollis,* two graceful native bunchgrasses, spaces between plants remain. Creatures like the snowy plover, which likes to lay its eggs on bare ground, and plants like the beautiful and fragrant *Lupinus chamissonis,* adapted to partially stabilized sand dunes, have opportunity to flourish.

Historically, various government agencies thought it would be a good idea to stabilize these dunes, to eliminate that shifting. Perhaps they saw it as a form of erosion needing correction. To solve this "problem," they brought in plants like the European beach grass, *Ammophila arenaria,* and iceplant, *Carpobotrus edulis.*

They may have regarded their actions as successful, because these species took hold. Dense masses of vegetation eliminated the impermanent nature of the dunes, which used to form right angles to the shoreline, allowing wind to blow freely through them. Dunes stabilized by European beach grass parallel the beach, blocking winds. Pieces of these plants wash into the ocean, drifting far from the original site. Where they land, they root from their vigorous rhizomes. Everywhere they root, they change the ecology of the dunes. Stillness settles where movement once prevailed.

In Monterey County, Smith's blue butterfly lives its whole life in the habitat provided by two buckwheats, the coast buckwheat and the dune buckwheat. Without the buckwheat flowers, there are no Smith's blues. The introduction and inadvertent spread of European beach grass and iceplant have eliminated the wind-blown shifting sands that created the bare areas in the dunes suitable for the growth and establishment of new buck-wheat plants. Seen in terms of dune buckwheats and Smith's blue butterfly, bare soil and instability are not undesirable.

In California, movement is the theme. Our cliffs erode and crumble into the sea, then rise back up again as marine terraces. Rivers and creeks change course, deepening here and widening there. Giants crash in red-wood forests, their dead bodies making fecund nurseries for the mycor-rhizal fungi and bacteria essential for plant growth. Tanoak, called the beautiful tree by the Pomo, moves into the clearings left by their demise. Sun-loving plants thrive for a time, then are shaded out.

Chaparral plants burn and resprout, making way more or less tem-porarily for grasslands, with their associated forbs. Flood or fire or earth-quake mixes it all up. Dynamic processes operate, not toward a fixed "cli-max" vegetation, but toward a rising and falling, a flourishing and decay. Edges shift. Change prevails. We learn the inherent dynamism of natural processes. It may be so in your garden too.

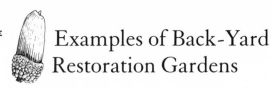 # Examples of Back-Yard Restoration Gardens

What gorgeous opportunity California has to work out a unique style of landscape gardening based upon her native trees, shrubs, vines and flowers. It is one of the richest spots on the earth's surface in variety of plants worth cultivating for their beauty. . . . Surely the most cultivated people of California must realize that there is something more refined than miles of scarlet geraniums, acres of callas and millions of crotons and cannas . . . which make California seem an imitation of other lands.   *Wilhelm Miller, 1913*

The real California garden will be born of California's sun-bathed earth; [the designer] will be free from the weight of traditions — Italian, French, English, or Japanese — so that his design will not be a patchwork quilt, but will grow out of an imagination that has been fired by the roll of our little hills, the weight of our mountains, the great spaces of our valleys and always the glorious sunshine, so that his design will never suggest a comparison.   *Alfred D. Robinson, 1913*

Thumbnail sketches of several California back-yard restoration gardens show how these gardens have been or could be realized by gardeners in different regions of California, each one deepened by slow work, additions and deletions, and response to the accumulation of information through time.

A Foothill Garden in the Bay Area

From the entrance, this garden rises gently. It is given order by beds defined by railroad ties. The beds are reminiscent of groves of oak trees, each dominated by a grouping of the large shrubs and small trees, such as holly-leaved cherry, *Prunus illicifolia*, that take the place of oak trees in this small garden. The mini-groves are underplanted with some of the drought-tolerant ferns, such as sword fern, *Polystichum munitum*.

At the top of the garden is a semicircular planting of coffeeberry, *Rhamnus californica*, grown as a small, sculptured tree, with other chaparral species like manzanita, wild lilac, mountain mahogany, and toyon. These shrubs are massed together, and through the spring, beginning with the pale pink bell-like flowers of the manzanita, something is always blooming.

Beyond this area can be glimpsed a small circular wildflower planting, backed by native grasses like foothill stipa and blue fescue. Brodiaeas and blue-eyed grass are in bloom now in the spaces between the grasses. Yarrow and mule's ear will follow them. A small creek, dry in the summer, runs through the property. Willows have been planted, as well as creambush, whose creamy, drooping panicles, sweetly fragrant, are in bloom. Indian lettuce has already gone to seed.

In midsummer this garden has a restful quality arising from the restrained, elegant nature of these plants of the semi-arid foothills. There are gray greens and olives, as well as deep shiny green foliage, and there are no invasive exotic plants, such as ivy or vinca. Chaparral odors are in evidence, from the pungent pitcher sage. It is a quiet garden, at home in the foothills that surround it and that it reflects. Colors come and go through the seasons; the browns, beiges, and golds of dormant plants are acknowledged as colors in their own right, given design status by the way they are used.

A Santa Clara Valley Redwood Grove

Fingers of fog drift down from the Santa Cruz Mountains, and although rainfall here on the east side of the mountains is less than half what would be expected in a redwood grove on the ocean side of the mountains, coast redwood, *Sequoia sempervirens,* was found occurring naturally in this suburban neighborhood. Many of these trees were removed when the street was widened, and others were outcompeted by the deodar cedars planted by homeowners. One front-yard redwood grove remains. It cools a snug little adobe house.

Most of the small houses on the once-peaceful street have well-groomed little front yards demanding constant maintenance in the form of pruning of exuberant shrubs and trees planted too closely, lawn mowing, watering, fertilizing, and the twice-yearly insertion of the standardized blasts of harsh color provided by local nurseries in six-packs. Our homeowner, however, has taken advantage of the redwoods in her front yard to transform a busy urban street into an environment of shade and filtered light. Some redwoods from the original grove were already growing there; others were planted. When too-large trees are removed, stump sprouts are allowed to grow. This house is many degrees cooler in summer than those surrounding it. In winter, the fireplace is well stocked with seasoned redwood logs. The Christmas tree is a graceful branch from a redwood tree.

The shade and moisture-gathering properties of the redwood make a congenial environment for some of the native ground covers, such as wild ginger, *Asarum caudatum*, redwood sorrel, *Vancouveria planipetala,* and redwood violet, *Viola sempervirens*. Redwood litter provides a natural mulch, and there is little weeding or watering to do. Even the slightest summer breeze stirs the leaves of the redwood tree, and harsh light reflecting off the city street is deflected from the living-room windows. A homeowner across the street has planted redwoods in his yard. Maybe the grove returns.

When I return ten years later to look at this little house, however, I find that subsequent owners have removed all the redwood trees. There is now no evidence remaining that, on this side of the Santa Cruz Mountains, on this street, redwood trees once naturally cooled the people and animals seeking relief from the heat of the valley summer.

The Orange Tree and the Oak

On the South Bay peninsula, I walk a suburban street. Not a spare inch of space here for people to gather or kids to play. Maximizing profit is written all over this development, a product of the 1960s.

In the space of three houses, I see a pistachio tree, a liquidambar, many junipers, palm trees, three birches, a cork oak, a couple of different kinds of cypress, yuccas, orange trees, a cactus, Lombardy poplars, lemon trees, flowering plum trees, and olives. Design-wise, it's a pretty restless example of collectors' gardens. Yet they have a lively individuality.

At the fourth house on the block, I come to an abrupt stop. Can it be? A huge valley oak looms over the back yard. How did it escape the leveling that preceded these thousand or so crammed-together houses? And how has it survived the irrigated garden that surrounds it? It looks to be 250 years old or so, with no obvious signs of disease, and it is obviously treasured; the pruning cuts look professionally done. Nearby, orange and lemon trees are loaded with fruit. Leafless in late winter, the valley oak allows the sun to penetrate to the citrus when they need it.

Next to it is a box elder, its leaves turning a pale gold. Two remnants! Imagine if every third or fourth house on this street had a valley oak in the back yard, how the disconnected, jumbled feel of this neighborhood would be softened. From the head of the block, one would sense the unifying presence of oaks. Property values would soar.

I'll check for acorns next fall, just in case.

A Central Valley Grasslands Garden

Probably more changed than any other part of California, the Central Valley offers a challenge to homeowners. Using the Jepson Prairie, a parcel owned by the Nature Conservancy, as a model, one couple have attempted to recreate around their home aspects of the vast bunchgrass and wildflower plant community that so entranced John Muir in his essay "The Bee Pastures."

After a year of extensive soil preparation to deplete the supply of weed seeds in the soil, bunchgrass plugs (*Nassella pulchra* and *Poa scabrella*) were fall-planted. In nearby areas, masses of wildflower seeds were sown, with the emphasis on yellow composites like tidy-tips and goldfields, as well as cream cups, owl's clover, and California poppies.

Although initially labor-intensive, the bunchgrasses were growing strongly by the end of the first year, and the wildflowers took on their own agenda, reseeding, moving around, and changing the original design. Frequent visits to the Nature Conservancy's Jepson Prairie, the Carrizo

Plains, and Bear Valley give this couple a wellspring of ideas for their own grassland, a natural oasis of complex vegetation and associated wildlife in an area dominated by monocrop agriculture.

A Coastal Garden

This garden was inspired by the low mounding shrubs and subshrubs of the coast, with their rich foliar tapestries of grays, silvers, blue greens, olives, and emeralds. Dotted in spring and summer with the oranges, reds, blues, and golds of coastal wildflowers, this plant assemblage, from coastal scrub and dune and grassland, proved to be easy to grow, required no irrigation, and went through many enjoyable seasonal changes.

Eschewing the use of trees as defining elements, the coastal garden bares itself to the coastal wind, sun, and fog. Instead of defined beds, certain plant groupings are used and repeated, including four important members of the coastal scrub plant association: coyote bush, sticky monkeyflower, California sagebrush, and lizardtail.

Woven into this tapestry are subshrubs and perennials such as seaside daisy, sea pink, bluff lettuce, coast wallflower, blue-eyed grass, checkerbloom, beach evening primrose, California fescue, and the coastal form of the California poppy. Narrow, mulched paths, like deer trails, wind unobtrusively through the garden. Where soil or drainage is poor, coyote bush is planted to improve conditions and unify the garden visually.

Walking through the coastal scrub nearby, the gardener notices subtle changes in plant combinations and the ways that different individuals grow. Such information is continually elicited from the wild and put to use in the garden.

Living at the Wavering Edge

We have a client whose back yard runs into a swale that cuts through a mesa before deepening into a creek that empties into the ocean. The other side of the swale is one of the nicest stands of coyote bush, shrub lupine, varied lupine, checkerbloom, and blue-eyed grass we have left. Our idea was to mimic that plant grouping in the client's yard, after removing the brambles and French broom that predominated, adding a few species that might once have been there, and organizing the plantings so as to provide a place to walk and sit.

Drainage patterns on this mesa have become confused, but some think that much of the land tilted gently toward the swale until the roads cut off this flow. Unprecedented rains the year of this planting flooded out the coyote bush on the client's side of the swale, and the appearance of sedges and rushes, wetland plants not seen there before, indicated that we needed to change the concept.

This client was sensitive to the delicate beauty of the sedges and rushes, and amenable to letting them be. We came in with some "edge of wetland" plantings of willows, elderberries, and Pacific reed grass, creek monkeyflower, grindelia, and coast plantain. A surprising amount of the coyote bush that we had planted came back after its drenching, but none of the California sagebrush or lizardtail survived. Dry years may follow, and the species composition may shift again. And we'll learn more about this particular wavering edge.

A Garden in the Sierra

The lodge owner complained that the growing season was too short for satisfactory bloom periods for the petunias and other annuals planted around the cabins every spring. She began planting native flowers that grew and thrived in nearby mountain meadows, perennials that did not require yearly replanting. Within two years, they were established and bloomed throughout the tourist season.

Each cabin took on the name of the flowers planted around it, including coneflower (*Rudbeckia californica*), leopard lily (*Lilium pardalinum*), columbine (*Aquilegia eximia*), and mountain spiraea (*Spiraea densiflora*). Privacy hedges were established with native shrubs such as spicebush (*Calycanthus occidentalis*), huckleberry oak (*Quercus vaccinifolia*), serviceberry (*Amelanchier alnifolia*), and local willows.

Visitors were delighted to have a close-by opportunity to identify and enjoy the local vegetation. People knowledgeable about montane flora began to visit her establishment, relieved to see native plantings instead of the ubiquitous petunias and marigolds. This mountain resident began a whole new interaction with the land that provides her livelihood.

GREG DONOVAN AND THE MISSION OAKS PROJECT   *I spent an afternoon looking around a development called Mission Oaks in Santa Barbara County, which is entirely landscaped with California native plants. Greg Donovan has worked on this project for eight years. The houses are surrounded by coast live oak, manzanitas, basketgrass, coffeeberries, and coyote bush.*

Greg's motives include a desire to "atone for patterns we've disrupted," but his goals must also take into account the expectations of his clients. "Standards of tidiness and neatness are the bane of my life," confesses Greg. But it's working. A casual interview with two homeowners revealed pride in their unique landscape.

Greg is aware of what he calls the "tendency to revert." Those who have been deeply imprinted with an appreciation for lawns may suddenly be unable to live without them any longer. Those for whom hybrid tea roses represent home may not want to be without them. Continuing education is required. But the framework of oak trees and native grasses and shrubs is strong at Mission Oaks.

A Recreational Equipment Store in the Northwest

This innovative store features fireplaces throughout, simulated rocks for trying out equipment and techniques, and showers for testing raingear. Outside, waterfalls are surrounded by plants from the great northwestern rainforests. Although a young planting, the cedars, ferns, sedges, and huckleberries are already holding their own, moving with the wind and pleasing the eye. The "bones" of this planting in its early days seem to be snowberry, *Symphoricarpos alba*, whose round blue green leaves are always attractive and whose white berries are an eye-catching design element in the fall.

A view from the second-floor restaurant reveals a typical downtown setting in the distance, but, in the foreground, the plants, water, and rocks that the store's customers love and seek out. Across the street is a typical planting of liquidambars and junipers. When the wind blows, they hardly move.

An Oasis in the Sonoran Desert

I know a guest ranch in the desert, operated by the same family for three generations, where reservations must be made a year in advance. It is a beautiful place to be. I have even enjoyed myself there when stricken with pneumonia one ill-fated vacation. Part of my enjoyment came from watching the myriad birds that flock to the bird feeders outside each cabin, and part from being surrounded by the desert itself, although at the time I was too weak to walk into it. The hedges and privacy barriers that separate cabin from cabin are native shrubs: ocotillo, mesquite, creosote bush, jumping cholla, and others.

Many guest ranches in the desert, and elsewhere in semi-arid California, strive to create a feeling of "oasis." Green lawns and colorful annuals accentuate the contrast between the dry desert and the lush, watered landscape of the lodge, motel, or inn. Feelings of luxury and privilege are supposedly enhanced by the ostentatious use of a scarce commodity, water.

It is rare, as a visitor to the desert, to have the opportunity to follow modest paths through the desert to your cabin, surrounded by plantings from the local plant associations. Ensconced within the unique ecosystem that is one of the reasons you came here in the first place, you experience the real desert vacation.

We Are Not the First

We have precedents for gardens that reflect and enhance local particulars. The Arts and Crafts Movement in California in the early part of the century looked to locale for inspiration, examples of which can still be viewed in such gardens as Charles Lummis's home, El Alisal, in Pasadena (recently redone by Robert Perry) and the Edwin O. Libbey garden in Ojai.

In his essay "The Conservation of Nature and the Preservation of Humanity," Wendell Berry says that there have always been two themes in America, a tension between "boomer and sticker, exploitation and settlement, caring and not caring, life adapted to available technology and personal desire and life adapted to a known place." These themes can be seen in the California garden as well.

In 1927, in her California book *Land of the Sun,* Mary Austin gave us "the sketched pattern of a suggested recovery." Gardeners from Lester Rowntree to Theodore Payne to Charles Francis Saunders have directed our attention to home. Whether it is time for this subtheme to gain dominance is anybody's guess, but at least we can say with Wendell Berry, "Anyhow, we have taken the side of care."

PART III

Doing the
Real Work

CHAPTER SIX

Along the Flower Trail

A humiliating fact in connection with our California wildflowers, is the average Californian's own indifference to them.
Not only does he not know their names, he does not even see
them. . . . why, the gardens of Europe are full of California
wildflowers, and have been for three generations, such flowers
as clarkias, collinsias, lupines, gilias, eschscholtzias, godetias,
phacelias, mariposa tulips, penstemons, and a score more.
Charles Francis Saunders, 1919

It is above you and I shall go
Along the flower trail you and I shall go
Picking flowers on our way
You and I shall go.
Wintu dream song

As I write this chapter on annual wildflowers, it is not wildflower time. In
wildflower time, spring through early summer, you will not find me inside.
All possible moments must be spent looking at, looking for, and being
among the wildflowers, at home and on pilgrimage, "along the flower
trail." For I am an aficionado of our spring wildflower displays.

In California, we are blessed with remnants of one of the greatest shows
on earth. Although it must regretfully be acknowledged that our wildflower fields are not what they once were, even in this diminished state, they
are still wondrous and worth seeking out as inspiration for the home
wildflower field, for the historical sense of what used to be here, and because
there may be something in our mental makeup that resonates with vast
fields of blooming annual plant life. Something in us that requires the glad-

---

Part-opening illustration: Coyote bush, male and female. Drawing by Ane Carla Rovetta.

dening of spring in order to cheerfully accommodate the quiet of our rain-less California summers.

Old California, from early reports, was a veritable heaven in the spring. What today can compare to the free-flowering, tremendously varied oak savannahs and grasslands of California before the arrival and full impact of European land use practices and weedy species? A little gem from a collection of reminiscences about the Sacramento Valley, written by Nicolus Hanson in 1944, gives a glimpse of what once was:

> This and future generations will never see this great valley as I have seen it, blanketed with thousands of acres of the most beautiful wildflowers.
>
> Snowdrops, a small white flower, would cover a field and make the field appear a great bank of snow. Another field of several thousand acres would appear like a bank of gold, covered with a small yellow flower. The stems of these flowers were fine and the pods were filled with a rich, fine seed. Cattle became fat and made excellent beef in June by grazing on that feed.
>
> Another field of red, gravelly soil would be covered with the state flower, beautiful yellow poppies. The next field would probably be bluebells and violets, and still another with redbells, a solid carpet of red. If you were fortunate you would see a field of the different varieties of soils combined with all the different varieties of wildflowers growing there in a great big bouquet arranged by Nature: poppies, Johnny-jump-ups, buttercups, primroses, modocs, purple lupine, bluebells, and many flowers I never knew the names of.
>
> And oh! the beautiful bouquets of wildflowers we gathered when we were a child. The fragrance never to be forgotten.
>
> In the spring shallow ponds of water would evaporate on the plains and a fine growth of vegetation would spring up and bloom thereon, the most beautiful velvet flower that contained all the colors of the rainbow. These flowers possessed the sweetest fragrance imaginable. All these beautiful pictures of Nature have been erased from this valley forever by civilization. Today we view the rice, barley, wheat, ladino and alfalfa fields, and the orchards.

Only one long generation ago, such scenes could still be viewed. Descriptions like the above provide priceless glimpses into the floriferous past. Jeff Mayfield, another early admirer of California's wildflowers, had this to say about his family's first view of the San Joaquin Valley in 1873:

As we passed below the hills the whole plain was covered with great patches of rose, yellow, scarlet, orange, and blue. The colors did not seem to mix to any great extent. Each kind of flower liked a certain kind of soil best, and some of the patches of one color were a mile or more across. . . . I believe that we were more excited out there on the plains among the wildflowers than we had been on the mountain the day before when we saw the valley for the first time. . . . Mother cried with joy and wanted to make a home right there in the midst of it all.

Note the impulse to be "in the midst of it all." There is something about this abundance of floral beauty that invites physical immersion, a twist on the concept "garden bed." John Muir, in his lyrical essay on the wildflowers of the Great Central Plains, describes nights spent on "glorious botanical beds" after intoxicating days of wandering through flower fields. He would wake to find "several new species leaning over me and looking me full in the face, so that my studies would begin before rising." Wildflower fields call for and reward such intimacy. When in the flower fields, whether at home or abroad, the "Muir's eye view," has much to recommend it. Muir, in his journey, became almost ecstatic as "the great yellow days drifted by uncounted."

The Great Central Plain of California, during the months of March, April, and May, was one smooth, continuous bed of honey-bloom, so marvelously rich that, in walking from one end of it to the other, a distance of more than 400 miles, your foot would press about a hundred flowers at every step. Mints, gilias, nemophilas, castilleias, and innumerable compositae were so crowded together that, had ninety-nine per cent of them been taken away, the plain would still have seemed to any but Californians extravagantly flowery.

The long and unusual life of Jeff Mayfield, born in 1844, was fortuitously recorded for us by anthropologist Frank Latta in 1928. When Jeff's mother died, he was informally adopted, at age six, by the Choinumne Yokuts of the Central Valley, with whom he lived for eleven years. He experienced and described many aspects of the Choinumne culture that would otherwise be unknown, including a single paragraph on their relationship with the wildflowers of spring and their names for individual species.

In the spring the Indians were always gathering flowers and fastening them in their hair. If there was a patch of wildflowers anywhere near camp, you would see up to a couple of dozen people sitting in them or picking them. Baby-blue-eyes [*Nemophila menziesii*] were called *lup-chen sub suh* or fish eyes. Another lighter lily (*Brodiaea* [*Triteleia*] *laxa*) was called *co-la-we*. Chinese houses [*Collinsia heterophylla*] were *tra-el-le enelo* or snake's dresses. Our paint brush [*Castilleja* sp.] they called *pawtch-aw-le.*

The languages of the fifty different tribes that inhabited California were rich with names for wildflowers. The anthropologist Anna May Gayton says, "Play with flowers, so incompatible with conventional notions about Indians, was widespread in the West." She describes another aspect of the Yokuts' relationship to the spring wildflowers:

Soon after this (late March, April, and early May) the lavish, colorful blooming of wildflowers engaged the Yokuts attention. Crowns of flowers, constructed like the shaman's feather crown, were worn by young and old of both sexes; armloads of flowers were plucked and danced to with special songs. Pleasure came from their beauty, their fragrance, and their indication of a plentiful seed harvest to follow. Winter rainbows forecast plentiful seed crops, for they were seen as four bands of color (magenta, blue, yellow, orange) of four flowers whose seeds were prized.

For the aboriginal Californians, the beauty of the wildflowers was literally mouthwatering. The abundance of spring-blooming flower fields was linked with hopes for a bountiful summer harvest of seed for making pinole — roasted, ground seed food.

Mary Austin, in her autobiography, *Earth Horizon,* describes her experience with poppies in the Owens Valley:

It was a dry April, but not entirely barren; mirages multiplied on every hand, white borage came out and blue nemophila; where the run-off of the infrequent rains collected in hollows, blue lupine sprang up as though pieces of the sky had fallen. On a morning Mary was walking down one of these, leading her horse, and suddenly she was aware of poppies coming up singly through the tawny, crystal-sanded soil, thin, piercing orange-colored flames. And then the warm pervasive sweetness of ultimate reality. . . . Ultimate, immaterial reality. You walk into it the way one does into those wisps of warm scented air in hollows after the sun goes down; there you stand motionless, acquiescing.

RED MAIDS AND TARWEED   *Red maids,* Calandrinia ciliata, *are an annual wildflower whose shiny black seeds are frequently found in archaeological sites, indicating its importance as a food crop and possibly for ceremonial use as well. This ground-hugging, sun-loving, four-petaled flower likes to colonize bare soil and is one of the few annual wildflowers that has moved into our garden of its own accord.*

Its shiny black seeds are tasty, its new leaves are edible, with a tang reminiscent of arugula, and on a sunny day, its small magenta flowers dot a wildflower field with color. Not individually large or showy, best grown with other low-growing wildflowers like sky lupine and sun cups, it is always a pleasure to see red maids.

The seed of tarweed, or Madia, *a group of late-blooming yellow flowers in the composite family, was also valued by indigenous Californians for food. Found amidst the dry grasses of late summer, tarweed's cheerful bloom reminds me of the painting by the late Grace Carpenter Hudson called* The Tarweed Gatherer, *in which a Pomo woman is depicted with traditional seed-gathering equipment. It seems to increase in abundance the year after a burn.*

One of the most insightful writers about native California flora was James Roof, director of the East Bay Regional Parks' Tilden Botanic Garden from 1940 to 1979. He fantasized an area within the regional park where California youngsters were specifically enjoined to gather and be among native wildflowers. His treatise on California wildflowers is an enjoyable combination of personal observation and passionate opinion, experimentation, and historical perspective. In it, he ranks play with wildflowers with any other respected recreational activity.

Seeds of California annuals sent to England provided material for the English practice of planting wildflowers as "bedding plants," annuals grown for their season of bloom and then replaced when done. To this day, while still a novelty in the American garden, California wildflowers are common in British gardens. Baby blue eyes, many species of clarkias, tidy tips, sky lupine, and of course the California poppy have been grown in England since 1889.

Wildflowers can be planted as one part of a complex ecological community (the California wildflower field), or they can be used horticulturally, as wonderful design elements for the adventurous gardener. They can be planted in containers or in fields large enough to provide bouquets for the house and flowers to sit among and put in one's hair, to enjoy as native Californians did. They can be grown for pollen, for seed food, for dyes, for medicinal properties, for baby-washing. They can be pressed, dried, drawn, painted, worn, and brought into the house. Lived with, loved, anticipated and remembered.

Yet in California, native wildflowers are almost the exotics, unfamiliar to many Californians, seldom seen in most gardens. Why is this so? Searching for clues, I delved into early garden books to uncover early attitudes toward our native plants in general and wildflowers in particular.

Edward J. Wickson, director of the University of California's Agricultural Experiment Station in the early twentieth century, had this to say of lupines: "These wild legumes in various shades of blue, also in white and yellow, are useful for large effects but not much grown in gardens, because one sees so much of them all over the state from the sand beaches of the ocean, across the plains to the mountain sides."

The quality of ubiquitousness, given here as a reason for exclusion from the garden, would now apply to many of the plants that Professor Wickson recommended for garden use, such as nasturtiums, petunias, pinks, scabiosa, daisies, impatiens, cosmos, and forget-me-nots. In the meantime, the fine sheets of blue lupine that transformed Marin hillsides, the masses of yellow and brown Johnny-jump-ups that older Oakland gardeners remember, and the fields of gold that John Muir strolled through are scarcely in evidence now. The balance has been tipped, gardeners putting a not-so-light finger on the non-native side of the scale.

What Has Happened to California's Flower Fields?

Once upon a time, wildflower fields were composed largely, although not entirely, of annuals, known as "spring ephemerals," setting seed in the summer to germinate with the fall rains and come into bloom in the spring. The disappearance of these fields makes this vegetation type one of the most endangered of all California plant communities.

The bee pastures extolled by John Muir, the painted hills, the fields of gold, what has become of them? Besides the obvious fate of submersion under asphalt, one major factor in the disappearance of native wildflowers has been competition from invasive exotic plants, whether ornamental or agricultural imports or inadvertent escapees. Many of these foreign weeds and grasses have adapted over thousands of years to European forms of land use, such as plowing, or heavy, year-round grazing. These plants thrive under conditions that have set the natives reeling. Here, too, they are freed from the natural controls that may occur in their native lands.

Spring ephemerals require rain or irrigation water to wash the water-soluble, growth-inhibiting chemicals out of their seeds before germination can occur. Following germination, growth is rapid. Leaves first grow flat on the ground in a basal rosette during the fall and winter rainy season. Then they elongate and produce flowers in early, mid, and late spring and early summer. Once the sun comes out and warmth increases, photosynthetic rates are high, and growth is swift. Annual non-native grasses, responding to the first rains of fall with a rapid upright growth spurt, easily smother tiny wildflower seedlings in the basal rosette stage.

Because of this phenomenon, a good wildflower year in California may occur the first year after a drought, but not the second or third year after a drought. In 1995, a year of record rains, many thought it would be a great spring for wildflowers. But the exotic annual grasses responded with such vigor to the additional rainfall that some areas considered wildflower meccas had poor shows. In our demonstration garden, excellent germination in January was foiled by the strength with which the annual grasses grew. Because the soil was too wet to walk on for several critical months, we were unable to weed, ending up with virtually no annual flower show. (An exception being some of the vernal pool annuals, including meadow foam, *Limnanthes douglasii,* and its subspecies *Limnanthes douglasii* var. *sulphurea.*) The perennials, already in place and growing when the second wave of rains hit, were a different story, in many cases thriving with the increased moisture.

Of all the ecosystems of the varied state of California that have suffered from the incursions of Europeans and their plants, the annual wildflowers are probably hardest hit. The second volume of *Conservation and Management of Rare and Endangered Plants* indicates that the most severe losses of plant species have occurred among lowland species and annuals. The loss of these annuals is also the loss of a particular habitat crucial to a whirling complex of associated fauna. The brightly colored flowers of the native wildflowers provide for many flying insect pollinators, unlike the mainly wind-pollinated, non-native grasses that have in so many cases taken their place.

Vernal pools, seasonal wetlands, are home to host-specific solitary bees, each seeking a particular wildflower for nectaring. Some are even named after the wildflower they pollinate, such as *Andrena limnanthis,* which pollinates only *Limnanthes.* Other insects also pollinate meadow foam, but seed production is thought to be more complete when pollinated by the bee — specifically co-evolved with that particular flower — that is "allegiant" to it. Restoration of these wildflowers is greatly complicated by the presence of invasive aliens. Which brings us to the question that we answer the most frequently: Can I simply throw wildflower seed out into an area of existing weeds and grasses? In most cases, the answer is no.

I have seen many disappointed faces upon imparting this information. The notion of such careless flinging of wildflower seed seems to be deeply imbedded in our gardening culture. If this procedure worked, wildflowers would be growing there now; in most cases, they are not. Seed thrown into an overgrown area often won't even hit the ground. If it is able to penetrate the thatch and weeds and make enough soil contact to germinate, the more aggressive non-native weeds and grasses will often outcompete it. Accordingly, in most situations, soil preparation is necessary to give wildflowers the best chance to germinate, bloom, and go to seed.

The nature of the dominance of non-native grasses (usually annual and from some part of the Mediterranean basin) is essential for the gardener in California who seeks to understand just what is going on here.

Creating a Native Wildflower Garden

SOIL PREPARATION

Like all seeds, those of wildflowers need warmth and moisture to germinate, elements that are aided by what is called "good seed-soil contact." For that condition to occur, a good seedbed must exist or be created. A good seedbed for wildflowers can be formed of many different kinds of soil, with different levels of fertility and different amounts of moisture, but it must be relatively weed-free.

If the area you wish to sow is weedy, there are a number of possible courses to follow. Just as nature has come up with multiple successful strategies for solving evolutionary challenges, so there are multiple ways to solve most gardening problems. The course you take depends on slope, drainage, soil type, rainfall, and which weedy species are present, as well as which method most appeals to you. Sometimes good results are possible with very little seedbed preparation. Every situation is different.

Perhaps the most common method of seedbed preparation is rototilling. Quick and easy, it may provide excellent first-year results. On the negative side, rototilling can bring existing weed seeds to the surface to create more weed problems. Grasses that reproduce from underground roots, such as Bermuda grass and kikuyu grass, may be chopped up by the rototiller blades, increasing the problem. Frequent rototilling can seriously degrade soil texture. The soil layers are disturbed, organic matter is used up more quickly, ruts may be formed that become permanent. Steep slopes may be unsuitable for rototilling, because of mechanical difficulties and erosion problems. You may decide to rototill only occasionally, perhaps every third year, using other methods of weed control as well. A shallow cultivator can be used on newly germinated weed seedlings without bringing up new weed seeds from below.

For a more thorough weed extermination, some use irrigation to germinate weed seeds in the summer dormancy period and then remove them as they sprout. They rototill in the first crop of weed seedlings, water until a second crop comes up, and rototill again. In areas where weed seeds in the soil are likely (particularly true in moister areas along the coast), rototilling should often be followed by a second weeding. Hand digging and tilling are useful procedures for smaller areas.

Another strategy involves waiting until weed seedlings have germinated with the first fall rains and then smothering them. Black plastic, clear plastic, old rugs, or organic mulch such as turkey bedding, sawdust, or wood chips can be used. When the plastic or other artificial smothering materials are removed, a bare and firm seedbed is revealed, perfect for seed sowing. One to three months is usually sufficient. Note that species such as Bermuda grass (but is there anything else like Bermuda grass?) will not be killed by this treatment.

A variation of the above plan, called soil solarization, involves clear plastic, absolutely level ground, and incessant sunshine for four to six weeks, usually not available to coastal or mountain gardeners. The goal is to kill weed seed present in the soil through intense heat; obviously, any existing wildflower seed will be killed too.

GLYPHOSATE

Many customers inquire about the use of the herbicide glyphosate, best known under the trade name Roundup, which is being used by the ton by gardeners and public agencies alike. It is a contact spray that works by translocating through the leaves and stems into the roots of the plant, where it mimics growth hormones, causing the plant literally to grow itself to death. I struggle with this issue on a daily basis.

Although glyphosate is considered among the least harmful of chemical herbicides, some citizen groups are concerned about it. The information necessary to evaluate the long-term effect on other aspects of the local ecology from the continuing use of this herbicide may not yet be available. Nonetheless, many restoration plans call for its use. Its opponents focus their concern on the unknown inert ingredients that are part of the formula, which are not required to be listed by the Environmental Protection Agency.

The advantage of glyphosate spray is that weeds can be selectively killed without disturbing the soil. Although Roundup is readily available to every homeowner, it should still be used carefully. I find its use most justified in removing those weedy species, such as bur-clover and sorrel, that cannot be eradicated by hand, as proved through twenty years of trying.

In James Roof's treatise on growing California wildflowers, written in 1971, he recommended the application of gasoline to weedy species, carefully applied by sprinkling from watering cans or with hand syringes. He called it "an effective weedicide and germinative stimulant of refractory wildflower seed," and claimed that it had "no bad or lasting effects on soils." In the light of what we now know about gasoline contamination of soils and ground water, we can see that he was operating under an optimistic delusion. Claims for the harmlessness of recently developed chemical herbicides might also suggest a certain caution.

The gardener may choose to combine the above techniques with good old-fashioned hand labor, which has many advantages if time and energy are available. "Hula hoes" are excellent tools for rubbing out young weed seedlings that are not rhizomatous; the gardener can remain upright, little soil is disturbed, and with the right kinds of weeds, areas can be selectively weeded fairly quickly.

Hand labor is our major form of weed control. A combination of techniques, rototilling one year and hand weeding or burning the next, will probably favor different species each year.

Addressing the weed problem thoroughly before planting your seed will increase your chances of a continuing wildflower show. One possible scenario involves digging and tilling the summer before planting and watering through the summer, removing weed seedlings as they appear. Then stop watering and let the ground bake until the fall rains begin.

Your mixture may change its composition from year to year, for reasons that remain mysterious. The combinations that delighted you one year may be replaced by others equally lovely the next year.

In order to distinguish your wildflower seedlings from weed seedlings, sow a small amount of your wildflower seed in a flat of sterilized potting soil. You can then see what the wildflowers look like at the seedling stage and avoid removing them from your planting in the ground. They are usually easily distinguished from weed seedlings. You may then have the pleasure of identifying clarkia, lupine, or poppy seedlings on winter walks through natural wildflower fields. Your back-yard wildflower project will help you to learn how to read the wildlands.

In few situations is it desirable or necessary to add any kind of fertilizer to the soil. Keeping as close to the unamended native soil as possible is the goal. Manures are not always helpful, for not only do they often contain uncomposted weed seed but the additional fertility only encourages unwanted weeds. I have seen native wildflowers grown in heavily composted soil for the cut-flower market reaching two or three times their usual height. Flourishing as they do in all kinds of lean and infertile soils, wildflowers don't need extra nitrogen. Researchers have begun to find that pollution from automobile exhaust becomes extra nitrogen in the soil, stimulating the growth of a suite of weedy grasses. Even on serpentine soil, the last refuge of annual wildflowers, nitrous oxide from the air can tip the balance in a weedy direction.

PLANTING TIME

Although October, with its blessings of rain and soil still warm enough for quick germination, has traditionally been considered the optimal time for planting wildflowers, we have found over the years that there is a fairly wide planting window. My experience indicates that wildflower germination and growth are not tied to day length.

Some people feel that the right time to plant is August, when seeds would have dropped from the plants in nature. It is thought that some species benefit from the long baking at the end of summer. However, the longer the seeds sit around unprotected, the more available they are for hungry bird populations.

We have had good results from plantings in late winter or early spring, particularly in coastal areas. There is often a dry spell in January, and planting when it is over has advantages. And of course, the later you plant, the later into the spring and summer your flowers will bloom. One central coast hillside was planted at two-week intervals through April and May. The soil was good, and the area received late afternoon shade, which made watering easier. Crowd-pleasing blooms were observed through October. At one point in early August, the most recently sown area contained the midspring blooms of bird's-eye gilia, owl's clover, and globe gilia, while another area was lush with clarkias, late spring bloomers.

SEED SOWING

Mix the seed thoroughly with a significant amount (at least four times the quantity of the seed) of weed-free compost or planting mix. Broadcast seed by scattering one-half of the seeds as you walk through the area. Make a second pass with the remaining seed at right angles to your first sowing.

If your soil is sandy, use the back of the rake to smooth the seed/compost mix into the soil. Ideally, seeds are covered by one-eighth to one-fourth inch of soil, or twice the diameter of the seed. With clay soils, raking will often bury the seeds under large lumps of soil. We suggest using a "pounding" motion with the back of the rake to jar the seeds into appropriate crevices. Protected but not smothered, the seeds can germinate in a situation resembling natural dispersal.

Good seed-soil contact is critical. In direct seeding of both wildflowers and native grasses, it is often observed that germination is improved where the tractor tires drove over the seed, or where the sower's footprints can be discerned. In a coastal cliff-planting project in West Marin, soil was packed into cliff crevices, in an attempt to forestall slumping. Wildflower seed sown in this 90 percent compacted soil made a marvelous show. In a direct-seeding experiment with native grasses, seed was sown and a herd of cattle was driven through the area, facilitating seed-soil contact through pounding hoof action. If such a herd is not available to you, good seed-soil contact can be created by laying large sheets of cardboard or plywood over the planted area and walking on them.

James Roof felt that all these elaborate procedures were unnecessary. He quotes his favorite wildflower gardener as giving the following advice: "I throw them into the hot summer dust," she said, "and I grind them in with my heel." This would certainly create good seed-soil contact, but a large area would require a daunting amount of heel-grinding.

Only experimentation with a particular site will reveal what procedures are best for that type of soil, exposure, and existing weed problems. We are flexible with our preparation, leaving an area to its natural reseeding one year, then rototilling the next year if weeds have moved in, or letting it lie fallow or under an arroyo lupine (*Lupinus succulentus*) cover crop for another year before resowing, while another area is sowed. The goal is not to let a spring go by without this ephemeral visual feast somewhere in close proximity.

PROTECTING SEED FROM BIRDS

To foil seed-eating birds (quail are notorious wildflower seed eaters) and soften the effects of pounding rain, mulch lightly with compost, hay, or straw. We sometimes lay twiggy brush over the seed, to be removed when seedlings have made good growth.

I have also observed that seed sown in gravelly or rocky areas, where the seed lodges in small crevices, suffers less bird depredation. One customer reports that he mixes granulated rock half and half with compost and spreads the mixture over the area to be planted, sowing into the mix.

Temporary sheeting materials used to facilitate vegetable seed establishment, such as Remay, are also effective in foiling bird depredation of both seeds and seedlings. The material is removed once the seedlings have made good growth.

If birds are a serious problem, consider delaying your planting till January or even February. In October and November, after the long dry times, quail are ravenous for succulent young seedlings. Migratory birds coming through in November may find your wildflower planting just the ticket. Better to let them concentrate on weed seeds and wait to sow wildflower seed till they have moved on.

One year we planted an area slated for wildflowers three times in succession with no detectable germination. Other areas planted at the same times showed a good take. After the third planting, I covered the seeds with brushy twigs from a raspberry pruning, and still no seedlings appeared. Getting up early one morning, I found that the hedge surrounding the seed-sowing area had begun to serve its purpose and sheltered hundreds of sparrows, who enjoyed perching on the raspberry twigs as they searched out and ate every single seed of all species sown except, for some reason, five spot, *Nemophila maculata*.

One January, we sowed wildflower seed — tidy-tips, desert bluebells, clarkias, and baby blue eyes — in four-inch pots in the greenhouse. Determined to see our carefully prepared plot full of wildflowers, I set out these pots into that area in early March. I also lifted shovelfuls of seedlings of meadow foam, tansy-leaf phacelia, and mountain garland from nearby successful sowings and planted them in the bird-invaded area. I watered the seedlings conscientiously for a month and mulched them well with composted sawdust. By April, there was a glorious show, which continued into the summer with clarkias and linanthus. Receiving the same concentrated attention as a garden bed, it responded with exuberant, weed-free bloom for a satisfying four-month period.

Although I think I understand the reasons why wildflower plantings can fail, I am still sometimes taken by surprise. By using different techniques at different times and in different places, I hedge my bets and learn a bit more each year. Perseverance pays.

WATERING

Some gardeners mistakenly assume that since California native wildflowers are drought-tolerant, their seed does not require moisture for germination. All seeds, including those of wildflowers, require moisture in order to germinate. Most native annuals might be considered drought-evasive rather than drought-tolerant, in that they grow during the wet times and then go to seed and die during the dry times.

Seed sown in the fall will receive sufficient moisture for germination if the fall and winter rains are consistent. Otherwise, supplemental irrigation is required. Water one to three times weekly, depending on your soil and evapotranspiration rate, until seedlings have made good initial growth. They will come into bloom in the spring and will not require further irrigation if you wish to follow their natural sequence. To prolong bloom, water once a week. Irrigation may, however, increase weed problems with such invasive species as Himalayan blackberry, English ivy, French sorrel, and bindweed.

At the end of the flowering season, when plants have formed seed, scythe your "wildflower hay" and allow for a dormant period in your wildflower garden. We encourage gardeners to take advantage of the late summer dormancy in the California garden to relax their gardening efforts. Take a vacation, enjoy the absence of weed emergence that unirrigated land can allow, do other things, and store up energy for the California autumn, when the rains come and the ground softens.

Once we were asked to do a wildflower planting in an area that had been disturbed in the course of installing septic-system leachfields. The planting was in late May, so we made it clear to the client that irrigation would be required and that summer blooms might not last as long or be as showy as spring blossoms. We had done successful sowings in this coastal area in April and felt that it had a chance.

The soil, brought up from eight feet below the surface, was not good (a neighbor was using it to throw ceramic pots on a wheel). The water supply turned out to be unreliable. The site was windy, so even when water was available, good coverage was impossible. That year, we had record hot days. The flowers that came up were pitiful stunted creatures, blooming almost at once, anxious to get on with it and shed this mortal coil.

This planting had too many factors against it: wrong time of year, insufficient moisture, high temperatures, and soil like concrete. The adaptability of annual wildflowers can go far, but apparently not this far.

As long as you supply the moisture, your annual wildflower seeds will germinate and grow most of the year. I have found it easy to germinate and grow wildflowers throughout the year in a coastal climate, but temperatures in hot inland climates may inhibit germination during the hottest parts of the summer. Water needs will increase with heat.

For irrigated summer sowings, plant in partly shaded areas. Wildflowers that come into bloom at the hottest time of the year will have a shorter bloom period and sometimes smaller blossoms than those blooming in the cooler spring. Some species particularly adapted to bloom on hot days are desert bluebells, goldfields, tidy-tips, and clarkias.

Bloom Period

Plants sown in the fall will bloom from February through July, longer in coastal regions. Here on the coast, a mild winter may leave clarkia blooming from July to January, effectively "lapping" the spring wildflowers. The first blossoms to appear are poppies, and the last are clarkia and linanthus. By removing spent flowers and providing supplemental irrigation, bloom can be prolonged, but be prepared for increased problems with perennial weeds. In coastal areas, the wildflower show begins in February and often does not end till October. As I write, in mid November, in my unwatered office garden, we still have clarkias, *Clarkia amoena,* and the white form of the California poppy we call "Moonglow" leaning on the fall-blooming perennial California aster, *Aster chilensis.* Seedlings of tansy-leaf phacelia, growing from seed that fell from last year's crop, are almost a foot high. Across the sidewalk, big yellow daisy-like blooms of gumplant, *Grindelia stricta,* entice late butterflies.

Choosing Wildflower Seeds

Wildflowers can be planted in combinations, bought either as "wildflower mixes," or in separate species, and I never can decide which I prefer. Mixes are a great education in wildflowers. Commercially available mixes are usually composed of ten to twenty species that will not, of course, all be blooming at once. Usually, four to five species are blooming at any one time, and many different combinations will emerge through the season. If you wish to control exactly what colors occur at the same time, buy individual species separately.

I enjoy planting in swathes — that is, using two or three different species in sweeps that merge and separate. For example, inspired by the spring wildflowers at Edgewood Park in Redwood City, I planted a mass of butter yellow tidy-tips with goldfields and poppies. First, I established a perennial planting of blue-eyed grass, *Sisyrinchium bellum,* and foothill stipa, *Nassella lepida,* and seeded the cream-to-yellow-to-gold annuals around them.

As for color choices, I could almost say I've never seen a wildflower whose color I didn't like. The magenta of red maids is not my favorite color, but when they spread through disturbed soil and open their petals to the sun, they become gay confetti. Add baby blue eyes for contrast, and suddenly it becomes one of my favorites.

All the pastels, the mid-season bloomers, including bird's-eye gilia, Chinese houses, grand linanthus, and Monterey clarkia, are pleasing together. One potentially painful combination that sometimes appears late in the season is the shocking pink of farewell-to-spring with the crayon orange of late-blooming California poppies. Add a blue purple penstemon, and it becomes rich and vivid, rather than nerve-wracking.

As the season progresses, each new combination becomes for a time the most beautiful of all.

Perennials in the Wildflower Meadow

A long-term wildflower planting might include native perennial bunchgrasses. Some natural wildflower areas show this combination, in which several species of bunchgrasses dot the fields, holding the soil and the territory when the annual wildflowers have gone to seed. What happens between the bunchgrasses is spectacular in season, but bunchgrasses can be the bones of the wildflower meadow.

Many perennial wildflowers, such as brodiaeas and other native bulbs, like calochortus, fritillary, and iris, will enrich the annual wildflower meadow. Indian pinks, *Silene californica,* sea pink, *Armeria maritima,* yarrow, penstemon species, checkerbloom, *Sidalcea malvaeflora,* yellow- and blue-eyed grass, and the native plantains all have their place, providing interest and food for pollinators when the annual wildflowers have gone to seed.

Wildflowers in the Small Yard

Native wildflowers can be used in traditional garden situations, wherever annuals are appropriate, as well as in a large garden or meadow. Parking strips are good places for wildflowers, and they can be effective in the formal garden. Clarkias, the workhorse of the wildflower garden, can be transplanted easily from one place to another and have, with or without supplemental water, an extremely long bloom period. Grand linanthus, *Linanthus grandiflorus,* with its fragrant pale pink and white blooms, blazing star with its satiny strong yellow petals, and bird's-eye gilia are excellent performers.

For areas of deep shade, such as under redwoods, I recommend the many perennial species that grow in that habitat, such as columbine, bleeding heart, redwood sorrel, wild ginger, or alum root. Not many annuals grow in deep shade, with exceptions like the two claytonias, Indian lettuce, *Claytonia perfoliata,* and peppermint candy flower, *Claytonia sibirica.*

The native wildflowers are superb garden subjects for the small yard, bringing delicacy and interest to the border that you won't find at the average garden center.

Wildflowers in Containers

I first began growing wildflowers in containers as germination tests and then as demonstrations for talks and shows. Now I couldn't do without our containers of five spot, *Nemophila maculata,* its purple-tipped white petals blooming year-round from successive sowings. Or baby blue eyes, *Nemophila menziesii,* cascading out of a large ceramic pot, contrasting with yellow Point Reyes meadow foam and backed up by the green of the slender hairgrass, *Deschampsia elongata.* The yellow subspecies of meadow foam is stunning in a deep-blue pot or a rough brown Chinese bowl.

In wooden flats eight inches deep, we cluster species representing different plant communities. The coastal prairie, for example, includes a thriving green mound of coastal hairgrass, surrounded by blue-eyed grass and tidy-tips. For an inland meadow, we included a permanent centerpiece of foothill stipa, a small and graceful bunchgrass, with globe gilia and owl's clover.

Sometimes I like to plant a wide terra-cotta pot with three different kinds of clarkias to show their similarities and differences. Or a Fourth of July pot with the red form of the California poppy in the middle, and around the rim the white form of the California poppy interspersed with deep blue desert bluebells. Some of our containers never need reseeding by us, since the flowers are allowed to go to seed in the container and appear again next spring. In that historically unprecedented rainy year when our fields were under a foot of water, it was the containers of annual wildflowers that let us know it was spring.

Flats and pots are an excellent way for beginners to get started with wildflowers. In the controlled environment of the container, seedlings may be observed and familiarity with their appearance gained. Seedlings can be transplanted from the container to a spot in the garden or from the large planting to the container, which we do with impunity. Native wildflowers in four-inch pots, although not yet seen at every garden center, are available from some specialty nurseries (see Resources).

One freak clarkia defied its classification as an annual, living and blooming in a large terra-cotta pot for almost two years. Contrarily, it bloomed in early spring instead of midsummer. Making rules about growing wildflowers should be gingerly undertaken.

The Cutting Garden

For the cutting garden, I recommend all the clarkias. Mountain garland, *Clarkia unguiculata,* lasted for an astonishing two months in a vase, its graceful arching stems making a dramatic show against a white wall. Blazing star, mountain phlox, bird's-eye gilia, globe gilia, and owl's clover are all useful for the flower arranger.

Bird's-eye gilia benefits from the close inspection a bouquet provides and makes a good unifier for an otherwise diverse bouquet. Weaker-stemmed species, such as baby blue eyes, tidy-tips, and five spot, can be displayed to advantage in a vase with a sharply flaring rim, of the kind found in florists' shops. Stiffer-stemmed species, such as linanthus, blazing star, or globe gilia, occupy the center of the bouquet, while the others drape themselves becomingly over the rim.

People are often dazzled by our bouquets of the California poppy, reputed to be a poor cut flower. Here is the secret. Pick them in bud, carefully strip most of the leaves from the stem, cut the stem on the diagonal and hold the cut place over a flame till it turns black and seems to seal shut. Change the water daily. The cream-colored variety of the California poppy is wonderful for toning down the vibrant colors of a mixed bouquet. I like to use a small round vase for the coastal form of the California poppy, whose petals open wide into an impossibly gorgeous yellow cup before they drop.

Wildflowers in Agriculture

Tansy-leaf phacelia, *Phacelia tanacetifolia,* an annual wildflower two to four feet tall, which grows in both sun or part shade, has fragrant, striking, purplish blue curling flower stalks. It has been used as a bee plant in Europe since the early part of the century. Interplanted with the seed crop, it draws bees to serve as pollinators. In the wildflower garden, tansy-leaf phacelia and meadow foam seem to be the stars for native bumblebees.

In 1988, researchers in integrated pest management interplanted tansy-leaf phacelia with sugar beets. They found that sugar-beet yields were significantly higher in plots grown with phacelia, possibly because adult syrphid flies, which feed on the floral nectar and pollen of phacelia, were significantly more abundant. These syrphid flies were credited with reducing the aphids on the nearby sugar beets. Hoverflies as far as 200 meters (over 650 feet) from the planted phacelia were found with the characteristic blue, star-shaped phacelia pollen in their guts.

Chia, *Salvia columbaria,* is a native wildflower with a long history of use on this continent. Found in burial sites throughout California, this pretty, upright blue flower, with grayish leaves and typical mint family floral structure, loves heat and drought. It produces large crops of a small, flat, brown seed that is nutritious and quite tasty. Researchers studying the dismaying propensity of Native Americans toward diabetes consider chia to have been an important part of the Western aboriginal diet and are using it in the modern treatment of this disease.

Collecting references to chia seed, I have read many times in various sources that Indians could be sustained on a twenty-four-hour forced march with one teaspoon of chia seed. The originator of this grim piece of information was Dr. Cephas L. Bard of Ventura. In 1875, Dr. J. T. Rothrock, botanist and surgeon of the Wheeler United States Geographical Survey, extolled its many virtues and uses. Added to water, he said, "it seems to assuage thirst, to improve the taste of the water, and, in addition to lessen the quantity of water taken."

AGUA DE CHIA   *Charles Francis Saunders writes of chia in several of his books about California. In* Western Wildflowers and Their Stories, *written in 1938, he describes the proper way to make "agua de chia," or chia water, which used to be served at chia fiestas in Mexico. This drink is enjoyed by many at our open houses.*

Recipe for agua de chia (serves 100): Pour one ounce cleaned chia seed into two gallons of water. Add the juice of eight lemons, one cup of sugar, and half a cup of cinnamon. If you are lucky enough to possess one, stir water and seed with a molinillo. Otherwise, a wire whisk will do.

I also like to add the delicate, nutty flavor of lightly roasted chia seed to a French butter cookie recipe or sprinkle it on rice.

Wildflower Viewing

Besides Edgewood Park in San Mateo County, famous for its unique serpentine-related flora and fauna, try Jasper Ridge Biological Preserve. San Bruno Mountain in Daly City is another unique Bay Area wildflower locale, as is the Nature Conservancy's Ring Mountain Preserve in Tiburon, Marin County.

Plate I. Planting of wildflowers on coastal bluff, including tidy-tips, goldfields, baby blue eyes, and owl's clover. Photograph by Saxon Holt.

Plate 2. Baby blue eyes, blooming in early spring. Photograph by Peter G. Smith.

Plate 3. Five spot, blooming in early spring. Photograph by Peter G. Smith.

Plate 4. Desert bluebells with goldfields in background. Photograph by Peter G. Smith.

Plate 5. Blazing star, with California poppies in background. Photograph by Peter G. Smith.

Plate 6. Farewell-to-spring blooming in late summer. Photograph by Peter G. Smith.

Plate 7. Cream cups from the Carrizo Plains, blooming in early spring. Photograph by Peter G. Smith.

Plate 8. Baby blue eyes and Point Reyes meadow foam with Idaho fescue. Photograph by Saxon Holt.

Plate 9. Ceanothus thyrsiflorus *'Snow Flurry'*, Ceanothus *'Concha', and* Baccharis pilularis. *Grier garden, Lafayette, designed by Lutsko Associates, San Francisco. Photograph by Ron Lutsko Jr.*

Plate 10. Native planting around the REI building in downtown Seattle, including cedar, huckleberry, snowberry, and salal. Photograph by Judith Lowry.

Plate 11. Larner Seeds demonstration garden, early spring. Red fescue and Douglas iris. Photograph by Saxon Holt.

Plate 12. Coastal prairie garden with Cape Mendocino reed grass, the coastal form of the California poppy, beach aster, Blair Fross, and bunny. David Fross garden, San Luis Obispo County. Photograph by David Fross.

Plate 13. Tufted hairgrass, California beach grass, and coastal poppy in Santa Cruz County. Garden designed by Ellen Cooper. Photograph by Ellen Cooper.

Plate 14. Larner Seeds demonstration garden, late summer, with Eriogonum *'Molly' in bloom, background of purple sage, California sagebrush, and coyote bush. Marin County. Photograph by Peter G. Smith.*

Plate 15. *Checkerbloom and California poppy cultivar 'Moonglow' blooming in early spring in front of a young coast live oak. Larner Seeds garden. Photograph by Saxon Holt.*

Plate 16. *Native succulents, including* Dudleya pulverulenta *and* Sedum spathulifolium, *with* Eriophyllum Nevinii. *Betsy Clebsch garden, San Mateo County. Photograph by David Fross.*

Plate 17. Gathering seed of California fescue. Photograph by Saxon Holt.

Plate 18. Enjoying Indian lettuce in early spring. Photograph by Judith Lowry.

Plate 19. Modeling a coastal scrub hatband consisting of coyote bush, cudweed, sagebrush, mugwort, and dune tansy. Photograph by Judith Lowry.

Plate 20. Evergreen huckleberry plant, berries, juice, jelly, and cleaned seed. Photograph by Peter G. Smith.

Plate 21. A day spent with cream cups. Photograph by Peter G. Smith.

In the East Bay, Sunol Regional Park is magnificent in the spring, with large stands of *Viola pedunculata* (Johnny-jump-up) and *Lupinus nanus* (sky lupine). Tilden Park Botanic Garden in Berkeley and the U.C. Berkeley Botanic Garden offer labeled, but still ebullient, spring displays.

Coastal wildflower gardens bloom well into the summer and can be enjoyed at the Point Reyes National Seashore, particularly at Abbott's Lagoon, Chimney Rock, and Kehoe Beach. In Colusa County, Bear Valley and Walker Ridge are spectacular. In Central California, try the Carrizo Plains. Sutter Buttes in the Sacramento Valley and Table Mountain near Oroville are meccas for wildflower lovers.

Spring wildflower shows are sponsored by various chapters of the California Native Plant Society. A long-standing event of fine quality is the April show sponsored by the Santa Clara Valley chapter, held at Foothill College. The Oakland Museum has a show in June, sponsored by the East Bay chapter, and others throughout the state are well worth attending.

Growing wildflowers, you will know them in the wild; seeing them in the wild may inspire you to grow them.

Time with Wildflowers

Once you have found your field of wildflowers, plan to spend the day. Subtleties will be revealed. Different wildflowers move with the wind differently, some from the stem, some delicately from the "neck." Some tremble at the slightest breeze; others are sturdily immobile till the wind picks up.

Note degrees of translucency of petals. I am drawn to flowers with "shine," occurring when petals are thin enough that the light comes through, like meadow foam and cream cups. Composites, such as tidy-tips and goldfields, don't have this quality, and I enjoy them in swaying masses. Because bees avoid darkness, many bee-pollinated, funnel-shaped flowers, like penstemons, are translucent at the base.

Details emerge as the day passes. As blossoms open during the day, the effect changes. From the top of the hill, they look different than when you are among them. Some spring ephemerals lean toward and follow the sun; others don't. Wildflowers such as goldfields that in small groups do not seem fragrant will sometimes reveal delicious aromas in large masses. Observing pollinators adds an extra dimension to the experience. Note pollen color; gilias have blue pollen.

Some flowers change color when they have been pollinated, which saves the pollinators a wasted trip. Researchers have found that scent also changes once pollination has occurred.

A Day with Cream Cups

Consider a changeful day spent with cream cups, *Platystemon californicus*. I have always been drawn to the creamy, silken texture of its six-petaled flowers, at the top of fuzzy, nodding stems, and its fascinating seeds, like many strings of beads twisted together. In masses, it brings food analogies to mind. One author found that "the field appears frosted with whipped cream." To me, a field of cream cups has the basic yellow-and-white appeal of butter on popcorn. (Other yellow-and-white flowers, like tidy-tips and meadow foam, also appear cream-colored from a distance.) It was no chore to spend time amongst them on a gentle hillside in the Temblor Range of San Luis Obispo County.

Early in the morning, partially opened blossoms, nodding at the end of stems, have a delicate form. As blossoms open with the sun, turning upward, the brushy white stamens, up to twelve in number, are revealed, influencing the perceived colors of the flower. Color variations in individual flowers range from pure cream, to cream with minor yellow markings at the base of the petal, to almost completely yellow. Such variability indicates that this stand is of the variety *crinitus*. In the coast ranges, the petals are a uniform cream.

A large beetle with green markings seems to be an avid pollinator, lurching from cup to cup. As the day progresses, a faint perfume emerges from the basking flowers, which I had thought to be scentless. Guilt about my personal impact on this glorious stand is mitigated by the fact that by the next day, traces of my lounging are scarcely visible.

Helen Sharsmith says this flower has been cultivated since 1830. But I have never seen it in a garden.

California Poppies: The Chalice of Gold

Enjoy the wildflowers but do not underestimate the power of their beauty. Take heed of a Chumash story collected by J. P. Harrington: "Advise your girls well. Tell your daughters that they will fare well at Capwaya, and should not place any belief in youthful talk nor in the enjoyment of poppies. People used to say that poppies were the ruin of girls. Boys would take girls out gathering poppies, and their beauty would overcome them and cause them to yield to the boys."

With its elegantly sinuous curve from flower base to rim and its dazzling color, our state flower, the most famous of our native wildflowers, is familiar to all. Beautifully named by the Spanish *calce de oro,* chalice of gold, it was early on sent overseas to be admired, grown, and bred into an exuberant assortment of hybrids and cultivars.

By the end of the nineteenth century, *Eschscholzia californica* was being used in wallpaper design (by the well-known designer Mary Ingalsbe Bradford), in architectural features, in jewelry design, and in painted ceramics. Dozens of poets and songwriters had tried their hand at extolling the beauties of the poppy, calling it "golden flower of the Golden West," "cup of gold," "heaven's gift of golden beauty," "copa de ora de California," "flower of flame," and other exuberances of the poetic style of the late nineteenth and early twentieth century. In many of these verses, parallels are drawn between the gold that drew the miners and the gold of the California poppy. Some years needed to pass, however, before poetry could draw its silken sleeve over the rough edges of mining days. (Now I'm talking like that!) Let's look at one such endeavor, chosen for its uncharacteristic brevity.

> O radiant and golden-hued poppy!
> Thou symbol and blossom of State!
> Could we without thee be quite so happy,
> Or failing thy smile, so elate?

Poppies aren't just orange anymore. The species *Eschscholzia californica* has been thoroughly manipulated by the breeder's art in Germany, England, and France as well as here, and we now have available an assortment of reds, purples, whites, creams, and pinks. Named hybrids, such as *Eschscholzia californica* 'Moonglow', 'Purple Violet', and 'Cherry Ripe', are available to the gardener.

The coastal gardener is lucky to have a local variety with great beauty and utility, *Eschscholzia californica* var. *maritima.* Although it is no longer recognized by the *Jepson Manual* as a separate subspecies, the coastal form of the California poppy is a perennial plant with mounding, blue gray foliage, a bright orange taproot up to two feet long, and petals of a strong yellow, with an orange blotch at the base. Since the orange, upright, annual *Eschscholzia californica* has been sown by the hundreds of pounds up and down California, the coastal gardener may see that poppy crossing with the coastal form. The orange blotch moves further and further up the petals the more outcrossing takes place. I urge gardeners to plant seed from local collections of poppies wherever they occur.

The foothill poppy, *Eschscholzia lobbii* (traditionally called *Eschscholzia caespitosa* in the flower trade), is a welcome addition to the flower border. It opens its pale yellow miniature flowers only to a truly sunny day; fog won't do. Diminutively pretty, and a less aggressive reseeder than *Eschscholzia californica*, with a neater habit, it is easily grown from seed.

The Wildflower Gardener as Researcher

Tuning in to wildflowers is a primary educational experience for Californians. Their ephemeral nature is one that dwellers in the arid west would do well to contemplate. Planting wildflowers to germinate with the fall rains, bloom with the spring sunshine, and go to seed with the summer drought teaches California gardeners lessons of seasonality.

Deepened understanding of the role of invasive exotic plants in California and in our native ecosystems throughout the country can emerge from working with wildflowers. The role of foreign invaders in complicated natural systems calls out for recognition.

Wildflowers serve as good public relations for California's native flora. Their beauty can serve to draw the gardener into the whole world of native plants. Events like the Wildflower Weekend, sponsored by the San Luis

Obispo chapter of the California Native Plant Society, are appropriate ritual occasions for Californians.

There is much to be learned about growing California wildflowers. Do not be intimidated or constrained by what the "experts" say. Some of my best ideas have come from customers operating on instinct or often blessedly ignorant of the rules. The spirit of playfulness often leads to discovery; this is particularly true in horticulture. So, experiment. With this group of plants, enticing for both their beauty and appropriateness, it is hard to lose. If you plant well, then, like the Yokuts of the Central Valley, you will have wildflowers in intoxicating abundance. If you plant well, you may find that, having been completely and totally saturated, dizzied, filled, and cleansed by the colors, textures, and forms of the annual wildflowers, you are ready to let them go. Sufficiently gladdened, you are ready for the flowers to go to seed and die, for the hills to go beige, for the string of sunny days to begin, as we move from spring to the long, rainless California summer.

 # The Land Wore
a Tufted Mantle

The Challenge
of Our Native Bunchgrasses

> Mr. Sherwood, who settled in 1853 in the valley which bears his
> name, and who was the first white settler there, took the writer
> to a point some distance from his house to point out danthonia
> (*Danthonia californica*) as the grass which was the most abun-
> dant on hillside and valley floor and which formed the favorite
> and most nutritious forage plant when he first brought cattle
> into the valley. This grass is now scarce in the vicinity.
> *Joseph Burtt Davy, 1902*

Time spent in native bunchgrass prairie has some of the same feeling as time
spent among old-growth redwoods, or in a place where aboriginal peoples
used to live. There is a haunting sense that mysteries await recovery and that
old relationships between soil and root, leaf blade and wind, are being
played out. The visual patterns of bunchgrass prairies are not ones that our
eyes are used to seeing, but they are the patterns of old California.

The Napping Prairie

It's late April, time for a hike to my favorite bunchgrass prairie in the
foothills nearby. Climbing the hill, I walk through non-native annual
grasses like ripgut brome and European wild oat. As I get closer to the top,
purple needlegrass, *Nassella pulchra*, appears, its long awns tipped with purple. Where traces of an old fire road remain, California oatgrass, *Danthonia
californica*, has filled in the tire ruts. In the spaces between, Douglas iris and
blue-eyed grass, poppies and Indian paintbrush flourish. In late summer,
pungent tarweeds add a haze of yellow that is almost chartreuse.

The hill levels off, then sinks down to a deep canyon with a creek running through it. Where it is level, the vegetation changes, forming a grassy strip four hundred yards long and fifty yards deep of almost intact coastal prairie. Running along the ridge, interfacing with coyote bush, ceanothus, coffeeberry, Pacific wax myrtle, and toyon, this is one of the most intact stands of native bunchgrasses I have seen. It is a place I like to be.

Tucked tightly into the edges of the coyote bush groupings is the graceful California fescue, *Festuca californica*. In the level stretches in between are foothill stipa, *Nassella lepida,* June grass*, Koeleria macrantha,* and more California oatgrass, *Danthonia californica*. Deep scarlet Indian paintbrush, purple Douglas iris, and the sweet smell of ceanothus. Later, *Triteleia laxa*, Ithuriel's spear, will be everywhere.

Here the Idaho fescue, *Festuca idahoensis*, grass of northern prairies, nears its southern limit. It forms a shining, rich green sweep along the ridge, clumps eighteen inches tall, blades soft and fine. Luxuriant growth. Almost nothing that wouldn't have been here two hundred years ago. I find myself yawning. There is no use fighting it. *Festuca idahoensis* is my favorite napping grass.

The Enigmatic Bunchgrasses

Writing this chapter, I imagine revising it until the presses roll, so continually are new information and perspectives about native bunchgrasses emerging. Which grasses where, and why, their evolution with megafauna from the Pleistocene, the role of grazing in restoring native prairie, techniques for restoring prairie, and local genotype purity are some of the issues revolving around this topic.

When I think of making generalizations about bunchgrasses, I am reminded of a quotation from Barry Lopez's *Of Wolves and Men*, in which he speaks of the Nunamiut Eskimo's belief "that each wolf is a little different, that new things are always seen. If someone says big males always lead the pack and do the killing, the Eskimo shrug and say, 'Maybe. Sometimes.'" This response would make an excellent motto for those seeking to make generalizations about our California bunchgrasses.

Our attempts to understand the dynamics of native bunchgrass prairies are a good example of the difficulties and limitations surrounding the scientific mind as it analyzes nature and elucidates our role in the transformation, both "forward" and "back," of the California landscape. I now see bunchgrasses as a heuristic device capable of humbling and occasionally bewildering us. Land use issues, political questions, real-estate conundrums, and other knotty problems surround attempts to understand their ecology.

None of that controversy lessens the beauty of our native bunchgrasses, or the possibilities for rich and comely meadows and interestingly textured grass gardens. Manifesting in many different sizes and growth habits, leaf widths and shades of green, seed and flower types, soil and exposure preferences, and even smells, California's perennial grasses are an aspect of the native flora neglected for years, even by the most dedicated students of native plants. Now every respectable native plant nursery carries a good representation of native grasses.

What Are Bunchgrasses?

Bunchgrasses, unlike the sod-forming grasses used for lawns, send up vegetative shoots every year from a central, perennial crown. Young vegetative stems grow upward with the enveloping basal sheath. Sod-forming grasses, by contrast, send up young vegetative shoots outside the basal leaf sheath. There is no distinct beginning or end to a sod-forming grass. The lawn, a smooth, velvet green carpet, suitable for playing croquet, the perfect sward at *Sunset* magazine's Menlo Park headquarters, this is the ultimate use of sod-forming grasses.

Another distinguishing characteristic of certain bunchgrasses, such as the handsome and adaptable California fescue, is the formation of a "skirt" at the base. While most of the stems are erect, some of the older outer stems bend over, thereby mulching, shading, and controlling erosion in between the grasses. This grass, with its graceful aprons of gold, green, and silver, often presents a neatly organized "staggered" effect on partially shaded banks. Craig Dremann, of the Redwood City Seed Company, from whom I first heard the word *bunchgrasses*, and who never shies away from controversy, believes that these skirts, which some call "thatch" and believe must be removed in order for new shoots to emerge, help to shade and protect new growth. It may be that in some situations, to some degree, some years, with some species, both are right.

Now that my eyes are tuned in to the subtle, complicated textures of a native bunchgrass prairie, a hillside of exotic annual grasses, no matter how luxuriant and spring green, is not enticing. I know that my chances are poor of finding wonderful surprises like the spring-blooming bulb pussy ears, *Calochortus tolmiei*, with its fuzzy petals, or mule's ear, *Wyethia angustifolia*. Acquainted with the challenges of reestablishing native grasses and all their associates in the face of these vigorous annuals, I now find the Irish green hills of spring only mildly enjoyable.

Are all native grasses perennial bunchgrasses? About 20 percent of our native grasses are annuals. Some perennials, like *Leymus triticoides, Festuca rubra,* and California beach grass, *Leymus mollis*, also spread through underground rhizomes, so they are at once bunchgrasses and sod-forming grasses. The majority of the species of native grasses in California used in restoration and in making grass gardens are, however, perennial bunchgrasses.

California Native Bunchgrasses

Native grasses and their associated plants used to account for around 30 percent of California's landscape. It is estimated that now remnant prairies account for less than 1 percent of that same landscape, and some researchers say that nowhere, except, perhaps, on serpentine soil, is there a significant sample of pristine prairie, entirely free of non-native species.

Putting together a picture of what the grasslands of California used to look like, how they functioned in the greater ecosystem, and how they varied from place to place requires the skills of many botanical detectives. We can only speculate now about the exact species composition for different areas. Observation of remaining stands, study of the writings of early observers of natural California, and work with restored prairies are all part of this imaginative recreation.

Work done with native bunchgrasses in the 1950s focused on their ability to function as range plants for livestock. Researchers at that time concluded that natives could not compete with the non-native species, which outproduced them in seed production, seedling vigor, growth rate, and ability to withstand constant grazing. In recent years, however, native grasses have become the focus of much interest from federal and state agencies, conservation and restoration groups, and homeowners.

For the student of native flora, the realization that the grasses that green our hills in winter are not the grasses that used to be there before European contact can be the beginning of a deeper search into the history of our land, including both aboriginal and modern impacts. Recognition of the crucial part that perennial bunchgrasses play in the California scheme of things has led to the formation of the California Native Grass Association. In addition to being what a friend calls a "fan club for native grasses," it is also an organization concerned with the fate of California's ranch lands. It seeks non-adversarial interaction with California ranchers, an approach with much to recommend it. Also in the past ten years, a number of seed companies specializing in bunchgrass seed have emerged.

The Disappearance of California's Native Grasslands

What happened to the formerly luxuriant stands of native grasses? As with the disappearance of California wildflowers, some obvious and some subtle factors have worked together to displace these vulnerable plant communities.

Historically, poor grazing practices involving sheep and cattle were a major factor. The Gold Rush, in particular, rang the death knell for much of our native grasslands, when one million cattle to feed hungry miners appeared almost overnight. Perennial grasses were stomped, tromped, and eaten out of existence. Year-round grazing, combined with drought, provided no opportunity to replenish carbohydrate supplies in their roots and crowns. In many areas, native bunchgrasses quietly vanished, to be replaced, perhaps forever, by annual grasses from other places.

Livestock grazing may have played a complex role in pushing the native prairies over the edge. Anthony Joern has hypothesized that hard grazing by cattle, by decreasing forage quality, made grasses more palatable to grasshoppers, whose populations soared. Grasshoppers actually prefer suboptimal, but not exceedingly poor, forage. Early patterns of cattle grazing tended to create just this kind of forage. Because perennial grasses are available throughout the life cycle of most California grasshopper species, they are continually available for depredation. Decreased above-ground foliage led to decreased root volume, which may have decreased allelopathy, or the ability of the bunchgrasses to retard the growth of other plant species. This provides one example of the complex plant, animal, and insect interactions whose results we see today.

Cultivation and its attendant changes in water patterns largely eliminated bunchgrasses from such agricultural areas as the Central Valley. The plow destroyed vast acres of native prairie in California, as it did in the plains states. Suppression of natural fires and cessation of man-induced fires, such as those previously set by California Indians, allowed, in some situations, the return of grasslands to shrub lands.

The rapid spread of European weeds and grasses that are adapted to the above conditions remains the single greatest challenge to those seeking to return large areas of California to the dominance of perennial bunchgrasses. The story of bunchgrass restoration is the story of weed control. Fire, controlled grazing, mowing, hand weeding, and chemical suppression are all techniques used to control weeds in bunchgrass prairies. In the Central Valley and other areas of California, experimental exclusion of grazing has not necessarily brought about a return of the natives. The hold of exotic weedy annuals is too strong.

Looking for Bunchgrasses

Although the percentage of California's hills and valleys covered by bunchgrasses has severely declined, they are still around. You may be passing clumps, masses, or even whole fields of them on most hikes into wilderness areas. The key to discovery lies in becoming familiar with their appearance. On hikes, it helps to know which species are most likely to occur in a particular area. Local floras can be consulted for that information (see

Resources for a list of regional floras). Trips with naturalists are also helpful. A visit to local botanic gardens, where each species is labeled, is an excellent way to begin your acquaintance. Many people say that all grasses looked alike to them until they began growing them in their own back yards, an easy way to gain visual familiarity. As with wildflowers, your back yard can be your grassy textbook.

Some botanists divide California grasslands into coastal prairie (dominated by *Festuca* and *Danthonia* species) and valley grassland (dominated by *Nassella* and *Poa* species). In the Central Valley, an example of the latter plant community, some feel that the hold of European and Eurasian annual grasses is so strong that it cannot be broken, and they are, in effect, "new natives." Relict stands of valley grassland can still be found in some areas, such as the Nature Conservancy's Jepson Prairie.

Along the coast, it has been said, additional moisture from summer fog favors perennial grasses over annuals. However, it also keeps the weedy annual grasses growing longer through the year. Still, many stands of native grasses can be found along the north coast, some surviving with livestock grazing, some where grazing has been discontinued, some where it never occurred. The seeker of native bunchgrasses will be rewarded many times in the Point Reyes area and up the north coast. Terraces along the Mattole River in Humboldt County present some of the largest stands of California oatgrass I have seen.

Serpentine soil presents a classic case of inhospitality to non-native weeds and grasses, and many serpentine areas are good homes for bunchgrasses. Ring Mountain in Tiburon, Mount Tamalpais around Rock Spring (and many other places on that mountain, which is rich in bunchgrass species), and Edgewood Park in Redwood City are all serpentine areas with wonderful native wildflower and bunchgrass displays. Other thin, infertile soils are likely spots to find bunchgrass colonies.

Partly shaded areas often shelter good bunchgrass stands, as many exotic annuals prefer full sun. In the redwoods, you may find vanilla grass, *Hierochloe occidentale,* with its pretty white and purple flowers and heavenly fragrance, or California bottlebrush grass, *Elymus californicus*, a handsome rhizomatous species. The foothill stipa, *Nassella lepida*, also likes part shade.

Places that, for one reason or a combination of reasons, have not favored the growth of weedy species are good bets for finding bunchgrasses. Figuring out these reasons is a major challenge. Soil type, exposure, land use history, available moisture, geology, and current circumstances are operative variables. Once your eyes have been opened to the growth habits and appearances of bunchgrasses, you'll wonder how you missed them.

The Ecological Significance of Bunchgrasses

Since the vanished bunchgrass prairies of California captured my imagination, examples of the far-reaching consequences of the demise of these ecosystems frequently catch my eye. Many such consequences will probably never be known, or fully understood, because the species changeover was so sudden and complete. Ecological roles played by native bunchgrasses may include the following.

POST-FIRE SEEDING OF ANNUALS

Seeding of annual grass species, particularly Italian ryegrass, has occurred throughout the state on a large scale in response to road cuts, fires, and floods. Recent findings suggest that this activity does little to prevent erosion and may even in some cases make the situation worse. Large stands of annual ryegrass encourage pocket gopher activity, which can increase erosion. Annual ryegrass may also secrete allelopathic chemicals that retard or prevent the reestablishment of native species.

The Natural Resources Conservation Service has found that annual grasses, even when recommended residue is left, are not preventing erosion on grazing land in some ranching counties. Ranchers, duly noting this finding, are reputedly becoming more interested in managing their land so as to favor native bunchgrasses.

FIRE PREVENTION

Native bunchgrasses have been evaluated for fire-resistance. In 1989, *Sunset* magazine did a "torch test" on *Bromus carinatus* and a non-native barley. The latter ignited instantly and was soon reduced to ash under conditions that had the bunchgrass barely smoldering. Since perennial bunch-grasses are alive, although dormant to different degrees, through the "fire time" in California, and since they green up earlier and stay green longer than the annuals, they offer more fire protection than annuals do.

OAK REGENERATION

Problems with oak regeneration may be related to the loss of the bunchgrass cover that used to be part of oak savannah. Bunchgrasses make good nurse plants for germinating acorns, providing snug nests where acorns can lodge and make protected early growth. Annual grasses, on the other hand, create an impenetrable mass of above-ground foliage that can prevent the essential seed-soil contact necessary for seedling establishment. The high rate of water use during the growing season by annuals also robs young oak seedlings of necessary moisture at a critical time in their development.

FOOD FOR NATIVE GRAZERS

The Point Reyes elk reserve consists of two thousand acres set aside for three hundred tule elk to graze, rut, and breed on, with a view to their eventual reintroduction to the National Seashore. Reintroduction has been hampered by disease for many years, but it was recently reported that with the improvement of the elk grazing range, including the recovery of native bunchgrasses, the Point Reyes elk herd is no longer testing positive for bovine tuberculosis. Perhaps the tule elk missed its longtime associate, the native bunchgrass. An interesting parallel situation has been observed on the Great Plains. There, big bluestem and other native prairie grasses retain their nutrition as they go dormant for the winter. Bison and elk clear the snow from native grasses to find nutritious, naturally cured "native hay" to get them through the winter. Now that the inadvertent spread of cheatgrass and the intentional spread of crested wheatgrass are pervasive, bison reintroduction programs are hampered by a lack of winter feed. It may be that California's native grasses have the ability to retain nutrition in California's "winter," the late summer and fall dormancy before the winter rains stimulate new growth.

Along with dense shrubbery for midday "hanging out" and trees for roosting, California valley quail like a mosaic of habitats that includes the complex of plants associated with bunchgrasses. The spaces in between the bunchgrasses provide the broad-leaved forbs relished by quail for greens and then seeds.

Habitat structure, the architecture of a home, allows for and encourages or prevents different activities for different creatures Here is a famous desert ecologist's description of the unforeseen consequences of an intentional introduction into the Mohave Desert of a foreign grass, red brome:

> Quite clearly, every horned lizard that emerged from its winter retreat into this new grassy world encountered a most formidable barrier in its search for food. The grass stems were so crowded together that these broad-bodied lizards were completely unable to move forward normally. To find food, and later to mate and produce young, the lizards would either have to develop leaping legs, or wings, or turn on "edge" and walk with two legs on one side or the other . . . starvation, because of inability to negotiate the newly hostile terrain, was staring the local population in the face.

While weeding in our coastal prairie plot, it was satisfying to spot a lizard lounging comfortably between clumps of coastal hairgrass, *Deschampsia caespitosa* sp. *holciformis*. Well-established deer trails in native prairie wind neatly and conveniently around bunchgrasses.

Microtus californicus, the California vole, is the state's most prevalent mammal. It is prey for everything, including hawks, owls, skunks, badgers, and coyotes. The black-shouldered kite is entirely dependent on vole availability, its population soaring when vole populations soar, plummeting when vole populations drop.

Voles, unlike gophers and ground squirrels, cannot survive in heavily grazed fields. Intact prairies are threaded with vole paths, because when the vole is not breeding, which it does practically from birth, it is scurrying around nibbling the tips of grasses. The more there is to eat, the more they breed. A chemical present in the growing tips of grasses triggers vole fertility, and good vole fertility means good black-shouldered kite, garter snake, and bobcat territory.

John Kelly and the staff at the Cypress Grove Preserve in Marshall have conducted vole studies in grasslands for the past five years. I asked John if he thought that their extensive grassland restoration projects were enhancing vole populations, a question to which there is as yet no definitive answer. He made it clear that vole population dynamics are linked to multiple factors. One might speculate that annual grasslands, with their flush of growth in spring and early summer and lack of food and cover in the fall, when the annual grasses go to seed and die (and when migrating hawks are looking for voles), would create a different cycle than a perennial grassland. In the latter, although growth diminishes in the summer and fall, food and cover are usually more consistently available throughout the year.

The canopy provided by perennial bunchgrasses throughout the year might make voles harder to find, which would be good for the voles, bad for the hawks. Still, what is good for the voles is ultimately good for the hawks, kites, and badgers.

BUNCHGRASS SEED AS HUMAN FOOD

As these last examples demonstrate, there have probably been many subtle and undetected long-term consequences of the demise of bunchgrass communities. Most of the devastation occurred so rapidly that some succeeding generations of native Californians lost knowledge of the existence of native bunchgrasses.

An anthropological exploration of burning patterns in California cites dozens of examples of the importance of grass seed in the diet of the California Indians. Burning was used to stimulate seed production and renew the bunchgrasses. It also served to make available to the grasses the nutrients stored in dead stems by reducing them to ash. Henry Lewis scoured early historical and anthropological literature for references to the practices of burning, concluding that Native Californians used fire as a semi-agricultural tool. Native bunchgrass meadows were actually quasi-agricultural fields, maintained by burning and harvesting. Parched and ground grass seed was frequently offered to early explorers. It seems that far from being a people without agriculture, native Californians had mastered a form of agriculture closely allied to some of the ideas gathered together in what is now called "permaculture." Crops gathered from perennial plants that do not require replanting were regularly and reliably available without the upheaval attendant upon the planting of annuals. Lucy Young of the Wailaki tribe said that native bunchgrass seed is more nutritious than the seed of the exotic grasses that have supplanted them.

Experimenting with this food source, I created a unique appetizer for parties: California prairie pinole, consisting of various native seeds roasted and ground, sprinkled with a little salt. I also experimented with a cracker made of roasted, ground blue wildrye seed, chia seed, pine nuts, and wheat flour, which I called the "California Cracker." It needs work but has potential, going down best with a cup of manzanita berry cider.

Bunchgrasses and the Homeowner

The growth rate of most California native bunchgrasses is what I think of as the "Californian" growth rate, "not too much and not too little." It is the growth rate appropriate for California's climate, soils, and priceless ecological complexes. Bunchgrasses belong in botanic gardens, nature preserves, wildlands, and also suburban back yards.

We get numerous queries from homeowners looking for a drought-tolerant lawn. Although bunchgrasses by their very nature will never make a football field or croquet lawn, let us explore what they can do.

BUNCHGRASSES AND WILDFLOWERS

Planting areas with annual California wildflower seed leaves the homeowner with dead annuals from mid to late summer. Including bunchgrasses in the planting creates a healthy meadow, the grasses providing the backbone of a viable and permanent wildflower field.

GRASS GARDENS

Some native plant horticulturists are designing "grass gardens," bunchgrasses grouped with an eye to their design potential. A backing of a group of handsome Pacific reed grass plants (*Calamagrostis nutkaensis*) in coastal areas or deergrass (*Muhlenbergia rigens*), one of the most versatile and handsome larger grasses, can be fronted by June grass or foothill stipa, with an edging of low, mounding deep green coastal hairgrass or Idaho fescue.

Or use small-flowered melic grass (*Melica imperfecta*), red fescue, or June grass to encircle the trees in an orchard. Cape Mendocino reed grass, *Calamagrostis foliosa*, graces the meridians in San Luis Obispo. Again, local botanic gardens provide samplers where texture, habit, and color of the different species can be seen.

In my experience, the toughest native grass is creeping wildrye, *Leymus triticoides*, which spreads from underground rhizomes. Known to frequent moist, even saline meadows, this grass is thought by some to have been at one time more widespread than *Nassella pulchra,* which is currently thought to have been the widest-ranging of California native grasses. At a recent conference, one speaker suggested that difficulties experienced in reestablishing native prairie arise from a misapprehension as to which species originally predominated.

I planted this tall (2–4 feet) grass in a native perennial border, where it gracefully waved behind a mix of yarrows and horkelias. When it seemed to be spreading too quickly, I dug it out. Afterwards, I missed its slender, quivering presence, but only a few weeks later, I saw that it was back, had never really been gone. This grass is ideal for a moist situation where it can spread freely. In drier situations, it is shorter and less eager to roam.

EROSION CONTROL

For road cuts, raw banks, and steep slopes, consider a planting of bunchgrass species local to your area. Blue green Idaho fescue, flowing red fescue, and the stately California fescue will all make stunning design statements on banks and slopes. Stagger them up and down the slope, mulch, and keep watered till established, and the bunchgrasses will form a strong, pleasing visual pattern.

LAWN SUBSTITUTES

Red fescue, *Festuca rubra*, is both a bunching grass and a grass that spreads through rhizomes. It is one of the most adaptable of the native grasses and makes an effective, natural-looking, drought-tolerant lawn. It can be mowed three or four times yearly, greening up with minimal water even at the end of the summer. Or it can be left to its own devices, letting its fine, blue green blades lie down in the direction of the wind. I have a gradually expanding section that is interplanted with the white form of the California poppy and Douglas iris. It is lush and beautiful throughout the year.

I get calls from clients seeking a smooth perfect lawn grass for a baby's first halting steps. But little feet can learn to make their way around the clumps, and a soft cushiony mound of red fescue or Idaho fescue makes a lovely spot for a crash landing.

WHAT USED TO BE

The back-yard restorationist forms a picture of what used to be where her house now stands. In some cases, it was a grassland or an oak savannah. In restoring grassland to a portion of your back yard, you create a situation where little maintenance is required once the grasses are established, and you are giving yourself up to that most delightful of gardening situations, the one in which your garden, taking on a life of its own, teaches you. Many heavy clay soils, whose drainage does not suit those mainstays of the native plant palette, manzanitas and ceanothus, will support a stand of bunch-grasses. Information gained from horticultural plantings of bunchgrasses can be a valuable source of information for the restoration ecologist.

The Controversy

Fremontia, the journal of the California Native Plant Society, recently devoted an issue to grazing concerns and ideas about bunchgrasses and grazing. In the following issue, the editor, Phyllis Faber, said that they had never in the history of the journal received so many letters about any issue. Where does the controversy come in?

Bunchgrasses are inextricably tied to land use issues. While the role of livestock in the destruction of California native grasslands is undisputed, some have suggested controlled livestock grazing as a tool in the restoration of these same plant communities. Whether such "restoration grazing" practices can work, and whether ranchers will find them economically viable enough to widely adopt them remains to be seen. For an interesting introduction to the whole subject, see *Beyond the Rangeland Conflict: Toward a West That Works* by Dan Daggett.

For example, cattle may graze noxious weeds, controlling them to some extent, but they also spread them. They may help to tromp seed into the soil, but they can also seriously compact soil structure, affecting the ability of the soil to retain water, retard erosion, and release nutrients to plants. Their grazing preferences may favor some weedy species. Mark Blummler, in a letter to a California Native Plant Society newsletter, summarizes it well: "No one management strategy will favor all natives. There are suites of alien species that respond to various levels of grazing pressure, so that natives will be under pressure no matter what. Under the circumstances, a diversity of grazing regimes (including enclosures) might be best."

Following the debate about native grasses, where they were and in what quantities, who ate them and when, what they grew with, and how we can best work with them, becomes a study in epistemology as well as botany, paleontology, and range management. Two researchers can look at the same plots, the same sets of Paleolithic megafaunal teeth, the same aerial photographs, and apparently come to different conclusions. There is humility to be gained from this, about the limits of our knowledge and the complexity of the natural world. How impossible it is to grasp all the aspects of any one chunk of nature, with its infinite interconnections. How careful we must be in our actions. How valuable is work done on a small scale, such as in the back-yard restoration garden. The attitude of indigenous observers, openness to variation and acceptance of ambiguity, seems to be among the things the native bunchgrasses have to teach us.

Interestingly, it is not just in California that prairies are the subject of fierce debate. In a book about the native prairies of the Midwest written in 1957, May Theilgaard Watts describes the issues of the historical provenance of prairies as "an old scarred battleground of midwestern botanists, where many a shiny theory has met defeat." Where California has advocates of grazing and exclusion, fire and no fire, seeding versus plugging, thatch and no thatch, in the land of the tallgrass prairie, a major question is: Why prairie here and forest there? Some say lack of rainfall creates prairie; others say it's soil texture and structure; some say drainage and depth of water table; some say age of rock; some say fire; others call prairie a deciduous forest temporarily without trees.

One researcher concludes: "We may never have definite answers to these questions. But they are tantalizing to ponder, and might even give some sleepless nights." But the back-yard restoration gardener need not lose sleep. The home garden can provide an uncontroversial opportunity for grassland restoration on a small scale.

Techniques for Back-Yard Grassland Creation

Since no one can tell the homeowner exactly how the native grasses grew in the place where she lives, the beginning grass gardener may find it helpful to bring a sense of play to this work. Looking at and thinking about the back-yard grassland, the homeowner can be his own researcher. By starting small and working carefully, he can engage productively in work with native grasses. Checking out local remnant grassland populations, perhaps with the help of local field trips with the California Native Plant Society, the Nature Conservancy, or any of a number of similar organizations, is a good way to start.

For the homeowner working in small areas, it can make sense to grow native bunchgrasses in flats and transplant to the site rather than to broadcast this relatively expensive seed. Weedy grass seed is frequently present in the soil, and it can be difficult to distinguish in the seedling stage which is a weedy grass and which the desirable native. For sites that lend themselves to direct seeding, the species that have been most successful for us are red fescue, purple needlegrass, nodding stipa, California brome, California meadow barley, and blue wildrye. Gardens that have been heavily herbicided for years, which is often true of urban lawns, can sometimes be successfully direct-seeded, since the weed population has been controlled over time.

We often recommend planting individual bunchgrasses, from plugs, four-inch pots, or even gallon-size containers, into the ground and then mulching heavily. The spacing for each species can be estimated based on the width of the mature plant. However, we have recently begun to crowd them. We plant our plugs at least half the width of the mature plant to facilitate complete cover and make it more difficult for weedy species to move in. Nassellas, fescues, and koelerias can all be planted eight to twelve inches apart.

The field can also include perennials appropriate to the situation, such as checkerbloom, Douglas iris, Indian pink, blue-eyed and yellow-eyed grass, California buttercup, native plantains, native bulbs like calochortus and brodiaea, and native clovers. The basic procedure is simple, no different from that of any seed-sowing project.

SOWING SEED IN FLATS

Special plug-planting plastic trays are available but not essential. Used by restorationists, they offer advantages for mass plantings, but they require a significant amount of plastic. The elongated shapes of these connected pots, originally developed for tap-rooted tree seedlings, may not be ideal for fibrous-rooted bunchgrasses. Suffice it to say that either will usually work, and plastic flats can often be obtained free and reused indefinitely. Cover the seed lightly with soil, tamp, and water. When the grasses have germinated and each seedling has three to five blades, transplant gently into four-inch pots. Keep well watered and provide some shade in the hottest time of the year.

Plug-growers usually seed directly into special plastic tube pots. Usually, each plug will contain more than one grass plant. Some prefer individual plants separately planted out; others let the plants work it out.

Most native grass seed requires no pretreatment, but we have observed the following exceptions. *Nassella cernua* (nodding stipa) germinates better with a fifteen-minute water soak and a two-week cold-stratification period. *Nassella pulchra* (purple needlegrass) with the awns attached is easier to handle after a fifteen-minute water soak. Most will germinate within one month. *Muhlenbergia rigens* (deergrass, basketgrass) can take longer, even up to two months, and prefers warm weather for germination. *Acnatherum hymenoides* (Indian ricegrass), formerly called *Oryzopsis hymenoides,* seems to germinate better with a two-month cold-stratification period. *Danthonia californica* (California oatgrass) germinates more readily following an after-ripening period of up to two years. It is cleistogamous, that is, it sets seed at the base of the flower stalk as well as at the top, and, interestingly, those basal seeds have higher germinative capacity.

TRANSPLANTING

When roots fill the pot, it is time to put the grasses in the ground. Good planting times are October through February, although this can be stretched a bit at either end. We use wood chips, sawdust, or other nonfertile mulch to maintain the advantage of the native grasses until they are large enough to hold their own. It is important to keep young seedlings well watered initially and through the first dry season. Bunchgrass seedlings are vulnerable to desiccation when young, although drought-tolerant species are tough and hardy once established. Some will thrive with an occasional deep watering in the hottest part of the summer. Too much summer water, particularly for those species from the Central Valley and other places that bake in summer, will lead to rot.

MAINTENANCE

Keep the spaces in between well mulched or hand-weeded, or both. I know of several prairies that have been established by borrowing techniques from permaculturists. Several layers of a combination of recycled newspapers and flattened cardboard boxes are spread over the area to be planted. Weed seed–free straw, such as rice straw, is piled on top of the cardboard, one foot thick. Small pockets are made in the straw, and sterilized potting soil is placed in the pockets. The bunchgrass plugs are then planted into the potting soil.

Some recommend spring or fall pruning to stimulate vigorous growth. Clumps can benefit from a spring raking to remove dead blades. It is said that setting fire to coastal hairgrass (*Deschampsia caespitosa* sp. *holciformis*) and burning it halfway down rejuvenates it. Other grasses that respond well to an annual shearing are Pacific reed grass and red fescue.

For large areas where direct-seeding is required, herbicide use is recommended by some to prepare the seedbed. Pre-emergent herbicides to deplete the weedy seed bank and post-emergent herbicides to control weedy competition are used. I leave this to your own judgment, but it is important to remember that the goal behind attempts to reestablish bunchgrasses is the health on all levels, including that of the soil fauna and the invertebrate population, of that particular piece of land.

Once the grasses are established, weeds can in some situations be controlled by fall and spring mowing; the theory is that this practice will prevent non-native weeds and grasses from going to seed, thus giving the perennial natives an edge. A disadvantage is that wildflowers growing between the grasses will also be prevented from blooming and going to seed. Also, many weedy species, both grasses and forbs, can respond to mowing by blooming and setting seed at a height of only three or four inches. Some weedy species may respond to mowing with renewed vigor.

The small scale of the back-yard prairie has much to offer. A little "napping prairie," a replication of the beautiful coastal prairie fragment in the hills near here where I love to lose consciousness, thrives close to hand between the house and the office. Idaho fescue, combined with California oatgrass and foothill stipa, makes a luxuriant bed. Constant nipping in the bud of weedy grasses and forbs, tender regard and careful pruning, and the opportunity for daily observations may all be factors in the greater success of the napping prairie than in some of our plantings not accessible to daily view.

When I hurt my back and couldn't get up to my favorite piece of wild prairie, I could still enjoy its spring green and summer multi-hued effect in comfort on a deck chair right outside my door. There are times for all of us when hiking to the pristine places is not possible, another reason to have these companions close at hand.

There may be a napping prairie near you, surviving against great odds, awaiting your discovery and appreciation, a repository of ideas for your back yard. The California grasses were an integral part of a complex ecological network, and their unprecedented retreat has had far-reaching consequences that we are only beginning to ferret out. At home and in the hills, may they flourish again.

CHAPTER EIGHT

To See All the Colors, to Hear All the Songs

Problems of Exotic Pest Plants

It was more than a year since he had trod this path, and as he found it growing fainter and fainter, and more and more over-grown with the wild mustard, he said to himself, "I think no one can have passed through here this year."

As he proceeded he found the mustard thicker and thicker. . . . The plant is a tyrant and a nuisance, the terror of the farmer; it takes riotous possession of a whole field in a season; once in, never out; for one plant this year, a million the next; but it is impossible to wish that the land were freed from it. Its gold is as distinct a value to the eye as the nugget gold is in the pocket.   *Helen Hunt Jackson, 1884*

The Bureau of Land Management recently completed a survey of plant communities on the 189 million acres under their administration. The data show that non-native invasive weeds currently occupy 3 million acres and are expanding their range by 14 percent each year; that is by 2300 acres per day. Once considered only an agricultural problem, invasive weeds are now the greatest single threat to natural ecosystems.
Report prepared by the California Exotic Pest Plant Council Biocontrol Committee, Summer 1995

"Unless greater actions are taken to control weeds, by the year 2000, weed infestations on Federal lands alone are projected to increase to 34 million acres, an area about the size of seventeen large national parks like Yellow-stone," Deputy Secretary of the Interior John Garamendi predicted in 1995.

When I attended my first conference organized by the California Exotic Pest Plant Council, I expected to hear about the magnitude of this problem, as well as about new methods to combat the spread of invasive plants in California. I hoped to be encouraged by success stories and to relax in the company of those with similar awareness of the astronomical growth of this problem.

What I didn't expect was that the conference would be among the most interesting I have attended. Because it was about relationships, between animals and plants, insects and plants, birds and plants, and fire and plants, dismaying news of the degradation of natural systems by exotic pest plants was balanced by a sense of revelation. Natural patterns were delineated in their complexity. The notion of their disappearance elicited despair while strengthening our determination that the world's play, the dance of many partners, not be lost.

We heard stories about volunteers who devoted their weekends to protecting California's ecosystems by pulling broom and removing Cape ivy from the Santa Cruz mountains. There were stories about new uses of fire in the control of broom and yellow star thistle. There were stories about careful, thirty-year-long studies of sagebrush land, of the desert tortoise, of the spartina invasions in our wetlands. There were stories about pampas grass, tamarisk, Cape ivy, arundo grass, pepperweed, iceplant, and cheatgrass, all involving relationships in the process of disruption.

Many of these plants are still sold by California nurseries and planted by California gardeners, whose back yards serve as springboards for the spread of such species as Cape ivy, capeweed, vinca, broom, iceplant, English ivy, passionflower vine, pampas grass, and acacia. Not a few gardens in my town consist solely of such species, often donated by other gardeners, who, understandably, "have more than they need." The time-honored sharing of plants between gardeners is a questionable practice in California gardens when it involves species like montbretia, calla lily, naked ladies, vinca, and iceplant.

Friends laughed when I said I was attending the California Exotic Pest Plant Council Conference, responding to something ridiculous about this specialized subject, but there is nothing funny about the 2,300 acres a day said to be lost as native habitat or to agricultural use through the spread and establishment of non-native pest plants.

Aspects of Change

Enmeshed in its unique web of interactions and resiliencies, each landscape will be interrupted differently by biological invasions. For example, in our California deserts, the course of events following the invasion of non-native annual grasses illuminates some of the ways in which invasive plants bring change. The characteristics of weedy grasses result in a change in fire regimes, which has consequences for the life history of the desert tortoise, a rare and endangered species.

CHANGES IN FIRE REGIMES

Unlike our western chaparral, the California deserts are not fire-adapted. Fires did not traditionally sweep through them. Spaces between shrubs were either bare or occupied sparsely by native herbs that, in the dry times, shrivel and shatter or are carried away by ants, providing little fuel load for the spread of fire. (*Fuel load* refers to the amount of flammable material available for burning at a given time). Unlike annuals in the chaparral, the seeds of desert annuals are not fire followers, stimulated by fire to germinate. Some important desert shrub components, such as creosote bush, long-lived and slow-growing, will not resprout after a fire.

When exotic grasses like red brome, *Bromus rubens,* invade the desert (or are actually planted by managing agencies), they do not shrivel or shatter after they go to seed and die, but remain in place, forming a thick cover of dead plant material. The wetter the year, the larger the fuel load provided by the exotic annual grasses. Intense fires began to sweep regularly through desert areas that had not known them before, killing shrubs like creosote bush, Joshua trees, and various cacti. Plants that live by washes are often better equipped to survive the disturbance of seasonal flooding, which allows them to adapt to this new fire regime. Consequently they begin to dominate, and the plant palette changes fundamentally. Food and shelter plants important for endangered species like the desert tortoise are destroyed, and ongoing plant successions are disrupted.

In areas that are fire-adapted, many creatures can either run from fire or burrow into the ground to escape it. The desert tortoise has no such capability. Changes in fire regimes are an important consequence of plant invasions, with different ramifications in each situation.

Whereas with strip-mining or clear-cut logging, major negative consequences are evident from the first, the disruption of natural processes that comes with the invasion of native plants may not be obvious for a while. Once it is too late, we can evaluate the loss of good grazing that follows the invasion of cheatgrass and yellow star thistle, or the compromising of dune ecology that follows the establishment of European beach grass, *Ammophila arenaria*. Continuity of experience is required, a return through time to note change. The "drive-by insight" obtained by driving at sixty miles an hour down a highway may not reveal the subtle processes transforming our landscape.

Slow, steady erosion of natural values resulting from the choices made by the land managers called gardeners is evident in many situations, from public lands to private holdings. Old house sites in national parks demonstrate the consequences of early horticultural choices. A hike into the southern end of Point Reyes National Seashore begins with a stroll through eucalyptus, Cape ivy, vinca, Klamath weed, and broom, and every year it takes longer to get beyond the plant community I call "old ranchhouse."

DEPLETING WATER AVAILABILITY

Eucalyptus planted by coastal creeks displaces willow thickets, elderberries, alders, and birch. Growing over one hundred feet high, eucalyptus act as a powerful suction pump, siphoning off water to support their quick growth and thus reducing creek flow and ground-water levels.

CHANGING VEGETATION ARCHITECTURE

Creatures that require a certain kind of spatial patterning for forage and shelter find their lives disrupted by changes in vegetation architecture. Take the example of the wide-bodied lizard, unable to negotiate the dense vegetation of *Bromus rubens* and consequently starving to death. These disruptions are noticed only if somebody happens to be looking. Few knew of the existence of the wide-bodied lizard in the first place.

Eucalyptus groves provide habitat for predators like the great horned owl, which includes other owls among its prey. Diminished populations of species like the much smaller saw-whet owl and others in the areas around the Point Reyes Bird Observatory are possibly attributable to the unnatural advantage given to great horned owls by the increase in eucalyptus groves in the area.

Nutritional inferiority can be a subtle yet difficult-to-detect factor in the slow diminution of resources. In a study by Harold W. Avery, captive tortoises were provided either native or non-native foods. Those fed *Camissonia boothii,* a native forb, had a greater rate of protein assimilation and remained in positive nitrogen balance throughout the study, whereas those fed *Schismus barbatus,* a non-native, experienced a significant loss in total body mass over the digestibility trial. Creatures may be seen eating non-native plants, but their ability to thrive on such fare cannot be inferred.

The face of California has been irrevocably changed by the invasion of non-native plants. Those who look now see a transformed landscape, often without knowing it. Adobe bricks used to build Spanish missions included in their composition seeds of non-native grasses, and from that time to the present, California has continued to host a succession of waves of invasive plants.

Habitat Restoration Begins at Home

Louise Lacey, editor of the *Growing Native Research Newsletter,* found a clear pattern of evolution in a survey of her readers. Most began gardening with widely available exotic ornamental plants, became organic gardeners growing their own vegetables, and then became interested in native plants. They have one-third of their gardens planted in natives and are slowly increasing the number of native plants. In informal observations of my employees, clients, and neighbors, I, too, have noticed certain developmental steps that apply once the interest in natives quickens, potential pathways for the back-yard restoration gardener.

First, the gardener becomes aware of some segment of the native flora that is visually appealing. Often, spring wildflowers, seen at wildflower shows, in natural displays, at nurseries, or in books, entice the gardener.

Planting annual wildflowers will in most cases lead to immediate success and pleasure. A tentative reach into other areas, such as shrubs and perennials, commences. More difficult subjects, such as native grasses, with their challenging ecology, and native trees, which require long-term involvement and delayed gratification, are subsequently tackled.

Somewhere in all this activity, the gardener notices that most of the work involved is weeding. The story of gardening in California, and indeed throughout the world, is the story of weeds. Possibly unique to California is the extent to which these weeds are offered in nurseries, bought, and taken home by gardeners. The gardener may begin to spend weekends removing French or Scotch broom from national parklands or replanting bunchgrasses on a San Francisco mountain.

As concerns beyond the fence develop, the learning will begin to flow both ways. Training in the use of the pulaski and other weed removal tools is available through various site stewardship and habitat restoration groups. Techniques learned on the trail can be applied to the home environs. Information obtained from a close back-yard scrutiny of plant characteristics can be turned to advantage on the trail. The gardener then may join with neighbors on local projects.

Removal and Control

An ounce of prevention is worth a pound of cure, and *a stitch in time saves nine.* Both sayings were made for exotics control. That lone pampas grass that could have been removed in an hour with a pick and shovel when it first appeared will now require a backhoe or a half-day's work. As Helen Hunt Jackson said of wild mustard, "one plant this year, a million the next."

Each species has its own characteristics, which determine how it can best be removed in various situations. Each species needs to be understood in order to be controlled with as little damage to non-target species as possible. (Non-target species are those plants and animals that we do not wish to affect.) As more information becomes available from controlled experiments performed by scientists and volunteers, techniques are continually fine-tuned. CalEppc has six different working groups, each focused on a particular pest plant, each with its own difficulties and protocols for effective removal.

MANUAL REMOVAL

Hand labor is the approach most frequently used by gardeners and also by our national parks. Various specialized tools have been invented or called into service for different weed problems. For example, the weed wrench (see Resources) was invented, manufactured, and sold by Tom Ness of New Tribe, one of the first to recognize and tirelessly wage the battle against French and Scotch broom, capeweed, and pampas grass in Marin County.

The weed wrench is a back-saving device that levers broom plants out of the ground. Another implement, called the root jack, also makes broom removal easy on the back. We used to think that all broom plants needed to be pulled out by the roots to avoid crownsprouting, but now the consensus of opinion seems to be that plants over one-and-one-half inches in diameter can be cut at ground level and will not sprout again. Those smaller in diameter must be pulled. Working when the soil is wet is ideal. Plants that require a tool when the soil is dry can be removed by hand when the soil is wet.

THE BRADLEY METHOD   *Two Australian sisters, working to restore native bush, devised this patient method of manual weed control. Weeding by hand, they locate the most intact stands of native plants and weed out from there. They are in essence protecting what is still intact. As John Seed, a fellow Australian, puts it, "They start from the strength."*

This seemingly simple way of tackling what can seem like overwhelming pest plant problems has worked for many. It offers a sensible way to prioritize activities and maintain the psychological equilibrium that the magnitude of such endeavors requires.

The pulaski, a combination pick and hoe, is the tool of choice for removing small pampas grass plants. For large clumps on flat land, tractors or trucks are sometimes used to pull the clumps out of the ground. On sloping land, where erosion is a consideration, the clump can be chainsawed off close to the ground, then covered with black plastic.

MOWING

Mowing prevents seeding and sets back invasive plants but may also result in the dragging around of weed seeds. Moreover, many weeds respond with vigor to mowing, regrowing with multiple stems and setting even more seed. Unless one uses a scythe, there is also the endless drone of the lawn mower, a highly polluting user of fossil fuels, to consider. And it is difficult to mow on sloping land.

Weedy areas in our garden are nevertheless kept rigorously mowed through spring and early summer. When dormancy commences in midsummer, we stop mowing. Mowing functions as a kind of holding action, preventing additions to the weed seed bank in the soil in parts of the garden that have not yet been planted. I appreciate the neatness mowing gives the garden — the quality of "being attended to" that distinguishes the back-yard restoration project from the wild.

Yellow star thistle is an invasive annual with massive seed production. A single plant can produce thousands of seeds. Yellow star thistle now covers eight million acres in California. If you don't have it yet, it's on the way.

It is not a problem on regularly plowed croplands, until they are let go fallow. On pasturelands and wildlands, or along roads, this plant can form a solid, thorny mass. Biological controls have been evaluated, and three insects have been released and established throughout the state. Although 70 percent of the plants in the test plots have been found to have seed-eating insects present in the flower heads, researchers believe that the capacity of this plant to produce seeds is so great that the remaining 30 percent of the plants forming seed are enough to keep this invasion on the move. It moves more slowly than if biological control insects were not present, but it moves. Such controls buy time to formulate other programs.

Other control methods include mowing and burning regimes. Experiments have shown that an effective method includes mowing or burning just at the point when the flower heads are beginning to turn yellow.

Pollination is prevented, so no seeds will form. However, the tremendous root systems often allow for a second growth of the cut plant, with even greater branching inflorescences and heightened flowering and seed production. A second and sometimes even a third cutting may be necessary.

The good news is that seed of yellow star thistle lasts only three years in the soil, so three years of treatment should yield eventual control.

BURNING

Large-scale burning can be used against broom and yellow star thistle. Complicated protocols have been worked out for deploying this useful tool to suppress invasive plants on a broad front, especially in fire-adapted ecosystems. Concerns include the effect on air quality, control of fire, especially in areas with significant residential presence, and the potential invasion of the burned-over area by exotics. Agencies controlling burn permits include air-quality agencies and local fire departments. A program including more than one burn is usually required.

One spring, I walked up the ridge to the napping prairie, model and seed source for my back-yard prairie. I knew that a controlled burn had taken place the previous autumn, and I had been back the previous winter to see the bright green leaf blades sprouting from blackened bunchgrass crowns, the new coyote bush sprouts within their hoopskirts of fire-charred limbs. The soil around the grasses was hard and crusted, but the rejuvenation of native plants seemed evident.

That spring, when I reached the top of the ridge, where the native grasses had held sway, stable for at least the eight years since my original discovery, I saw that the weedy grasses previously found only on the hillside below had moved into the napping prairie. The bunchgrasses were not flourishing, but the weedy grasses were. Two years after that day, what had been a perfect example of native prairie is now almost indistinguishable from the degraded grasslands around it. I don't nap there anymore.

Although California grasslands are fire-adapted, changes in the land may make fire less than a friend to some native plant communities. Huge weedy seed banks exist nearby, easily spread by equipment or somehow given an edge by fire. Our soil is different now, depending on its land use history, and may react differently to fire. I can only hypothesize about the reasons, but the prototype of my back-yard napping prairie is no more. A friend working with the Park Department asked me to map any other such pristine grasslands, so that they could avoid them in future burns. But I know of no other such place.

Fire is an appealing tool. It involves lots of toys — trucks and flame torches, helicopters, radios, balloons, lots of organizational apparatus, and a natural process that might seem to do our work for us. I cringe when I see a controlled burn, soil blackened and bare, with just a few fennel plants left at the edge, loaded with ripe seed. Because the protocol did not include the simple hand removal of nearby weed seed sources, that burned area will soon be a fennel field. Fire requires follow-up, and if the plant community is not broken, don't fix it.

SMOTHERING AND SOLARIZING

For small areas, black or clear plastic as well as a number of organic materials can be used for weed control. Clear plastic is used to solarize the soil, killing seedlings and, in optimal conditions, providing some kill of seeds in the soil as well. This technique is not useful where the land is not level or on the coast, where it rarely gets hot enough to provide significant kill, and solarizing instead creates a kind of greenhouse.

We have mulched for years with both turkey bedding and whatever chips were made available by tree-removal crews. Weeds like French sorrel and Bermuda grass, which spread vegetatively, will not be killed by even a foot of mulch but can be removed more easily when their roots move through this mulch layer.

In the process, however, we are adding unknown quantities to our soil. Ideally, chipped coastal scrub plants would be used to mulch coastal scrub plantings, but we accept chipped eucalyptus, pine, or cypress, with no apparent harmful effects.

BIOLOGICAL CONTROLS

This method of weed control consists of the introduction of natural enemies of weeds from the home range of the weed. The famous success story in the arena of biological controls is Klamath weed, *Hypericum perforatum*. A poisonous weed from Europe, it had infested more than two million acres in California alone when biocontrol insects from Europe reduced it to less than 1 percent of its former abundance in California and Oregon.

Predators must be selected that will confine their attack to the target species, and mass rearing and release into the environment must be carefully controlled. It takes years to verify host plant specificity. Rigorously controlled by extremely complicated, demanding, and time-consuming USDA regulations, biological management is possibly the best way to go, turning pest plants into team players rather than dominant species.

HERBICIDES

Some of the hardest questions in the field of restoration relate to chemical use. Herbicides are widely used, although efforts are made by many to use them as infrequently and as precisely as possible. Still, there is no doubt that policies requiring the control of exotic pest plants are a boon to the chemical industry.

Restorationists must consider that many native plant gardeners have an organic gardening background and find the use of herbicides unacceptable. The back-yard restoration gardener, usually working on a smaller scale, may more easily rely on other methods.

Proper Disposal of Debris

When dealing with pest plants, debris disposal is as important as removal. In my town, residents have treated our coastal cliffs as dump sites, simply unloading their garden debris over the edge. This often consists of those plants they wish they had never planted — just the ones that can best take advantage of being dumped in unmanaged areas. Cape ivy, most nefarious of vining plants, has spread in this way over cliff faces. It smothers the willows that hold the cliff's wet places and kills the coyote bush that digs deep in dry soil, disrupting the plant associations that give us our best shot at cliff stability along California's shaky shores.

When a group of volunteers working in the coastal mountains removed masses of Cape ivy from a creekside, they piled the plants in heaps and left them there. A rainy winter caused the creek to rise and sweep those piles downstream, where it is likely that many rhizomes and living roots colonized new areas.

Beware of seeds remaining on the plant to ripen and fall where the plants are taken, or nodes that can root in contact with the soil. Removing the problem in one area should not create it in another. I learned this from personal experience when a debris pile on an adjacent vacant lot became a nightmare of tangled branches, old junk, wine bottles, baby shoes, and re-sprouting Cape ivy, expanding down the block.

When we remove Cape ivy, we place it on double-ply black plastic and cover it with another sheet of the same. Eight months later pink rhizomes are still alive, with the potential to root and grow. We also have special composting strategies to use with rhizomatous weedy species like sorrel and for plants growing from corms and bulbs, like yellow bur-clover, naked ladies, and calla lilies. Unless they are managed and monitored for high temperatures, compost piles should not be the repositories of rhizomatous weeds.

"Junky" areas, part of many rural scenes, are natural homes for the spread of invasive plants. Every rural locality has its own particular configuration of pasture lands, protected public lands, neglected and ignored lands, agricultural lands, and intensely gardened lands. Yours will be unique, with its own weedy species, its own species to protect, its own "native nightingales singing its native songs."

In urban and suburban areas, where high standards of neatness prevail, potentially invasive plants like ivy, vinca, and Bermuda grass are often regularly pruned and controlled. In semi-rural and rural areas, where maintenance is often more relaxed, such plants may prove ruinous to vacant lots and open land.

Sometimes removal of one invasive plant opens the way for another. Broom gave way to eupatorium in one situation, sorrel in another. Both are rhizomatous spreaders, harder to remove than broom, which has the advantage that once you pull it up, it's gone, except for seeds waiting to sprout for twenty to eighty years. We've been working on French sorrel for ten years, without (as James Young of the USDA said of cheatgrass) having done it any serious damage. It seems less daunting, in terms of sheer biomass, than eucalyptus or cotoneaster, yet it may be the ultimate victor.

Ann Young of Marin County spent one day a week for some years removing broom on nearby Mount Tamalpais. She always came back glowing, with stories to tell of what she had seen — a pileated woodpecker, a beautiful fog bank, spider tubes, calypso orchids.

Ann is a deliberate person, mindful of all her actions in the garden. The larger, exuberant habitat restoration teams were not suited to her style of working, so she began a relationship with the nearby state park in which they allowed her to work either by herself or with one or two other people. They brought her tools, removed debris, and respected her methods and persistence.

Looking back on the two years she was able to go regularly to the mountain for broom and thistle removal, she concluded that if you persevere, working carefully and slowly, the results will justify effort spent. Her major concerns were to disturb nothing native and to leave the soil as intact as possible. She emphasizes the importance of working with somebody who knows the plants, has watched the land through the seasons, and can tell you where the calypso orchids will be next spring.

"Now that I'm not doing it anymore, I miss it," says Ann. "I'm somehow lesser. I would prefer to still be doing it."

Getting the Concept

A stand of French broom grows along the road to my house, between the road and the soccer field. *Genista monspessulanis* spreads rapidly, and its seed is said to live twenty-five to eighty years in the soil; it is adaptable to almost all habitats in the coast ranges, but its root system is usually shallow, and in wet or damp soil, seedlings can easily be pulled up. Every year it bloomed, sometimes twice, set seed, and ejected its seeds five to ten feet from the plant, spreading itself down the road.

One year some of us decided we didn't want to watch this increasing degradation of the land every time we played soccer or drove home. We publicized a broom-removal day, explaining in the local paper what we were up to, borrowed weed wrenches and root jacks, put up signs, and met with lunches, children, and a willing spirit.

Along with publicity and support, we also received our share of letters criticizing our efforts. I read the letters at the chiropractor's office, where the strenuous activity had sent me. Although I ended up lying down, I didn't take those letters that way.

Some colleagues recommended ignoring these critics. I thought their feelings and attitudes needed to be considered, and I continue to find that controversy, though not pleasant, forces me to continue investigations of these issues, to my own ultimate benefit. My search for the reasons to control biological invasions has taught me as much as any other part of my work.

I often hear the statement, "I'm not native here either." The hint of longing to belong somewhere rings a bell with me. It's as though our human feeling of homelessness is so great that compassion must be extended to recent immigrants of the plant world, as one hopes that it will be extended to oneself. Being not native here, does it not behoove us to begin to know this land where we find ourselves, to honor it with a clear look rather than collude in its continual diminution?

We broom-pullers were mightily abused. We were called genocidal, racist, and, worst of all, "well-meaning." One of our critics extolled the beauty of wild lilac blooming along the roadside, companioned by yellow broom. She used the "drive-by insight" to prove that broom is a friendly invader that can co-exist with native plants, even enhancing their beauty. The reality is that ceanothus, in my experience, does not reseed into stands of broom, and since most ceanothus is relatively short-lived, in twenty to thirty years there will be no blue contrast to the ubiquitous (although by no means unappealing) yellow of broom blossoms.

There will be no honey-sweet fragrance emanating from fragile ceanothus blossoms, no strange dry black seeds dropping in midsummer. Deer, who don't fancy broom, will miss snacking on the ceanothus. Tortoiseshell butterflies will not be laying eggs on shiny ceanothus leaves, nor will the ceanothus moth make its cocoons, prized rattles for traditional dances. There will be no swishing the blossoms in a bucket of water to make suds to wash with, as the Pomo did, and wreaths made for the Strawberry Festival will no longer include ceanothus. There will just be yellow.

The drive-by writer might get out of the car and follow a trail back into the woods. There she will find redwood violet and peppermint stripe candy flower carpeting the woodland edge, with a bit of broom from the roadside finding its way in. She needs to come back next year and see if there are any violets and candy flowers left. She needs to count plants over a span of fifty years before drawing conclusions about the amiability of Scotch broom.

THE SCAVENGING GARDENER   *A gardener who occasionally buys plants from us is an inveterate garden scavenger. He is thrilled by the idea of getting anything for free. Once he told me triumphantly that he had dug up some western columbine,* Aquilegia formosa, *from the edge of the coast road. "Wait a minute," I said. "Not only is that illegal, and they'll cut off your hands if you get caught, but I look forward to that patch of columbines every spring." He was unrepentant, insisting that he had only saved them from death by car tires.*

Turns out he was right in a way. When I checked out that patch the next spring, I saw that fennel, Foeniculum vulgare, *had moved in on it, and there were almost no columbines in evidence at all.*

Interfering with Darwin

It is hard to imagine that it will be possible to entirely eliminate broom, or any other exotic weed, from California. Those who fear the complete extermination of invasive plants can rest easy. The most we can hope for is containment.

Another common strain of argument goes something like this: Who are we to interfere with the dispersal of plant species, ongoing for eons? Who are we to make presumptuous choices, favoring what we call native plants over the newcomers, which we ourselves also are. If broom plants naturally outcompete the natives, they say, it is interfering with evolution, the survival of the fittest, to remove broom.

This laissez-faire argument is called by one naturalist "letting your dog pee on a person after you've knocked him down." On agricultural lands, we plow and weed and irrigate with impunity, managing for the plants that feed humans. Does it make sense to maintain a hands-off posture in our wildlands, even as we see the plants we have introduced, and continue to introduce, move over the landscape like a conquering army, destroying food and shelter for those voiceless species we may not have heard from yet? Roads spread weed seeds, and disturbed land makes a hospitable seedbed.

Most of the food products we eat are produced on intensively managed land. Even on organic farms, the soil is plowed, fertilized, or manured, and predators, including weedy species, are in some way controlled. The organic farmers in this town use burning, hand weeding, and smothering to control weedy species in their annual salad crops. The end result is a food product that we, gastronomically still European, consider edible. Land is being "managed" to feed us.

By removing broom and other invasive exotics, we are managing land to feed the others: the native insects, animals, and birds that were here before we arrived. In both cases, the land is being managed; in one case, for our gastronomic benefit, in the other case, for the stomachs and shelter of native creatures.

It may be that in a thousand years, broom and pampas grass will have found natural enemies, will have become part of the game instead of dominating it. By then, so many players will have been eliminated, both among those we know and those we don't, that it will be a much less interesting game.

In the edge communities that are increasingly common, those bordering on open-space land or national or state park land, it is critical to educate gardeners. One lone gardener planting a hedge of French broom on the flanks of Mount Tamalpais created the vast stands of French broom now being expensively tackled by controlling agencies. Disrupting habitat for miles and creating fire hazards that seriously concern nearby residents, this plant invasion began because someone thought that planting events are isolated occurrences.

"Miracle" Plants

The infamous gypsy moth was introduced to this country to begin a silkworm industry. European beach grass, now dominating a thousand miles of coast, was introduced to stabilize dunes. French and Scotch broom were introduced to stabilize old quarries. Kudzu was brought in to revegetate mined lands. Eucalyptus were brought in for quick-growing firewood and lumber. Bermuda grass, kikuyu grass, and other weedy grasses were brought in as "miracle" lawns. Capeweed, iceplant, and Cape, Algerian, and English ivies were brought in as speedy ground covers. These disastrous introductions should influence future decisions about "the right plant for the job."

In many cases, native plants were rejected for these jobs because they were not as "miraculous" — meaning not as fast-growing. Fast growth usually means weedy growth, and in the case of trees and shrubs, may also mean short lives. Monterey pines grow forty to sixty feet in twenty-five years in California coastal climates, and the sapling that cost a dollar in 1968 will cost $2,000 to remove in 1998.

A friend owns ten acres in Redwood Valley. Most of it is in grapes. There was one little corner where some remnant blue oaks, *Quercus douglasii,* put out a good annual crop of acorns, which I collected if I was there at the right time. My friend wanted to grow his own firewood, so he planted a "miracle tree," a species of poplar said to grow quickly, in the corner with the oaks.

They did grow quickly, but they made terrible firewood and were a disappointment to my friend. Before they were removed, they overtopped the oaks, stressing them to the point of no return. If that grove of oaks had been managed properly, it might have produced enough BTUs to make the poplars unnecessary.

People want fast-growing hedges and screens, instant lawns, quick vines, and instant landscapes, and, in too many cases, the species that fall into those categories become invasive.

A Biological Desert?

My daughter was asked to do some drawings of our hometown for a school project. She did a series of tree drawings, all eucalyptus. When I protested she said, "That's what I see in this town." I had to admit it was true. There are some oaks and an occasional buckeye, but the landscape, and the skyscape, is dominated by eucalyptus.

Because they surround me, I set myself the task of learning to be more positive about eucalyptus. A painting by a local artist helped me to see the silvery blues and creams of its peeling trunk. Sitting in a grove, I learned that it is not true that eucalyptus forest is a biological desert, as some have called it. I hear rustlings and chirpings and see a hawk raising babies in the tall branches of a eucalyptus. Before the monarch butterfly population crashed in 1995, the eucalyptus groves on California's coasts were roosting sites for monarch hordes, and they may be again.

We need to be careful before we call things a biological desert. I was startled to hear that once foresters had so classified old-growth redwoods, as part of the justification for clear-cutting. Yet now we know that that is far from the case, that old growth is crawling, leaping, and scurrying with life.

A controversial speaker at the CalEppc conference challenged the policy of removing tamarisk, salt-cedar, from arid and semi-arid riparian areas. It does provide some compromised bird habitat, and this speaker had tested the soil in which some tamarisk was growing. His data showed the soil in some places along the Colorado River to be saltier than ocean water, incapable of growing most plants. He concluded that tamarisk might be better than nothing.

Among those who criticized his conclusions were those engaged in removing tamarisk from relatively pristine desert riparian areas, where it is pushing out native vegetation. To leave it in severely damaged lands, from whence it can spread to less damaged lands, or try to remove it completely? Many questions, many decisions.

It would be inaccurate to conclude that exotic invasive plants are completely out of the loop. Bees like broom, and butterflies enjoy the nectar of yellow star thistle, blooming in the fall. But the quality of the nectar that native insects derive from non-native plants may be inferior. In some instances, it will not contain a chemical that makes them repellent to predators. Perhaps, too, the sugar content will be less or inferior. It may be food, but not necessarily good food. Exotic plants are not as likely to foster the whole range of humming, seething, flying, slithering confusion that is the necessary background for the richest human life.

Hawks and vultures and owls like eucalyptus. Remember, however, the case of the East Bay salt marsh sculptures. Artists were encouraged to express themselves in this area of marsh, between a freeway and San Francisco Bay, with sculptures made from found objects. It was subsequently observed, however, that their sculptures provided a place for hawks to launch attacks on the slower-moving shorebirds, like the endangered rails. They were given an advantage by this change in habitat structure.

In spite of the uses of eucalyptus, the understory in a eucalyptus grove is almost always confined to other invasive exotics, like Cape ivy, broom, or brambles. Should there be a fire, the chemicals released into the soil by eucalyptus leaves will change the way in which this land recovers from fire, the way in which it can absorb water. A eucalyptus grove on fire, tall flaming torches, presents an entirely different fire-control problem than coastal scrub or even oak groves do.

The predatory hawks the eucalyptus shelters may not have been here when all our trees were relatively low-growing native species like oak and buckeye. The balance is tipped in an Australian direction, but we don't have koala bears for control. It is not that non-native plant species are completely useless as habitat, but that they are less full in relationship. Anything that tends to obscure the specificities of where we live tends to diminish biological diversity, and our life experience is impoverished, whether we know it or not.

Restorationist's Heaven

Sometimes those of us who work in this field ask each other, "How many years of your life would you give to be able to see California as it was, to have the questions answered that we try so hard to figure out?" Such as, what was the bunchgrass with grains as big as wheat, which the Luiseno tribe is said to have harvested, and which no longer exists? Did the elk really migrate, like caribou, from the Central Valley to the coast every year, as Point Reyes naturalist Jules Evans speculates? Was *Nassella pulchra* the dominant grass of the Central Valley, as some claim? When did the Indians in the north, south, and west burn the prairies, and how frequently? What was it like to avoid the grizzly trails through chaparral and river grove? What was it like to revel in endless miles of wildflowers every spring?

On the trail collecting seed one spring, I had a glimpse. I was bending over to gather the seed of some low-growing plant, and when I straightened up, I was dizzy. Momentarily disoriented, turned around, I didn't know where I was. The shallow bank behind me was solid with the pink of checkerbloom, the blue and purple of two kinds of lupines, the gold of mule's ear. For a moment I felt a hint of an old glory.

Leslie Marmon Silko says that her elders counseled waiting, that answers will come. "The old-time people always told us kids to be patient, to wait, and then finally, after a long time, what you wish to know will become clear."

No Limits?

A commercial sponsoring the 1996 Olympic games showed athletes performing impossible feats, leaping the Grand Canyon, flying over the plains. The message flashed on the screen at the commercial's end reinforced the image: no limits.

An important part of the idea of California, so appealing to newcomers, is its ability to allow so many different plants to flourish here. Freed from the constraints of harsh winters, new California gardeners are loath to limit themselves. Gardening is supposed to be for pleasure, one of the few areas where choices can be made based on whim and personal preference, with no immediately apparent price to pay for casually made decisions. Gardeners may understandably resist limitations, given how few arenas are left to us where we can play without consequence.

We don't always know which species have the potential to become invasive or suddenly to increase their destructive capacities. Showing restraint, resisting the plumelike flowers of pampas grass until we know for sure whether the supposedly non-invasive species really is so, forgoing the purple stalks of loosestrife until we are sure it will not invade in California the way it has in New England, doesn't seem much to ask. I often hear clients say, "But I like pampas grass," or, "I like Scotch broom." When I protested a good friend's introduction of calla lilies into a field of coastal scrub she had purchased, she silenced me with "I want it."

I suggest another kind of play, different toys, different rules, different pleasures. When we draw certain boundaries around our gardening activities, we cause ourselves to go deeper. That lifetime deepening is what our planet needs from us. Perhaps, too, whether we know it or not, it is what we crave.

When my daughter was three, she would bring me a book, climb on my lap, and open it in front of us. "My eyes need you to read me a book," she would say. In the same way, I believe that our eyes and our senses need all the colors, songs, textures, light refractions, leaf litter patterns, spatial configurations, and branching structures of the life forms of the book of this land. Invasive plants unchecked leave it simpler, and us poorer, our eyes with less to see, our minds with less to grasp.

News of the Trail

I have always been enchanted by Mary Austin's invitation in *The Land of Little Rain* to come visit her in "the little brown house under the willows." There, she says, news of the trail will be shared.

There is an undercurrent of such news in town these days, nothing new, but maybe swelling. It's about bringing the salmon back, fixing a trail that is eroding into the creeks, burning the Scotch broom, sending the winter waters back into their original pathways, controlling the eucalyptus groves, taking down the pines, and replanting with local native species.

Recently, I took three walks. On the first, I came to a willow grove along a creek being invaded by eucalyptus. The willows were just beginning to leaf out, and a ruby-throated hummingbird called pugnaciously from the top of one. How long before it is no longer evident that once willows grew along that creek? The jobs that willows do, and their beauty through the seasons, those are songs that could be sung, stories to tell.

The second was in an oak grove at the head of a canyon. I reclined along the length of one almost horizontal oak trunk, diverted by the patterns of oak limbs, when the blue gray colors of a eucalyptus sapling grabbed my attention. No big eucalyptus groves were in the area, but somehow one seed had found its way to this oak grove. How long before no remnant of the unusually contorted growth habit of these oaks remains?

The third walk brought me to the coastal scrub at the ocean end of Jack's Creek. A large eucalyptus sapling had appeared in the middle of the coastal scrub. How long before it reseeds and that story, about how coastal scrub holds the bank of a creek where it meets the ocean, is lost? The land tells stories, how plants hold cliffs, how willows grow by creeks, how oaks make homes for many. Invasive plants, unmanaged, represent the reduction of many stories to few.

It is my job to talk of it now. I am of the ones old enough to remember. Because I saw that oak grove, that willow thicket, that stand of coastal scrub, I will write it and I will tell it. And I will garden to give it a place in that piece of land that I see when I wake up, and in my rustling dreams.

 # Wildland
Seed Harvest

When my grandmother started out to gather seeds,
she would say, "Father, give me lots of seeds."
She was thinking of Coyote.
Maria Copa, Coast Miwok, 1932

I have been a wildland seed collector for twenty years. Information has accumulated behind my plucking, picking, gathering hand.

Once, on the trail, it was foggy, and I thought something might happen. I thought somebody might appear.

Maybe another woman, also gathering seeds. She would give me a song, show me how to thank the plants.

Maybe we would trade: my badminton racquet and paper bag for her willow seed-beater and hazel gathering basket.

The fog might bring that.

This work has taken me to the woods, by the creeks, in the grasses, by the ocean, in the dunes, up the mountains, in the hills, down the canyons, by the rivers, and to the places where those places meet. I bring paper bags, envelopes, pen, badminton racquet, stainless steel bowl, day pack, and optional snake-bite kit or prayer, "Snakes, stay far away from me."

I began seed collecting twenty years ago, motivated by a sense that this would be a valuable way to spend time. I didn't understand, in the beginning, how deeply my life changed the day I first took hold of a paper bag and dropped drying seed capsules into it. I have a better idea now of what I hoped to do and can more easily extricate my intentions. I hoped to rewire unused pathways in the brain, connections having to do with setting out looking, with matching the image in the brain to what was hanging from bushes, drooping from trees, swaying with grasses in the wind.

The natural world might sometimes say no and sometimes yes to me. I wanted to learn what that felt like and how to live with it. My goal was to fill seed orders, not bellies, but the orders filled bellies, so I cared. It mattered, in that way, what the answer was.

I wanted to see what it would be like to accumulate data from the natural world — about what, where, when. I wanted to see how my brain would hold what used to be told, and retold, as an aid to memory. I would tell who wanted to hear.

I wanted to use the activity as a way to slow down. I couldn't articulate at the time why I liked the plucking, the putting in the labeled bag, the taking home. I knew it was a gift, sensed that I wanted to put myself in the way of receiving that gift.

I remember once, when I was new to the endeavor, finding myself at an elegant breakfast with three lawyers. Eggs Benedict, sunlight pouring in on a civilized table, and they were curious. One asked me, "How do you do it? How do you actually collect seeds?"

I mimicked the action, the plucking and the putting in, and they all, including me, laughed. How could anything so simple, so slow, put food on anybody's table, and why would anybody want to try? So slow, so tedious, so limited to the capacity of the hand. Regarding history, our human history, maybe it's not so funny.

Outside my office door, we build the compost of California, the poppy capsules, buckeye husks, acorn caps, and redwood cones. A bowl of acorns is left outside for the scrub jay, who is not averse to coming inside for them if necessary. In recent years, people have been finding oak seedlings around here. Jay is the planter. Most of the acorns he retrieves, but those he does not have often been well planted and will turn into acorn-producing trees in some thirty-five years. Or sooner.

Semiconscious rules have slogged around in my brain, things I only half knew. Seeds are a gift. Be optimistic but not disappointed. Julia Parker (Kashia Pomo) said, "Even if it's a bad harvest, still pick some. So the trees won't be offended, and will produce better the next year." Collect not thoroughly. Be sloppy and inefficient. Never strip a plant. Don't get too good. Keep the balance and share the harvest. If what I set out to find isn't there, something else usually is. If what I set out to find isn't there, that's interesting, that it's not there. That's information on a real event. Even if it seems as though nothing has happened, something has always happened.

Acorns and Oaks

If I keep records for the rest of my seed-collecting life, maybe twenty or twenty-five years, I shall still not have enough data to justify drawing conclusions about acorn-crop variability, the multiplicity of factors that affect growth, connections between rain and wind and seedling survival, and fire. We lost thousands of years of information when the aboriginal oak stewards were denied access to their trees. Some questions, although not all, may remain unanswered. Genocide and land seizure weakened (although never entirely broke) the links of knowledge and relationship to the oaks and the land.

On the case, however, are researchers at the Hastings Reservation of the University of California. For the last fifteen years, they have studied 250 trees of five different oak species. They found what any deer or acorn jay could tell you, that acorn crops vary widely in size from year to year. They found no significant correlation between the acorn crops of different species, with the exception of valley and blue oaks, two closely related species in the same subgenus. In other words, a good year for coast live oaks is not necessarily a good year for black oaks or canyon live oaks:

> For valley and blue oaks the most important single factor is weather in April, the peak month for pollination, with crops being heavier in years when April temperatures are warmer. This suggests that conditions favoring more efficient pollination are the key to annual variation in acorn production by these species. For other species, acorn production is correlated with rainfall occurring one or two years earlier, not in the same year as acorn production.

A Question of Ripeness

A significant characteristic of most wildland plants is that they ripen seed sequentially. Domesticated crops, grains and the like, ripen all at once, making it possible to harvest them efficiently. Wildland plants often have an indeterminate flowering pattern — that is, they flower from the bottom of the flower stalk first. It is common to see lupine flower stalks with a perfect flower at the top and well-formed seed capsules at the bottom of the stalk. Since once a flower is pollinated, it stops making nectar, a long period over which buds open to flowers is desirable for hummingbirds and other pollinators. Wildland collecting won't be efficient. You will be unable to harvest all the seed at once, which is good for the particular stand of plants. On the other hand, you stand less chance of missing ripe seed altogether. Usually, you will be able to collect something. Never a total hit but not a total miss either.

Many seeds can be picked before they are completely ripe and left to finish ripening in paper bags (never plastic, which fosters rot and mold). A cut stalk of ripening lupine will often finish the maturation process in a bag, an important piece of information for the beginning seed collector, who soon realizes the unlikelihood of always being in the right place at the right time, there at the exact moment of ripening. A little early will usually yield good results (although there are exceptions).

Points of Attachment

Seeds are connected to plants in different ways. These points of attachment can be more or less tenacious tags of plant tissue. The scar left on the seed at the place of detachment from its base or seed stalk is called the hilum. The sounds seeds make as they detach are distinctive. Lupines opening their seed capsules (a process called dehiscing) in the hot summer sun make a sharp popping noise. Poppies also dehisce — that is, split along a seam in an explosive manner. Once, driving in a hot car, I thought I was being shot at, but it was a bag of wisteria capsules, dehiscing in the heat.

Other seed capsules (of monkeyflower, clarkia) open sequentially and quietly; seeds drop noiselessly to the ground. The wings of the maple and the plumelike outgrowths of the willow seedcoat send seeds flying on the wind. The berry, the drupe, the achene, and the nutlet all have different ways of being attached, and of detaching.

Pine cones formed by some pines have coarse fibers inside each cone scale that shrink as they dry, pulling the scale open to reveal the seed inside. A jay, a human finger, a pair of pliers, or even the wind can remove it. Bird pines such as the whitebark pine don't have that coarse fiber to pull open the scales. Years after harvest, they remain obdurately closed. Clark's nutcracker, a resident of the high mountains, has just the right kind of bill for shredding the scales of whitebark pinecones and removing the seeds. Caching the seeds in the ground for winter harvest, the nutcracker landscapes the forest.

In our coastal live oaks, when the acorn grows heavy on the tree, the cap's attachment to the twig becomes tenuous. A good breeze, and we hear the thud of acorns hitting the ground. In a year of abundance, it's a click, as acorns drop onto other acorns, piled in beige, brown, and golden heaps on the ground.

Appearances

Seeds are jewels, pretty in different ways: dull, shiny, small, large, round, irregular, flat, speckled, plain, black, brown, beige, reddish, smooth, pitted, or fuzzy. Seeds can be circular, compressed-ovoid, asymmetric-reniform (with one end arched over only partway toward the other), truncate-cylindric (like sawed-off segments of a solid cylinder), or rounded rectangular-solid. The seed of every species is distinct, particular, and words exist to describe those particularities.

Seeds can have blotches or not, have a caruncle (outgrowth of the outer seedcoat) or not, have impermeable or permeable seedcoats, have awns or no awns, be winged with samaras or not. They can be with or without a pappus (a tuft of delicate fibers at the tip of a tiny fruit). They can be dormant or ready to germinate.

Lupine seeds are as varied as birds' eggs. *Lupinus chamissonis,* growing on partially stabilized dunes, has seeds with a pale, creamy background speckled with light brown blotches. They are a match for the shells of the snowy plover's eggs, also seen near dunes, and pale with light-brown blotches.

Some seeds are food. *Pinole* is the Spanish word for many different kinds of seed food, flour made of roasted, ground seeds. Here are some California plants whose seeds were used for pinole by aboriginal Californians: blue wildrye, creeping wildrye, red maids, tidy-tips, hemizonia, mule's ear, chia (most famous today), clarkia, islay, California brome, California oatgrass, miner's lettuce, tarweed, ceanothus, California buttercup, and purple needlegrass.

In Search of Seeds

Sometimes I collect with friends, but usually I am alone. Sometimes a wind blows through that sounds strange. Early Russian explorers once came upon a Pomo woman out gathering seeds by herself, singing at the top of her lungs. She explained that she was singing to keep the bad spirits away. "They listen pretty good to me," she said. Regarding bad spirits, and the occasional evolutionarily imbedded feeling of unease, she thought she knew what to do, what was needed, and what would work.

Sent out for seeds of Douglas iris, *Iris douglasiana,* my apprentice tells me that at first he could not find them. After a while, he developed "iris eyes," also called the "search image." Then he saw that irises were everywhere.

Running into me with my pack full of seed bags, friends ask, "What were you collecting?" Sometimes I am at a loss; I can't remember. It's not exactly as if I were in a dream, or meditating. It's a concentrated and relaxed feeling, with many thoughts. Somehow, back in town, at the post office or the grocery store, I can't call on the names of the plants, can't recall what I was so recently engaged in, can't access the information from that other place.

E. O. Wilson talks of the distinction between those tropical predators that are "searchers," such as jaguars and pumas, which take whatever animals they meet, and "pursuers," such as cheetahs and wild dogs, which select a few kinds of animals and chase them down. Seed collectors can be categorized in this way as well. Sometimes I go out after something specific. At other times, I go out to collect what is ready to be collected at that place, at this moment in time. Most of us do some of both at the same time.

In *The Shirley Letters,* Dame Shirley, an early observer in the camps of the Gold Rush, provides a rare description of a seed-gathering scene. Although she is an appreciative and interesting writer about those times, her negative point of view regarding California Indians is such that she is surprised by the beauty of their seed-gathering baskets:

> Shaped like a cone, they are about six feet in circumference at the opening, and I should judge them to be nearly three feet in depth. It is evident by the grace and care with which they handle them, that they are exceedingly light. One of these queer baskets is suspended from the back and is kept in place by a thong of leather passing across the forehead. The other they carry in the right hand, and wave over the flower seeds, first to the right and back again to the left alternately, as they walk slowly along, with a motion as regular and monotonous as that of a mower. When they have collected a handful of the seeds, they pour them into the basket behind, and continue this work until they have filled the latter with their strange harvest. The seeds thus gathered are carried to their rancherias and stowed away with great care for winter use.

John Muir largely perceived the wilderness as something one experienced, hoping to affect or interact with it as little as possible. He brought his loaf of bread and his blanket, and he seems to have only rarely partaken of the culinary possibilities the landscape offered. In *Mountains of California,* he describes a gathering scene and one tentative taste of California:

> Five miles below the foot of Moraine Lake, just where the lateral moraines lose themselves in the plain, there was a field of wild rye, growing in magnificent waving bunches six to eight feet high, bearing heads from six to twelve inches long. Rubbing out some of the grains, I found them about five eighths of an inch long, dark-colored, and sweet. Indian women were gathering it in baskets, bending down large handfuls, beating it out, and fanning it in the wind. They were quite picturesque, coming through the rye, as one caught glimpses of them here and there, in winding lanes and openings, with splendid tufts arching above their heads, while their incessant chat and laughter showed their heedless joy.

To the Indians of California, the mountains, plains, and foothills were a domestic scene, where known herds of deer were carefully harvested, where grass fields were burned to stimulate seed production, where basketry materials were pruned, burned, and managed. Plants and animals were harvested, inventoried, evaluated, gathered, appreciated, checked on, noticed, observed, handled, sought, discussed. People used to talk about seeds.

Humans evolved amassing and sharing complex information about the surrounding plant, animal, and mineral world. Elders were valued as repositories of such knowledge, all communicated orally. It's another kind of local gossip, the many and continuing conversations, the passing back and forth of local data and experiences.

Seed gathering to restore native plant communities, and their attendant animal and insect communities, is a way of reentering the garden, of managing a way to take and give at the same time, a reason to be there. I'm not lucky enough to know a thanking song, but I can take some of that plant's seeds and help them grow.

I met somebody on the trail once, while I was standing dazed by the bounty, deciding which seeds to gather first. He stopped to ask what I was looking at, put a finger out to touch the plant I mentioned. The seeds were ripe and instantly dropped off the plant. He drew back. "I shouldn't have touched it," he said. I wanted to cry out after him as he walked away: "It's okay! I think it's okay. We can touch them."

My daughter, at age eight, asked me, after listening to a presentation on environmental problems, "Are we bad for the earth? I mean, if we didn't have cars and dams. I mean we, just we."

She is worried, this one. Where do we belong if not here? I felt that just by the skin of my teeth had I begun to know the answer, for the wind, and the seeds, have hinted that, yes, we are part of it. I mean we, just we.

 # Seed Propagation and Planting Techniques

> I have great faith in a seed. Convince me that you have a seed
> there, and I am prepared to expect wonders.
> *Henry Thoreau, 1860*

It was work with seeds that first drew me into this field, and to this day it is
an integral part of my life, collecting, cleaning, sowing, transplanting, and
watching plants in various stages of growth. Life would seem quite empty,
almost unimaginable, without such accompaniment. Some believe that
plant propagators are long-lived — all that new life every day.

The back-yard restorationist's involvement with seed work can be more
or less complex. You can stick with annuals and easily germinated "colonizer" plants, like certain coastal perennials, or try your hand at some trick-
ier species, bulbs, shrubs, and trees. There is nothing particularly difficult
about any of it. When I first began propagating at a native plant nursery, my
scariest days were those when I had to deal with sulfuric acid to break seed
dormancy. I would wake in the morning thinking, "Now, is it the acid that
can't be poured into water, or the water that can't be poured into the acid?"
(Acid into water is correct; water into acid creates an explosion.) Not too
many propagators use sulfuric acid anymore. In most cases, other, equally
effective techniques have been found.

Why is growing plants from seed so rewarding? To know a plant from
seed stage to seedling deepens the relationship between gardener and garden. What many of us seek these days is an enhanced sense of connection
with the earth and its nonhuman inhabitants. Although buying a plant in a
container and putting it in the ground does involve watering and weeding
and watchful tending, to participate in the progression from seed to seedling
to mature plant adds an extra, intangible but undeniable dimension to the

human/plant relationship. It's the "I have known you since you were a baby" relationship. What's more, there is nothing hard about growing plants from seed.

It is mostly a matter of assembling appropriate materials and learning simple techniques. By becoming comfortable with these techniques, you can expand your ability to grow interesting, rare, and worthwhile plants for a small expenditure of time and money. You have begun a great adventure.

After obtaining the seed, look up the species to be sown in Dara Emery's *Seed Propagation of Native California Plants* or in Jeanine de Hart's *Propagation Secrets for California Native Plants*. Both books list species-by-species propagation requirements. You will be told whether the seeds can be sown immediately without treatment or whether they require treatment before sowing. Sometimes a particular species does not require treatment if the seed is fresh, while stored seed must be refrigerated.

Note that definitive methods for the best way to propagate a given species are not always available.

Germination requirements for many wildland plants reside in the brains of propagators of native plants all over the state. They may be extracted in some cases. The best way to do this is to become a customer. Information laboriously acquired by an experienced propagator should not be requested casually.

Broadcasting Seed

Seeds of annuals — that is, those species that germinate, grow, blossom, and make seed in one season — are often broadcast, or direct-sown, meaning that they are planted directly in the area where they are to grow. Most perennial plants, including trees and shrubs, are started in flats and transplanted into gradually larger and larger containers, till they are ready to go into the garden. For the best use of your annual seed, establish a good seedbed before sowing. That means a section of ground where, among other things, weed competition has been eliminated or severely set back. Weed competition is one of the major reasons for failure of broadcast seed.

Sowing Seed in Flats

Many customers ask about broadcasting tree, shrub, and perennial seed where it is to grow. In some cases, this may be an effective technique, as with acorns that are carefully protected from predation with screens both above and below ground, but it often requires large quantities of seed for acceptable results. For the most economical use of relatively expensive perennial, tree, and shrub seed, we recommend sowing in flats for later transplanting into containers and then into the ground. Here are the simple methods we follow.

1. A light, porous, seed-sowing mixture is placed in a wooden flat, clay seed pot, peat pot, or any fairly shallow container with drainage. The slotted plastic trays available from nurseries, used to hold small pots, can be lined with newspaper and then filled with a soil mix. Commercial potting mixes may be used. We use a combination of peat and vermiculite, also commercially available, or a homemade combination of one-third each compost, good garden loam, and sand. Seeds don't need rich soil to germinate. The mixture is tamped down in the container with a flat board or brick.

2. The seeds are evenly sown on the flat surface and covered with an appropriate amount of soil mix. The rule of thumb is to cover the seed to twice its diameter. Obviously, nature is not so finely tuned. Another rule of thumb is to cover the seed till you can't see it anymore. (In some rare cases, seed needs light to germinate and does not need to be covered.) The soil is tamped firmly over the seed. For tamping, we use an 8" x 6" board with a simple handle on one side. Any large flat surface will work.

3. Water gently and thoroughly. Many hose attachments are available that create a fine spray. You may wish to place the seed container under plastic to retain moisture. A pane of glass may also be used. Do not allow the flat to dry out. It should be kept evenly moist but not soggy.

4. Place in a warm, protected place to germinate. Bottom heat may speed germination but is usually not essential. Seeds may be germinated in the house but should be moved as soon as have they have germinated, or the

seedings may begin to lean in the direction of the sun and become etiolated from insufficient light. We use an unheated greenhouse attached to our office that is warmer than simply being outside, because of protection from winds and heat retention from the sun. For most situations in California, unheated greenhouses work well.

Some propagators, including those at the Tilden Park Botanic Garden, find that they get the best results by placing screened flats outside the greenhouse in fall and winter, where they can experience the normal changes of temperature and the advantages of real rainfall. Protection from animals is critical. Germinating in flats outside eliminates problems of "damping off," a fungus resulting from the combination of heat and warmth. For the back-yard restoration gardener, I think it is ideal.

5.   To sow very fine seeds, place sifted sphagnum moss one inch deep over normal seed-planting mixture. Scatter seeds over the top and water gently to wash seeds into the upper level of moss.

6.   When they are about one and a half inches tall, check seedlings every two weeks to see if they are ready for transplanting. Test root development by carefully scooping out an individual seedling from the flat using a knife or dibble. If it has a good fibrous rootball, with numerous tiny hairs branching off from the main root or roots, it is ready for transplanting. Be sure, especially with taprooted trees and shrubs, to transplant seedlings before the roots hit the bottom of the container.

Preconditioning Treatments for Germination

Some seeds require special preconditioning treatments. None are beyond the scope of the home gardener who has access to hot water, refrigeration, and a local drugstore.

REFRIGERATION

Many trees and shrubs, and some alpine perennials, require a cold period to overcome internal dormancy before they can germinate. Cold-stratification, or refrigeration, is probably the most common treatment used by professional propagators to enhance or enable germination. There is nothing tricky about it.

Place a mixture of peat moss and vermiculite in a plastic bag. Add seeds. Shake the bag so that the seeds are distributed evenly throughout it and cannot be seen from the outside. If they can be seen, add more mixture. Dampen the contents of the bag slightly (when squeezed in a fist, water should barely come through the fingers). Seal the bag, label it, and place it in a refrigerator (not a freezer) for the specified length of time (it varies from one to six months, as indicated on the seed packet or in your resource book).

When the time is up, spread the entire contents of the bag over the surface of the container. Cover the contents with a little more planting medium to ensure seed coverage, and lightly tamp down. Water carefully.

Sometimes seeds germinate while in stratification. In this case, make no attempt to plant the seeds individually. Simply spread the whole contents of the bag gently over the container, cover, and lightly tamp down the planting medium. Water carefully so as not to expose any sprouts. Don't worry about putting the roots down and the shoots up. The plant will orient itself properly.

The seeds of maples, fremontias, pines, and cypresses are among those that like cold-stratification.

HOT WATER SOAK

Equally simple, hot water treatment may be used to soften impermeable seedcoats. Bring water to a boil, pour it over the seeds, and leave for the specified length of time, as indicated on the packet or in your resource book. Drain the seeds but do not allow them to dry out before planting in containers. This procedure is used for shrub lupines, fremontia, sugar bush, and some other trees and shrubs.

PRE-GERMINATION IN A PLASTIC BAG

Plastic bag pre-germination treatment is used for large seeds, such as acorns, which produce a taproot before the shoot arises. Place seeds in a 5 percent bleach solution for five minutes. Drain. Mix the seeds with peat moss and vermiculite mix, and place in a large, clear plastic bag. Close the bag tightly and keep it in a warm place. Check weekly for germination and to be sure that the mix is still damp but not soggy. Upon germination, remove the seedlings and transplant to gallon cans.

HYDROGEN PEROXIDE SOAK

Place seeds in a container, pour a 3 percent hydrogen peroxide solution over them, and let stand for half an hour. Then rinse, drain, and sow the seed.

WHITE GAS SOAK

Place seeds in a container, cover them with white gas (Coleman fuel), and let stand for an hour. Then rinse, drain, and sow the seed. Used for bush poppies, violas, and others.

Transplanting

1. Set yourself up with the materials you will need so that everything is at hand. Scoop individual seedlings up with a spoon, stick, or widget. Gently lift from the flat, handling and disturbing the roots as little as possible. Root-prune the seedlings, snipping off a small amount of root hairs to promote fibrous rooting.

2. Hold the seedling over the container so that the point where the stem begins is about half an inch below the rim. Pour the soil mix, which may often be richer than the seeding mix, in around the seedling till the soil covers the rootball. Possible containers may be two-inch or four-inch plastic pots, depending on the size of the rootball, a peat pot, or a clay pot. In our experience, we have the fewest watering problems with plastic pots, which can be reused almost indefinitely.

3. Water gently and thoroughly, until water runs out of the drainage hole. We do not recommend plugging the drainage hole with a piece of tile or putting a layer of broken crockery in the bottom of the pot. Water as necessary; schedule will vary according to the intensity of the sun, day length, and wind. Remember that soil in pots dries out much more quickly than the soil in your garden. I find that even on the coast, plants in small pots benefit from some shade protection.

4. Place seedling in a sheltered area, out of direct sun and wind, for at least a month. Check to see if the plant needs transplanting by holding it upside down with the fingers on either side of the stem. Tap the edge of the pot on a table until the plant slides gently into your hand. If the roots have filled the pot, it may be transplanted into a larger container. In some cases, you may now wish to transplant directly into the field.

    Each time a plant is transplanted, it may be pruned back to produce a bushier specimen, if appropriate. Cut always to a node, the point at which new growth will emerge. The rootball may also be pinched back an inch or so at this time.

5. When the plant has filled a larger can with roots, it may be planted out in the field. Dig a roomy hole twice the diameter of the root ball, if possible, making sure that all the roots can comfortably stretch out. It is no longer recommended that soil amendments be added to the hole. However, in situations where the existing soil is extremely bad, such as rocky fill, soil without humus, or subsoil, mix some soil that resembles the mix in which the plant has been growing in with the existing soil.

6. Remove the specimen from its container. Make sure that none of its roots are circling around the root ball, which could eventually strangle the plant. Plant it slightly higher than it was in the container to allow for settling of the soil. Firm soil around the plant and water deeply.

In most situations we depend on mulch to provide nutrients, leaching slowly into the soil the way nature intended. In extremely poor soil, however, slow-release fertilizer pellets are sometimes placed in the bottom of the hole, where the roots can reach them. If the container-grown plants are "fresh" — that is, in a state of vigorous growth — and the soil into which they are placed is reasonably good, no fertilizer is necessary. Excess fertility may cause overly vigorous initial growth followed by an early demise.

Mulching

Once your plants are in the ground, you may want to mulch them. Mulching is a well-known gardening technique involving the placement of organic material on the surface of the soil around the plants. It is not the same as amending the soil, in which case the material is put in the planting hole rather than on top. Often used in association with organic gardening, this practice serves to suppress weeds, retain moisture, equalize soil temperature, and improve the soil from the top down, the way nature does it. It can make a messy planting look neat and "attended to."

URBAN CHIPS   *I was thrilled while staying with a friend in an urban area to see trucks going by loaded with chips headed for the dump. My chip-obtaining reflexes were activated. When I asked for the chips to be dumped in my friend's driveway, offering a six-pack as inducement, the crew complied with alacrity and some surprise. Imagine my host's delight on coming home from work to find an elephant-sized mound of steaming wood chips in his driveway.*

The pile included some lumber-sized pieces, as well as an old rake, and the chips were mostly long and stringy, but after several weekends spent hauling them from the driveway into my friend's back yard, they were neatly piled in the shape of a berm for planting with native perennials and grasses in the fall. (The extra height of a raised bed improves drainage for native species that require it.) Meanwhile, the old lawn was being smothered and the soil improved.

The neighbors laughed at the size of the pile, but I bet they won't laugh for long. Soon they'll be staying home from work on tree-trimming days, six-packs at the ready.

Mulch can visually define planting beds. It can mark the placement of tiny plants that might otherwise be lost. A neat job of mulching lends unity to the garden while waiting for the plants to grow. Paths can be marked and kept walkable with mulch. It can also gently shape a flat garden, providing slightly raised planting areas for species, like ceanothus and fremontodendron, that like good drainage. Although the rise in elevation of such beds is probably only about eight inches, it can be a crucial eight inches.

Ground wood chips or leaf litter from the same species as the planting are the ideal mulch for native plants. For example, oaks would be mulched with oak-leaf litter, Pacific wax myrtle with its own cinnamon brown leaves, redwoods with redwood duff, coastal scrub with chipped coyote bush and sagebrush. Since such opportunities rarely arise, we use almost any mulching material we can get, including eucalyptus, pine, and cypress chips, the most common chips in the Bay Area.

When I started my coastal garden, I could get wood chips for free from the local tree removal crews, who were happy to have a place to dump them instead of taking them to the nearest landfill. Now, people line up, addresses in hand, when they see a tree crew working for the utility company, bribing them with six-packs of beer or promises of easy unloading situations. The local tree crews, wise to the situation, all charge for chips now.

Planting Tricks

Where weed problems seem insurmountable, I have learned to plant closely, not waiting for plants to reach their ultimate size, and I have learned to use coyote bush where not much else is growing. I have learned that, contrary to the "rules," spring and even early summer are good times to plant along the coast. If I wait until fall, the standard recommended time for planting in California, I find myself digging into soil that has received no rain for six months and is powdery dry, hard to wet. (Mulch applied in spring can make early fall planting easier.) In the past few years, once the winter rains started, they were relentless, making planting difficult. Newly planted specimens, their roots not yet established, may drown with heavy rains, whereas those planted the previous spring have formed good root masses by the time of heavy rains, surviving the onslaughts with equanimity.

Along the coast, planting in springtime requires only a few months of watering till the fog appears, followed by fall rains. This scheme sometimes doesn't work with those perennials that go dormant in the summer, like Indian pink, *Silene californica,* mule's ear, *Wyethia angustifolia,* and native clover, *Trifolium wormskioldii.* Planted in the spring, they go into summer dormancy, I speculate, before their roots have taken hold. Once they disappeared, they were never seen again.

Every site has its own tricks to be learned through attention and time.

Pruning

Just as in nature there is no one right solution to how to survive a summer drought, but multiple solutions, so in gardening, many things will work. Growing is what plants want to do. In my experience, water at the right time and elimination of weedy competition are the two keys to successful transplanting. Third comes pruning.

Grooming plants, we provide services that fire or herbivores might ordinarily provide. We use spring rakes to remove dead leaves from bunchgrasses, and clippers and shears to cut perennials like gumplant, California aster, and perennial buckwheats almost to the ground in early fall. Shrubs that are fire-adapted, like California sagebrush, get cut to one foot above the ground every two or three years. The island bush poppy also usually resprouts tidily after severe pruning.

Some coyote bushes get cut back to about a foot above the ground every four or five years; others don't seem to need regular pruning, particularly if the wind is keeping them shapely. Our pruning efforts with coyote bush have never been as successful as controlled burning. In a nearby burned area, every coyote bush displays a cage of blackened limbs encircling a clump of green leaves sprouting along the base. Nutrients released by the burn or the reduction of pathogens and predators through fire may account for some of that post-fire vigor.

Oaks we leave alone, except eventually to remove limbs growing close to the ground. Pruning the tree too early to a lollipop shape will prevent the desired thickening of the trunk.

Watering

In the California floristic province, most native plants are adapted to a three- to six-month-long drought. (This rule does not apply to montane species, which get summer water.) Plants from most of California will require water through their first dry season but then usually benefit from an adherence to our winter-wet, summer-dry climate. Accordingly, fall, winter, and very early spring are the best times to plant in most parts of California. The earlier plants are established before their first dry season, the less water they will need to get through it.

Drip irrigation should not be installed in the native plant garden without careful consideration, useful though it may be in commercial agriculture and in annual vegetable gardens that receive constant attention. I regularly arrive at job sites to be told that the drip system is not functioning. I have seen many hillsides threaded with black plastic tubing that is no longer delivering water to the intended spots. Vulnerable to damage by animals and to the tendency of complicated systems to have problems, drip irrigation requires maintenance, and when people move or gardeners change, the secrets of individual drip systems are often lost.

Moreover, our soil is meant to dry out in the summer, and keeping it in a continually moist state will necessarily change its inhabitants, leading to disease problems that occur only with the un-Californian combination of summer heat and moisture. Native plants of the kind adapted to our winter-wet, summer-dry regime will in many situations require only enough water to become established. Hand watering through the first dry season may be all that is necessary, so installing a complicated drip system will not pay off.

I breathe a sigh of relief when I am told that the client wants to hand water. I know then that the plants will be looked at regularly. Automatic timers and drip irrigation can create the illusion that aftercare is not necessary. I have seen plants on drip irrigation that were buried beneath debris falling from trees, and no one knew. I have seen them swamped by weeds stimulated by the moisture, and no one knew. The months just after planting are the most critical for long-term survival.

Hand watering with the right tool is a pleasant, undemanding activity. A good watering wand eliminates soil splash, and if it is held close to the base of the plant, the diffuse flow will not compact the soil and goes right where it is needed.

Where possible, I recommend hand watering for initial establishment, deep mulching, and occasional summer watering for those plants that look more gardenworthy with it. The rule of thumb is that new plantings require one inch of water per week, to be supplied by the gardener if the rains don't provide it. Plants in damaged soils may have greater water requirements both initially and thereafter.

An informal survey of native plant landscapers indicates that drip systems are not widely used for native plantings anymore. Overhead sprinklers or soaker hoses are preferred.

The gardener in California's "fifth season," August through October, that long, luxurious warm spell with no rain, has for gardening tools the hammock, a book, and a glass of lemonade. With no moisture, the weeds (most kinds) will be at rest as well, so the gardener can make his leisurely way through the garden, watching pollinators at work, watching flowers turn slowly to seed.

Staking

Staking should be done in such a way that some movement is possible. Where movement occurs through force of wind, certain chemicals are activated that stimulate the production of more tissue at that point. Staking so that the upper portion of the tree moves while the lower part does not will create an unstable, top-heavy tree. Stake so that the entire trunk gets some play. As Bill Mollison of permaculture fame says, "Wind makes wood."

Fertilizing

When I first planted fruit trees on our rocky New England hillside, we dug large holes and filled them with imported soil. The trees did well for some years, then abruptly died. Horticultural theory now recommends that the roots be allowed to get accustomed to native soil, in which they will ultimately be growing, from the start. Some transition from the loamy, porous potting mix in which the plant has been growing to the native soil is desirable, so we mix native soil with a small amount of soil amendment to fill in the planting hole.

Some landscapers recommend placing a slow-release fertilizer in the bottom of the planting hole. Others say it depends on how "fresh" the plant is. If it has not been in its container too long and is in a state of vigorous growth, obviously still feeding off whatever fertilizing program the nursery provided, it may not require extra fertilization.

Native plants, once established, usually do not require fertilization. Mulch, slowly decomposing around the plant, should be sufficient.

Growing Native Bulbs from Seed

Few plants are more beautiful than California native bulbs, such as calochortus, brodiaea, dichelostema, and fritillary. Although their requirements are specialized, the varied markings and exquisite clean lines of these flowers make them worth the trouble. They are strictly adapted to the Western dry summer / wet winter sequence, and to grow them successfully, it is best to follow their natural schedule. Since these native bulbs are rare, growing them from seed is often necessary. Here is our procedure.

1. Plant seed in the fall or winter, using deep pots to minimize transplanting. We use a porous soil mix, with additional sand or gravel when the particular species is from such an area.

2. Some growers sow into large containers like fifteen-gallon plastic pots or large wooden planter boxes. The seeds will sprout and send up leaves during the rainy fall and winter. They will need to be kept evenly moist and protected from slugs and snails during this period.

3. In summer, yellowing foliage will indicate the need for a dormant period. Without this dormant period, the plants will probably not survive. Stop watering, but to avoid excessive heating and drying of bulbs in containers, keep them in a filtered-light situation during the summer.

4. To transplant into the ground, wait until September or October. Plant in the ground as you would transplant any container plant. To plant corms, wait till the bulbs have been baked by the summer sun and the tops have disappeared. Remove the corms and let them ripen in a shady place for several months. Then plant them where you wish them to

grow, three inches deep and spaced closely. Protect from gopher predation with wire baskets.

The corms of brodiaeas and calochortus, called "Indian potatoes," were relished by the California Indians and taste somewhat like water chestnuts.
Many calochortus species make excellent cut flowers and will actually ripen
seed in the vase, which can then be collected and sown.

Bulbs of California natives are becoming more readily available, particularly at Native Plant Society sales. You will save yourself three to seven
years' time by taking advantage of existing bulbs. These have often been
grown by tissue culture, and not infrequently in Holland, where they seem
to do a better job with our native bulbs than we do.

Why Grow Plants from Seed

That seeds with their varied colors and shapes are beautiful and fascinating is evident to anybody who works with them. The attraction in a flat
of newly germinated seedlings, fresh in their recent emergence from the
seed, must be experienced to be understood. Here, as well, are some practical reasons for growing plants from seed.

One inexpensive packet of seed can produce dozens of mature plants.
One seed capsule of some species can produce hundreds of seeds. Nature is
profligate with seeds, and we can benefit.

Although much work has been done on plant propagation, it is surprising how much remains unknown. Information on collecting and propagating is simply unavailable for many species. If you have an opportunity to
watch a favorite plant bloom, check on it at regular intervals. Watch the
flower develop into the pod (members of the legume family are particularly
fascinating to watch). If you keep records on the length of time between
bloom and seed maturity, you will, in many cases, be collecting original data.

The best pre-germination methods for different species are by no means
established. It was not long ago that many more-cumbersome methods of
propagation were in practice, such as scarification (nicking seeds individually with a file), burning (setting fire to flats of sown seeds to simulate na-

ture's fires), and soaking in sulfuric acid, a dangerous and unpleasant chemical to work with. All these techniques have, in many cases, been replaced by less intimidating but equally effective methods.

The Case for Cultivars

Some who grow native plants take to the trails, searching for individual specimens with characteristics that might make them gardenworthy. Looking for larger flowers, or the flowers of a different color, a smaller leaf or a neater habit, these patient, discerning plant hunters wander with a mission. Cuttings of selected plants are brought back to nurseries to be grown and tested. Many of the native plants in our gardens are cultivars being propagated vegetatively. Talks given by speakers who look for and introduce cultivars of California native plants bring the faint scent of dusty trails, each introduction representing a special day in the field.

Some call Bart O'Brien, horticulture director of Rancho Santa Ana Botanic Garden in Claremont, California, the king of cultivars. Bart's fascination with this particular human/plant interface and his ability to trace the histories of plant introductions and selections is legendary. Bart's calling is to honor the many distinctions, such as leaf size, twig rigidity, flower shape, size, and color, that distinguish different cultivars. For example, the cultivar garden at Rancho Santa Ana Botanic Garden gives an opportunity to view and compare five different cultivars of coyote bush growing right next to one another.

The goal behind much of this work is to make natives gardenworthy, so that they will have characteristics that appeal to the gardening public. My own approach is more "restorationist," but I am grateful for those who have developed and made available such useful cultivars as *Baccharis pilularis* 'Pigeon Point' and *Fremontodendron* 'California Glory', as well as dozens of manzanita and ceanothus cultivars that reliably grace our urban gardens. Some of these cultivars have proved to be of astounding showiness and utility.

When the Mount Vision fire of 1995 burned populations of *Ceanothus gloriosus porrectus,* we knew that many representatives of that form existed in gardens, where they are known as *Ceanothus gloriosus porrectus* 'Mt.

Vision'. Cultivar names that commemorate the location from which the plant was collected have great potential use; the native plant garden can be a warehouse of restoration possibilities for public lands.

Since growers of native plants are usually at least somewhat interested in restoration, it makes sense to include some seed-grown plants in their nursery inventories. The current trend in horticulture, in which cultivars are propagated vegetatively, results in clones of a single favored plant being planted by the thousands all over the state. Selection criteria, such as flower size or color, may be too narrow to ensure the survival of the species. Only seed-grown plants can do that.

The back-yard restoration gardener, growing locally collected seeds, can play a role in resisting the depletion of local gene pools and maintaining healthy and adaptable populations of the flora of home.

PART IV

Resources for the Back-Yard Restoration Gardener

 # Naturalists and Field Trips

Users want and need clear, neat, simple answers to their questions. Experts want to convey their evolving, complex, and dynamic perspectives, which are often neither neat nor simple. The primary goal of The Jepson Manual Project was to find the fine line that best accommodates these diverse wants and needs.   *The Jepson Manual, 1993*

The dark vision cannot come to reality, the thrush seems to be telling me, because the continuum of wild nature is even stronger in humans than the continuum of greed. Even the agribusinessmen will understand, once the wilderness areas they escape to are all paved with traffic jams and populated with de-animalized bears eating human garbage. Then everyone will be convinced that the only "escape" is to make all the Earth over into the various realms of the Great Garden.
Gene Logsden, 1994

Under the oak tree, in this wet year, the Indian lettuce grew unprecedentedly tall, its flower stalks rising six inches above the last tier of leaves. Now the seed is ripe. Shiny black and about the size of an ant's head, they drop from their stalks, out of their little green enveloping sepals, onto the saucer-like leaves underneath the flowers. The quail take advantage of this easy way to eat seed: handed to them on a plate, so to speak. Birds connecting with plants.

These are things I see. Sometimes I want to see more. I want the information and perspective that I don't have, that comes from a lifetime of focus on a different part of the picture. Through our modern ceremonial exchange of information called the field trip, my tunnel vision widens.

Part-opening illustration: Native blackberries and grasshopper. Drawing by Ane Carla Rovetta.

While I spent years preoccupied with plants, only peripherally noticing the insects fluttering at the edges of my vision, and the near and far calls of birds, others have focused on birds, butterflies, beetles, or snakes. It was not plants that first drew them into the natural world, but birds, or bugs, or rocks, or mammal tracks, or damselflies. Hummingbirds have wide appeal, and much is known about bees, particularly the honeybee. Voles provide a field of study, requiring devoted experts, and those experts probably have parties, gatherings of vole experts, where conversation centers on voles, and spouses smother yawns. Spiders have their aficionados (although fewer), and beetles (of which there are several million species, 30,000 in California alone) fewer still. Yet they have their experts, their field guides, their national associations, trade journals, and allies, those who warn us of their endangerment.

It used to be that elders were valued for their accumulated knowledge of the land, which would be made available to the members of their community. Ceremonial sharing of knowledge was one way. Or an elder might sit in the sun, telling those who came to ask where various plants or animals might be found, calling on some mixture of intuition and experience. Now, elders sitting in the sun may be hard, although not impossible, to find. Instead, we have public and private research institutions, field researchers, naturalists, books, data analysis, scientific journals, and, for the general public (including the back-yard restoration gardener), field trips.

The Field Trip as Tool

Field trips are an important resource for the back-yard restoration gardener. This weekend, a casual look at such events in my region shows, within an hour's drive, two bird walks (one shorebird and one land bird), one look at serpentine grasslands, a tidepool ramble, a grass identification workshop, a talk on insects and plants, and a butterfly walk, all free. Next week there will be an opportunity to look at mushrooms and lichens and migrating birds. True, I live surrounded by national parks, nature preserves, and a national seashore, but most Americans, even in urban areas, have access to regions of protected land, whose protecting agencies have public education as a goal.

Schedules for field trips can be obtained from the visitor centers of national, state, and county parks. Most environmental organizations, from the Nature Conservancy to the California Native Grass Association, regularly publish newsletters that list upcoming field trips. These listings, and such access to experts, are among the perks of membership in many of the organizations listed in Resources. It is usually not necessary to be a member of the sponsoring organization to participate in field trips. These people want to share what they know. They want you to know what they are up to, and to bring it into your life.

CARL SHARSMITH   *To Yosemite-loving Californians, of which, in spite of crowd control problems, garbage trucks, and feral bears, there are many, one naturalist above all has had an impact out of all proportion to his size. The late Carl Sharsmith led field trips in Tuolumne Meadows for sixty-three years, till his death at age ninety-four. The video documentary on Yosemite called* The Fate of Heaven *ends with a shot of Carl falling to his knees in the snow to examine something more closely. The resemblance to a man struck suddenly by the need to pray is unmistakable.*

I am indebted to Dave Fross for the following story about Carl. Once, mid–field trip, in his beloved Tuolumne Meadows, Carl stopped abruptly by a sedge plant.

"You'll have to excuse me for half an hour," he said to the participants. "I've just met an old friend, and we need to spend some time together."

He proceeded to fill his pipe, after which he sat down by the side of the trail, next to the plant, and puffed away, leaving the field trippers to mill about on their own.

"And he took every minute of that half-hour," recalls Dave.

In the name of the field trip, I have sat in a laboratory passing bottles of animal feces around, held up traffic with birders on the lagoon, measured bobcat tracks, tapped at rocks, and scrambled after butterflies. I have walked with birdwatchers, plant lovers, bug aficionados, geologists, butterfly specialists, hummingbird lovers, and scatologists.

Leaders may be employed by universities, by junior colleges, by research institutions like the Point Reyes Bird Observatory, by national parks, and by all kinds of organizations, from the California Native Plant Society to the North American Butterfly Association. They may be Ph.D.s or just interested laypeople. Participants on hikes range from beginners to experts, from the mildly interested to the obsessed. I have walked with charming people and a few annoying ones, elders and the middle-aged, and never enough, although always some, young ones.

RAY PETERSON   *Ray Peterson is the resident biologist at Audubon Canyon Ranch. In this position, which he fills with relish, he writes weekly pieces for the docents, small "alertings" to what's on the trail. His longtime acquaintance with the canyons and his deep reservoir of information make walking two feet with him opportunity for myriad teachings. The layers above the plants are seen to be full of insect life. Detail and relationship abound in his talk.*

As an example of the combination of insight and perception that is his trademark, Ray talks about the four "smell seasons" in the canyon. Winter rains bring the season of the fragrance of loam. The honey-sweet fragrance of ceanothus is the spring smell. The lingering odor of huge buckeye blossoms represents summer, and in the fall, the spicy fragrance of coyote bush marks the season.

Ray specializes in making information about the natural world accessible to people through his own brand of mnemonic devices, crowd-pleasing spectaculars of natural facts, and humor. "Stories," says Ray, "are the pegs on which information is hung."

To avail yourself of the freely offered information provided by field naturalists on walks and treks, bring a relaxed, absorbing attitude, much like the attitude you bring to your back-yard restoration garden. Unlike in school, you are not required to maintain a rigorous level of total attention at all times, and you will not be tested at the end of the day. What is important is to come away with some new information and a feeling of connection, which, like most gifts, may be hoped for but not coerced.

Many things separate us from access to the natural world, from lack of training to the increasing remoteness of nature's manifestations. It takes time to retrain eyes, ears, and brains. Simply being around people whose attention is directed in a certain way provides an important model. You can learn from and study field trips themselves, as well as those who lead them and those who take them. Watch the watchers. Note the joy and focus of their study, the ways they acquire information, the degrees of uncertainty attendant upon conclusions.

I Have Always Been a Plant Person

It has always been easier for me to learn the names and habits of plants than the names and habits of birds or beetles. The learning process in this area is almost unnoticeable for me, partly because I work, talk, and think every day about plants. When I step outside my field, I seem to require almost endless repetition of information before I "know" something. In recent years, I have made a low-key commitment to this expansion, mostly through attending field trips with naturalists.

For years, most of the field trips I took focused on plants, my way into the nonhuman world. Plants hooked me. They drew me in and on. Their stillness calmed me. Plant growth seemed like something for nothing. A tiny seed, its needs relatively easily met, providing flower or food, or both. A bargain, a gift. I began drawing plants, hoping that in recording the special curve of a fluted petal or the detail of a fern's fronds, I would find a moment of connection and honoring recognition that would bring me in, where I wanted to be.

Growing came next. Interacting with plants by growing them provides an intimacy, familiarity, and camaraderie. Learning the seeds of many plants, their collection times, and germination requirements, their peculiarities and particularities, I came slowly into more complex relation with plants. I knew gossip about them, could remember when and where I first laid eyes on a particular species, and all the places I had seen it. My seed-collecting envelopes became the records of my life, reused for years, listing dates, locations, companions, thoughts.

The Plant People

Once, while giving a talk at a native plant conference, I mentioned the first bird walk I'd ever taken. I had appeared sans binoculars, assuming in my ignorance that we would be concentrating on characteristics visible to the naked eye. My lack of apparatus was not a problem: Everyone else on the trip had at least three pairs of different kinds of binoculars, so I was easily supplied.

My audience of native plant people laughed at the overgearing foibles of the bird people and their love of long-distance magnification, identification, list-making. Birders are sometimes hilarious to nonbirders, although not to themselves. By the side of the road with the birders, I too become intent on finding that quick singer in the trees, oblivious of the stream of cars going by, with their freight of curious, envious, or amused passengers.

Not long afterward, I was on a plant taxonomy trip. We were looking at tiny flowers. At one point, everyone around me flung themselves to the ground to examine flower structure through hand lenses, counting stamens, assessing the angle of curl of pedicellate hairs. Would the bird people have laughed to see us?

Plant field trips often focus on plant identification. Plant taxonomy is a subject with great fascination for some, but it is not necessary to be able to key out a plant with a taxonomic key in order to identify, enjoy, and know how to grow it. Botanical names, meant to codify a stable labeling of plants, are changeable, creating the ironic situation wherein common names are sometimes more helpful in conversation. Lumpers, those who tend to group plants under a single name based on similarities rather than marking them off by differences, fight with splitters, and new floras seem to be controversial for the first ten years after their appearance.

At the Santa Clara County CNPS wildflower show, wildflower samples are brought in from all over the state. Of all the dedicated volunteers who create this show, probably 3 percent do the actual keying out. It's a specialized and fascinating way to know plants, but not essential for significant involvement with native plants. Embracing the human-created systems for talking about plant species is only one way to engage with native plants.

The California Native Plant Society has focused on particular endangered species, doing untold good in education and conservation. In 1990, the CNPS's board of directors recommended a shift from focusing on individual plant species to focusing on plant communities. One issue of the society's journal included an invaluable article on the pollinators of vernal pool flora, and a following issue was almost entirely devoted to pollinators. Maybe the day will come when plant descriptions in our state floras will include some mention of pollinators.

Bob Stewart

When I began to look outside of my field, I sought out the field trips of a local naturalist, Bob Stewart. Bob has led over 2,000 field trips in various parts of Marin County. Like other naturalists, he has his "groupies," people who are indebted to him for the patience and good humor with which he teaches. Bob leads not only plants walks, but bird walks, butterfly walks, insect walks, lichen walks, mushroom walks, and what he calls "habitat walks," in which everything is looked at.

After years of this work, he has started to notice that the specialists are beginning to broaden their interests. Avid birders have begun to appear on his plant walks, and plant people on his bird walks. He himself is an example of this ongoing expansion of fields of knowledge. His goal, as he defines it, is "to keep learning, go deeper, and broaden." When wishing to take on a new area, he hires an expert in the given field, lichens or spiders or native grasses, a naturalist's naturalist, to lead him on a field trip.

"To begin learning in a foreign area, you need somebody to show you what to look for, to help you out of the place where you don't know anything at all," said Bob. The experts tell what books to get, how to distinguish one thing from another, how to get a handle on the field of study. Bob is aware of how hard it is for beginners to "break through confusion," getting past the threshold of noncomprehension, because he puts himself in the beginner's place constantly in his own systematic acquisition of new knowledge.

The Bird People

It is early morning on California's north central coast. Bob Stewart and about fifteen bird-watchers have gathered for a May field trip billed as "Bird Song and Bird Nests." There is no guarantee that Bob, a Renaissance man of the natural world, won't talk about insects, plants, bats, or geology as well.

It is sunny after days of fog. Some participants have driven two hours to arrive at 8:00 A.M. on a Sunday morning. Predictably, only two of us are local. I swell with pride to think that people have taken so much trouble to arrive by eight in the morning at a site only two miles from my home. It is typical that hikers will be from somewhere else, so programmed are we to value that which is elsewhere over that which is local. The back-yard restoration gardener will want to seek out nearby trips, which will provide information more relevant for your garden. You will learn which birds might nest or pass through there, which endangered butterflies might be provided with a nursery, which lizards might come to do push-ups on your rocks.

Three experienced regulars have brought spotting scopes. They are cumbersome to carry, but when one is set up, I am able to see the rufous-sided towhee as though it were right next to me, its throat vibrating with song. I am grateful for the contribution of this tool. These impassioned viewers amaze me with their skills. No sooner was a bird spotted than the scopes would be set up, focused, and made available to the rest of the group, while I still ineffectually searched the brush with my binoculars. A courteous little line would form behind the scope, each taking a brief moment to look.

The morning of that bird walk with Bob Stewart in late May, I heard a plethora of bird song, overwhelming in its complexity, but at the same time reassuring to those aware of the perils faced by birds these days. Bob told us it was okay to be confused. Although I had hoped for more information on specific bird behavior, the particular coastal canyon and scrub land we were walking through was profuse in species. Just identifying the different songs was challenging and exciting.

Reason to Know

That afternoon I sat down with a tape called *Bird Songs of California* to try to cement some of this audio information in my brain. My cat lay peacefully by until the tape came to the section playing the calls of birds of the coastal scrub, the ones in our garden, the ones that she has reason to know. At that point, she became agitated, leapt off the couch, and went in search of the tape player.

"A reason to know" is often the missing ingredient for modern people, removed as we are from the necessity of knowledge of nature. The ongoing creation of the back-yard restoration garden gives the reason to know. I want to know which birds are coming to it, what they are doing while there, which species I am most likely to attract. Then I can intelligently make choices about what the garden should be like. Or at least make more interesting, informed guesses.

The Insect People

It seems that some people begin with a natural inclination in one direction or another. I get the casual impression that entomologists are frequently inclined in that direction by the age of six or seven. While their friends shudder in repulsion at beetles and bugs, these incipient entomologists are gazing with awe at the varied bumps and horns and legs of caterpillars and centipedes. "I always liked to be surprised," one entomologist friend explained.

Butterflies, like wildflowers for native flora, can serve to draw people into the world of insects, which needs all the public relations it can get. A culturally reinforced dislike of insects is evident, from Kafka's *Metamorphosis* to the use of DDT, sevin, malathion, and, for the gardener, outside bug zappers, indiscriminate insect killers, killing millions of insects. Yet flowers, which most of us love, are linked extensively, through all aspects of their lives, with those very insects, which relatively few of us love.

Once I went to hear a talk about termites, seeking information on non-chemical cures for termite problems. The entomologist giving the talk took the opportunity to show some slides of native bee pupa at the end. Each one looked out of its own snug little hole in the cliff. For the first time, a face emerged for me. A cute little buggy face with big eyes, looking something like my dog. In this complexity of wings and appendages and fierce stingers, I saw creatures with appeal. When observing insects in my back yard, I now make an attempt to see the eyes, which give them a face.

After this experience, this opening into the insect world, I attended a special field trip on insects at Point Reyes National Seashore. This very crowded field trip required reservations. On it, I learned that 85 percent of the bee species in the world are not hive bees, like the much-studied European honeybee, but solitary bees. In California, all the native bee species are solitary. Some, like the vernal pool pollinators, are completely host-specific. Their host plant can be pollinated (although possibly not as well) by other insects, but the bee itself will nectar from only one species. The continuing destruction of vernal pools, with their specialized flora, drags along with it the evolutionary end of those species of native bees that sip nectar from one, and only one, species of vernal pool wildflower.

The co-leader of the trip brought along a little wooden box with a homemade display to illustrate one point of the walk. It included a picture of a desert cliff wall in which a species of desert native bee lives. Pinned to the bottom of the box were specimens of those native bees, and specimens of the tiny wasps that parasitize them, and specimens of the tinier wasps that parasitize them.

Forty percent of all insects are parasitized by other insects. The complexities of the relationships between plants and insects are compounded by the complexities of the relationships between insects and insects. Parasites have parasites that have parasites.

On the morning of a field trip, I try to avoid last-minute frantic scramblings, making sure that I have my day pack ready in advance, clear directions to the meeting place, and a realistic idea of how long it will take to get there. I might bring a field notebook and pen, water, sunscreen, hat, collecting envelopes, magnifying lens, binoculars, and lunch. Robert Michael Pyle, an eminent butterfly-watcher and educator, even reminds his fellow naturalists to wash their eyeglasses. He also tells us what to wear: beiges and browns (although he has found that certain butterflies are attracted to bright red sweaters).

The subject of what to wear when butterflying falls into the category "Nobody really knows for sure." The natural world teems with items in that category. Once, on a field trip where posters warned that ticks abounded, animated discussion of the best way to remove them ensued. When consensus could not be reached, a doctor on the trip commented, "That's because nobody really knows."

Take the example of lists of deer-resistant plants. In some California counties, the question most frequently asked of nursery people is what plants deer will not eat. On many lists of deer-resistant plants, bush lupines, *Lupinus arboreus* and *Lupinus propinquus,* are prominent, but on other lists, bush lupine is described as important browse for deer. Some deer, some time, must have disregarded lupine in someone's garden. Salvias are also regularly listed, yet our deer eat them with relish. California fuchsia, *Epilobium canum,* ranks high on several deer-resistant lists, yet on a recent job, it was munched almost to the point of no return as soon as we walked away.

Where relationships among living things are concerned, a multiplicity of factors operates, reflected by contradictory advice. Field science is less easily controlled than lab science. That wonderful complexity means that you can take many statements with a large grain of salt. Just one more opportunity for the back-yard restoration gardener to develop the ability to identify, tolerate, and enjoy uncertainty and complexity.

On field trips, two categories of information can be presented. One involves naming and identification, and the other is about relationship. Note the epistemology of the subject matter — that is, how do people know what they think they know about bird breeding behaviors or the pollinators of certain plants? Is it from direct, personal observation? If so, how was that obtained? Through what complex of tools and measuring devices is information garnered?

Bird banding and mist-netting are two techniques that have contributed much information to ornithologists. Mist-netting, in which birds are caught in nets for banding, weighing, and recording, is a tool invented by the Point Reyes Bird Observatory. It enables birds to be tracked throughout their lives.

Think of the countless hours it takes to make even one good inference about the behavior of birds, as they swoop away from us and disappear in the trees. Is the careening flight of that butterfly a search for a mate or a search for just the right larval food plant to lay an egg on? Or a nervous response to possible predation? Is that particular call of the quail a response to perceived danger to the flock or a call to move on to another area for browsing? Should your observations not match the conclusions of scientists, salute the unknowable and don't assume you are wrong.

Barry Lopez describes Alaskan biologists discussing polar bear migration paths, with an eye to predicting them. The Inuk hunter sitting nearby gives his view of such endeavors: "Quajijaujungangitut. *It can't be learned.*" (Emphasis added.)

Epistemology in the Garden

Biologists are continually refining the questions they ask and their methods for obtaining answers. Nature defies the quick glance and the easy conclusion. It behooves the back-yard restoration gardener to judge any information about the natural world accordingly. Birds don't come forth to explain their behaviors, nor do tidal scours come labeled with impact statements. Information must be teased out laboriously over time.

I had a client once whose goal was to return eight hundred acres of overgrazed grassland, dominated by yellow star thistle, to a state of health. "Nobody in your field really knows what they're doing," he said. "Everybody's just got a little piece of it." He seemed disgruntled by this state of affairs. Other aspects of our lives support the notion that "fields" should be knowable, and that once goals are established, protocols should be clear. But the field of restoration ecology has been thriving for not much more than fifteen or twenty years, while ignorant and destructive land use practices in the West have prevailed for over two centuries.

Learning what we need to know to reverse this state of affairs is neither simple nor easy, and it is probably not even possible within our lifetimes. Natural models may no longer exist to guide us. Scientific studies may contradict each other. Variables of soil, climate, exposure, and land use history make all information site-specific.

In an example of continually refining the questions being asked, John Kelly, of the Cypress Grove Preserve in Marshall, California, makes the point that data on songbird feeding patterns have often been lumped together, without distinctions between time of day, time of year, or gender. The naturalist looking for clues to what the common yellowthroat is gleaning in the Olema Marsh must lug ladders through the marsh, making observations morning, noon, and night, taking into account all these factors, and individual preferences as well.

Ways of Learning

Early one Saturday morning, I found myself contemplating vials of mammal scat being passed from hand to hand. It was an opportunity to learn a bit about how mammalogists draw conclusions about their elusive subjects. Scatology is one way.

Context is critical in the field of scatology. An informal study showed that scatologists agreed only 60 percent of the time when identifying unlabeled scat samples in a laboratory setting. Shape, texture, color, and contents are not always sufficient. Guesses are best made in the field, where the situation in which the scat is found provides crucial information.

Witnessing wildlife events, even those as frequent as bird song, requires patience and time in the field. The optimal way to learn to identify bird song is to witness the open mouth of the bird who pours forth the song. Those who study scat are rarely present when scat samples are produced, and they must therefore make educated guesses. Students in this field are able to tolerate this uncertainty. Each field has its own requirements for such tolerance and its own ways of finding things out.

Some ways are indirect. Biologists study the rise and fall of vole populations by estimating the number of vole runways in use, rather than by direct observation of vole activities and individuals. Voles, like people, build new highways when the old ones become crowded. The more trampled, chewed highways visible in a prairie, the more voles are busy making them.

Less invasive techniques are on the rise. Butterflies that used to be killed and pinned on boards are now dabbed with a marking pen and released. Jeffrey Glassberg of the North American Butterfly Association promotes the advantages of butterflying with binoculars as well, an advance over the collected butterfly, pinned forever to a board. Binoculars have also taken the place of shooting and stuffing birds for identification purposes.

Reading so often of the detailed knowledge that indigenous peoples had and have about the movements and habits of animals and plants, I compare them to modern naturalists. How could the former compete, without our advantages of the scientific method, binoculars, magnifying glasses, rulers, and calculators, in drawing conclusions? One advantage is time spent observing. Indigenous students of nature were not paying taxes, writing a thesis, reading books, watching TV, waiting in line, buying new vests, paying credit card bills, applying for grants, or calling the plumber. They were engaged almost continually with the material.

The Butterfly People

"All time spent with butterflies is quality time," says Robert Michael Pyle, an eloquent and impassioned public relations man for the lepidopteran world, whose *Handbook for Butterfly Watchers* tells you what to look for, how to think about it, and also what to wear while doing so. Butterflies are definitely his way in.

Pyle appreciates their value as linking entities. Once you become interested in keeping butterflies around, recognizing an aesthetic and emotional contribution to the garden, you will think more about their basic needs, which involve the plant kingdom. Butterflies exploit the environment in two major ways: one as caterpillars seeking leaves of a host plant, the other as nectaring adult butterflies.

Some butterflies in the larval stage require as food the chemical com-

*Once I fell asleep reading an obscure text about basketry among
the Indians of California's northwestern coast and dreamed
about the plants in the book, including alder roots, used to dye
fern fronds red. The next morning, I went to my favorite swimming hole, a small, exquisite pond fringed with alders, willows,
and huckleberries. The water there makes my arms look reddish
gold, and my feet, farther down, a deeper red. Making my
way up the muddy bank, climbing over alder roots, I suddenly
thought: "The alder roots are dyeing the water, which makes my
skin look red."*

*This conclusion appeared from nowhere. I wasn't searching
my brain for reasons why the water might have a faint, lovely
reddish cast. Sometimes water looks red because of dissolved
minerals like iron. Or it may be for an altogether different
reason. I enjoyed the way this understanding came unbidden,
perhaps an older way of drawing conclusions about the natural
world. Reading and dreaming provided a different way in.
Dreams are a time-honored source of song, prophecy, and information for native peoples. The use of datura as a psychedelic
(a significant pharmacological achievement: datura is highly
toxic in any but minute doses) may first have been dreamed.*

*I have a friend who knew a botanist studying plants with
the peoples of the rain forest. When this botanist fell asleep, the
tribespeople would rub her forehead with leaves from a specific
plant about which they wanted to know more. She would wake
up to find them gathered around her bed, waiting to be told
what it was that she had learned from this plant in her dreams.*

position of the leaves of a specific host plant. Such butterflies are called *host-
specific*. Others may lay eggs on a host plant that will not give them the
chemical protection from predation they require. Because you see a butterfly

or bird nectaring from a non-native plant or laying eggs on a non-native host plant, do not conclude that all is well. They may not be getting what they need.

You Are What You Eat

Thomas Eisner at Cornell University has been studying the moth *Utetheisa,* which is poisonous to birds and spiders. When the moth in its larval stage is able to feed on the genus *Crotolaria,* consisting of poisonous plants, both the caterpillars and the butterflies are avoided by predators. When larvae were raised on substances devoid of the poisonous alkaloids found in *Crotolaria,* they were devoured by spiders.

These researchers found that, not only had these moths evolved to be able to eat poisonous plants, but they were able to incorporate the alkaloids into their own bodies for their own defense. They also found that parents, both male and female, contributed to the presence of alkaloids in their eggs, which also protected the eggs from some of their enemies. Female *Utetheisa* can, after multiple matings, select the particular sperm they wish to fertilize their eggs, and it is almost always the sperm of the larger males, more richly endowed with the poisonous alkaloids, that they choose.

This piece of research demonstrates the intricacies that science can begin to tease out. For the back-yard butterfly gardener, the message is to provide the plants with which butterflies have co-evolved. Because a species may nectar from or feed on many non-native plants, it does not necessarily follow that they are getting what they need to continue the subtle maneuvers, choices, and ways of thriving of which they are capable.

The kind of protection, shelter from sun, wind, and predation, afforded by the host plant at the particular time of year when the butterfly is in the larval stage is critical to its survival as well. The seemingly random flutterings of the adult female butterfly once she has mated are in part actually a search for the particular host plant on which to lay her egg, which will require this particular "nursery" when it hatches.

The disappearance of the host plant may take the host-specific butterfly with it. This is what has happened with a number of extinct or almost extinct species. Other butterflies do not have such specific requirements; some lay eggs on a number of different, readily available plants, and some have adapted handily to non-native plants. But if we want the colors of the Bay checkerspot, the Mission blue, the San Bruno elfin butterfly, the El Segundo blue, Lange's metalmark, the California pipevine swallowtail, and the Palos Verdes blue, we must provide the right plants for their egg laying and the right food for those caterpillars when they hatch.

TOLOWIM WOMAN   *"Tolowim Woman and Butterfly Man" is a Maidu story, one of my favorites from the collection made by Malcolm Margolin in his book* The Way We Lived. *In this story, Tolowim Woman is seed collecting with her baby on her back. She sees and pursues a beautiful butterfly, leaving her baby behind. During the pursuit, she discards, piece by piece, all of her clothing. She falls asleep when night comes and wakes to find that the butterfly has turned into a handsome man. He tells her that she can stay with him always if she can follow him through a valley, the southern side of which is full of beautiful butterflies. (Butterflies, in their search for sun, are indeed found on the southern side.)*

But Tolowim Woman is so distracted by the beauty of the other butterflies that she lets go of her husband and tries to catch them as well. The story ends in disaster, her love lost, her baby abandoned, and herself dying in the valley. It recognizes the intoxicating, potentially overpowering beauty of the natural world (and the danger of greed).

Lange's Metalmark Butterfly

This butterfly lays its eggs only on the naked-stemmed buckwheat, *Eriogonum nudum.* The butterfly and the buckwheat historically occupied the dunes near the confluence of the San Joaquin and Sacramento rivers.

Located in populous and growing Contra Costa County, this butterfly's habitat has been compromised by mining, vineyard development, and the encroachment of non-native weedy plants.

Ironically, the crowds that were drawn to view the off-course humpback whale "Humphrey" in 1985 trampled many stands of naked-stemmed buckwheat, the host plant essential to the development of Lange's metalmark. Subsequent attempts to remove weedy species and replant with naked-stemmed buckwheat have been successful, allowing the butterfly to recolonize some of the restored sites. The population has grown from fewer than two hundred in 1986 to nearly two thousand in 1991.

What does this mean for back-yard restoration gardeners near the towns of Antioch, Concord, and Walnut Creek? You might want to include a good planting of naked-stemmed buckwheat. This species, like all eriogonums, has much to offer the gardener. Felted, silvery foliage and striking flowers in shades of white to pink are followed by interesting seeds in rich shades of browns and rusts. Eriogonums are low-growing, easy-to-grow, drought-tolerant native perennials. They provide bloom at the end of the summer, when not much else is flowering, and it is then that adult Lange's metalmark butterflies can be seen nectaring from them, as well as from shrubby butterweed, *Senecio douglasii,* and broom snakeweed, *Gutierrezia sarothrae.*

You don't want just a smattering of eriogonums. You will want at least fifteen plants, a good mass, a design element that can be repeated throughout the garden. Other, less host-specific, late-summer butterflies and bees as well enjoy the nectar of eriogonums, which are always a buzzing, fluttering spot in the garden. They blend beautifully with other low-growing, nectar-producing native perennials like beach asters or grindelias.

Even if Lange's metalmark butterfly doesn't come, you will know that you are honoring an endangered plant/insect relationship local to the area. You set the table; let the guests come if they will, maybe tonight, maybe next year. The movements of butterflies are complex, varying from species to species, and even from local population to local population.

Many books have been written on butterfly gardening. The best ones admit that it may not work. You may have the right host plant and nectar plant, the right mix of sun and shade, and good supplies of puddles, yet still not draw those capricious, unpredictable butterflies. Wet years can create fungal problems; dry years can create food problems for larvae. Their predators may be enjoying a good year. Learn to rest easy with the many factors beyond your control.

Many plants, both native and non-native, can fulfill nectaring requirements for butterflies. Nectar plants are not usually the limiting factor in butterfly survival. Some scientists have raised questions about the nutritional value of certain well-known non-native butterfly plants, so sticking to native offerings ensures that subtle nutritional aspects we may not be aware of are being provided. Open, simple flowers are best.

THE GRINDELIA BY THE OFFICE DOOR   *Gumplant,* Grindelia stricta, *blooms in November by the office door. Numerous butterflies, bees, and hoverflies nectaring from its sticky yellow flowers form a buzzing background to the day's work. This plant seeded itself in the middle of a small prairie recreation. Although we planted grindelia elsewhere in our garden, it was in an obscure corner, and I never noticed what a sensational draw it was for insect life.*

This wet year, we have been particularly interested in late-blooming nectar plants, since that is when most of the butterflies finally appeared. After witnessing the amount of insect activity this plant attracted, I decided to plant it successively through the winter. Bunchgrasses within the range of this plant are noticeably greener, larger, less completely dormant than other grasses in the prairie. Craig Dremann of Redwood City Seed Company observed that burned grasslands returned more quickly to health and vigor when grindelia was one of the components. Hmmm, grindelia.

After a butterfly field trip, I see them better in my own garden. I notice when they're there and when they're not and can speculate about what they might be after. Watching butterflies "puddling" in a shallow mud puddle on a field trip, I noted its similarity to the puddle in my yard, formed by a faulty gray-water system draining the kitchen sink. I decided not to fix it for a while, to see how it might serve the butterflies.

This last wet year, they came late. A late March planting of wildflowers bloomed in August, when such flowerings are usually long over. It was available for them when they finally turned up. Two out-of-sync events meshed.

Elders in the Field

Naturalists like Bob Stewart, Carl Sharsmith, and Ray Peterson, whose eyes are everywhere at once, are able to honor all aspects of the nonhuman world with the constancy and breadth of their regard. They have something precious to offer us. Our naturalists are the high priests and priestesses of ecological literacy. When we began to read books, and the written word began to speak, the nonhuman world became increasingly silent to many. These men and women help it speak again.

David Abrams describes indigenous shamans and magicians in a way that might apply to the modern naturalist: "The traditional magician cultivates an ability to shift out of his or her common state of consciousness precisely in order to make contact with the other organic forms of sensitivity and awareness with which human existence is entwined. . . . His magic is precisely this heightened receptivity to the meaningful solicitations — songs, cries, gestures — of the larger, more-than-human field."

I asked Bob Stewart if he ever felt bored with the prospect of yet another field trip, and he admitted that occasionally that was the case. "But when I'm actually out there, it can't be boring," he said. "It's a movie I want to be part of, to go out into and watch. I never know what we're going to see. I am open to what we're going to see. One or two little things will always happen that I never saw before, that make my day. That, to me, is having fun." As Ray Peterson puts it, "No two days are ever alike."

Bob describes his personal motivation as "needing to honor as many life forms as possible in my lifetime. That means knowing their names and seeing how they fit together. I'm willing to do the hard work that it takes to help me distinguish among them."

Knowledge of the natural world has always represented control, security, and ultimately survival to human beings. In a relatively stable culture, it provides a reason to honor the old. Transmitting knowledge provides a reason to stay alive once you are old. In the fields of natural science, obsolescence is held somewhat at bay, and age still brings honor, wisdom, and continued learning.

Many people in this field lead notably long and productive lives, working and teaching into their nineties. Animated by a lifelong desire to see the natural world, Carl Sharsmith lived to be 94 years old. Lester Rowntree died at 101, after years of solitary trekking through the mountains and valleys of California. Gerda Isenberg of Yerba Buena Nursery, who died at 96, was growing, raking, and propagating till 93. Willis Linn Jepson was hunting, classifying, and studying our native flora till age 79.

Some degree of ecological illiteracy is a given for most of us. "Nature study," which came into being with the Industrial Revolution and is now called "environmental education," is an attempt to remedy a situation unique in the history of humankind, in which a life lived with no knowledge of or direct connection to natural relationships is not only possible but common.

The back-yard restoration garden can serve as a corrective, a kindly textbook, bringing nature home, where it can most easily and comfortably be absorbed. That includes the contradictions, the exceptions, and the surprises: the dynamic flow of seasons and soil change, the movement of insects, the sudden whims of birds. Here's to the rich complications and the dynamic interaction of countless factors. Here's to the mystery, and to those who send into it the searchlight of a humble human attention.

 Tools and Tricks
of the Trade

Greek amphoras for wine or oil,
Hopi vases that held corn, are put in museums
but you know they were made to be used.
The pitcher cries for water to carry
And a person for work that is real.

Marge Piercy, "To Be of Use"

For twenty years, I have watched and attempted to facilitate the process
whereby gardeners become seized by the kinds of activities and attitudes
that will tend in the direction of making their piece of land a diverse, rich,
and healthy part of the ongoing evolution of life.

Here are some organizations and techniques to fuel the vision and
hone the skills of the back-yard restoration gardener, useful tools to help you
find out what is growing near you now and what might have been growing
near you once, and how to bring it back in close.

Maybe it is obvious that you are in an oak woodland, or maybe it is not
so clear. Miles of asphalt may separate you from the nearest wildland, but
there are resources that can help you get the picture you need. Such information can be pursued to different levels, from going to the nearest nature
preserve to checking herbarium specimens at the California Academy of
Sciences or Sonoma State University to verify historical locations of a particular species.

Native Plant Societies

A good place to begin, local native plant society chapters are gold mines
of information. Here, some of the elders of the native plant world gather.
Dedicated volunteers, both laypeople and professionals, share lifetimes of

memories of field trips, plant discoveries, good and bad wildflower years, and conservation-related legislation successfully enacted.

In California, most areas of the state have their own chapter of the California Native Plant Society, membership in which includes monthly meetings with a wide range of speakers, monthly newsletters, field trips, and conservation projects. Every member receives a bimonthly copy of the organization's journal *Fremontia,* a scholarly but readable compilation of new discoveries, descriptions of individual species and plant communities, and information on garden uses of native plants.

Each chapter has a unique flavor. The East San Francisco Bay chapter organizes and grows plants for the biggest native plant sale in the state, held annually at Merritt College in October. Native plant aficionados line up early in the morning of the first day of the sale, where volunteers wait tensely to facilitate the thousands of dollars worth of plant sales that will support the efforts of the society.

The Santa Clara Valley chapter sponsors a spring wildflower show, involving dozens of volunteers in a statewide collection of samples to be keyed out and labeled for the education and enjoyment of hundreds of viewers. This chapter has also been successful in preserving a priceless piece of serpentine grassland and wildflower fields.

Wilma Follette of the Marin County chapter developed the wildflower poster project, which has netted the organization thousands of dollars. The Dorothy King Young chapter in Gualala was responsible for successfully eradicating invasions of French broom before most chapters had begun programs concerned with invasive exotic plants.

In southern California, the San Gabriel Mountains chapter seriously engages in restoration projects. The San Diego chapter is known for its conservation activism. The South Coast chapter is responsible for the native plant garden at the Point Vicente Interpretive Center, which features plants from the Channel Islands.

Although a variety of people belong, I note the development of one type of member in particular, the dedicated, knowledgeable layperson — computer programmers expert in a particular genus of wildflower, secretaries who specialize in wildflower photography, surgeons who love taxonomy. I am often in awe of these dedicated amateurs, people whose love for the flora of California invigorates their lives. On CNPS field trips, I relearn how an interest can sustain a human being through a lifetime.

WILMA FOLLETTE   *On a field trip she is leading, Wilma brings out her copy of* Marin Flora, *by John Thomas Howell. Twice rebound, it is dog-eared and crammed with notes and supplements. She ordered it in the late 1950s, hearing that it was about the wildflowers of Marin County. When she received it, she couldn't understand a word. "It was written in another language," she said, "but I knew it was trying to tell me something."*

Wilma learned that language so well that she has taught college courses in plant taxonomy for eleven years. For the past twenty-one years, she has led weekly walks in the spring through the coastal hills and inland mountains of Marin County. On such occasions, attendees are treated to Wilma's walk, an unpredictable combination of speeding up to cover ground and slowing to a crawl for minute examinings.

The Society for Ecological Restoration

This organization, based in Madison, Wisconsin, sponsored the conference where I first realized that what I did had a name. William Jordan II, the editor of its quarterly journal, *Restoration and Management Notes,* is an articulate spokesperson for the field. Wide-ranging philosophical issues are tackled in his editorials, and the journal includes complete reports on restoration projects, as well as abstracts of articles in the field of restoration ecology. Their yearly conferences, held all over the country, are exciting events.

California has its own state branch of SER, called SERCAL, and its newsletter and annual conference focus on the concerns of Californians involved in restoration.

The Nature Conservancy

Nature Conservancy preserves are dotted all over California, and most of them provide opportunities for volunteers to be trained in restoration techniques and attitudes, which can then be applied to their own land. Docent training provides an opportunity to become fluent in the flora and fauna of nearby preserves, demonstrating that the best way to learn is to teach.

Botanic gardens, such as Strybing Arboretum in San Francisco, and organizations like Audubon Canyon Ranch at Stinson Beach also have well-organized docent training programs. Audubon Canyon Ranch's docent training program is the equivalent of the best college course you ever had.

Neighborhood Organizations

The Bernal Hilltop Native Grassland Restoration Project, the Potrero Hill Association, Friends of Codornices Park in Berkeley, the Greenway in El Cerrito, and Friends of Nipomo Mesa in Arroyo Grande are all organizations formed by neighbors to protect and enhance land held in common. Workdays for all organizations involve controlling escaped exotics, planting site-specific seedlings that volunteers have grown, maintaining plantings, and enjoying and learning about the common neighborhood.

Floras

Every thirty or forty years, a new California flora, a dichotomous key listing all the state's plant species, is produced. This massive tome is usually controversial at first, lumping or splitting species to the displeasure of those who liked or had become used to the old classifications. Eventually, it becomes the bible till the next production.

Willis Linn Jepson's *A Manual of the Flowering Plants of California* was published in 1925, becoming the standard reference for California's plants for over twenty-five years. Born near Vacaville in 1867, Jepson was a lifelong bioregionalist who loved his hills of home and believed in meticulous, thorough observations in the field, seeing each species within its own particular environment. The back-yard restoration gardener in or around Vacaville might profitably look into Jepson's early writings and notebooks for inspiration from his descriptions of how it used to be. In 1991, the Vacaville Museum put together a rich display of Jepson's diaries and later work. "Man is too ignorant of the earth on which he lives to take such a responsibility as to kill out completely any species," Jepson said in 1928.

When I first became interested in California native plants, in the early 1970s, the taxonomic bible was *A California Flora* by Philip A. Munz, published in 1959 and reprinted with supplement in 1968. In 1993, a new flora, *The Jepson Manual: Higher Plants of California,* was published after ten years of work. It involved over two hundred volunteer authors, experts in each area, and the stated goal was "to follow Jepson's lead in making the extraordinarily diverse world of California wild plants available to the widest range of people possible." Four years before publication of the complete manual, a taste of what was to come was provided by an attractive shorter book, *Introduction to the Jepson Manual,* paving the way for comment on and acceptance of the changes in the final book.

In the *Jepson Manual,* horticultural information on native plants used in gardens is for the first time systematically included in a major flora. Necessarily terse, its inclusion nonetheless validates the importance of this aspect of the flora of California, bringing horticulturists and taxonomists together. I hope that the next flora of California will also include the pollination path for each genus.

The new *Jepson Manual* has met with both appreciation and controversy. Munz's *A California Flora* initially met with similar reactions, but by the time I encountered it, twenty-five years after its publication, whatever controversy it had engendered was perhaps noticeable only among plant taxonomists.

Some species and subspecies have been eliminated or combined in the *Jepson Manual*, names have been changed, and some new species are described. The *Manual* explains it this way: "As taxonomists learn more about the complexities of variation patterns, their best taxonomic assessments automatically change. It may become more difficult to represent what is known in a taxonomic scheme. Scientists continually work toward a more integrated perspective but probably will never be fully successful in the search for simple answers. The more we explore and learn, the more intriguingly complex we find the natural world to be."

The Jepson Herbarium offers a series of workshops for those with a serious interest in taxonomy. For those not so interested in studying the plant world as filtered through the minds of taxonomists, I recommend local floras, of which there are many. Some, like *Marin Flora,* by John Thomas Howell, first published in 1949, and again, with a supplement, in 1970, are local by county. These are "must-haves" for the back-yard restoration gardener. *Marin Flora* is a good example. An early chapter describes the different life zones and plant associations found in Marin County, with a brief plant list for each one. These plant lists could be the basis of a garden planting.

Other floras, such as John Hunter Thomas's *Flora of the Santa Cruz Mountains* and Helen K. Sharsmith's *Flora of the Mount Hamilton Range of California,* focus on a specific region rather than a county. The City of San Francisco has its own flora, written in 1958, in which one can trace the further demise of a unique and beautiful assemblage of plant communities. Floras for national, state, or local parks, sold in visitor centers, are often helpfully specific. You might want to try your hand at a neighborhood flora, a way to share what you've learned with your neighbors.

A new resource recently published by the California Native Plant Society is *A Manual of California Vegetation,* by John Sawyer and Todd Keeler-Wolf. The California back-yard restorationist can use this manual to put together a plant list for his garden. For example, if he knows that woollyleaf manzanita is an important species in his area, he can look up the "Woollyleaf manzanita series" to determine that it is also found with black sage, California buckwheat, California coffeeberry, chamise, and possibly birchleaf mountain-mahogany, as well as others. He can garden with the plant palette listed in what this book calls a "series" rather than a plant community. Smaller plant groupings are known as "associations" and are based on characteristic species in the understory layers, reflecting more localized variation in soil and climate.

Other Places to Look

Regional museums, historical societies, and museums of natural history are a good place to do some casual or strenuous firsthand research. Gems of information can be gleaned from oral histories. Our local regional museum, for example, is mandated to expend a certain amount of its resources, including curated shows and research projects, on local history, which inevitably includes some land use history.

From oral histories at our local museum, I learned the extent of the cutting of oaks for firewood in this area. I heard one rancher's memorable view of the effect of ranching here: "We have left a disaster for our children." I found the early photos that might explain our widely held local view that the mesa most of us live on was originally a treeless prairie. Taken shortly after the Gold Rush, these pictures show the results of the kind of grazing practices that characterized that period. The oaks, wax myrtles, buckeyes, willows, elderberries, toyons, and alders, as well as the large patches of coastal scrub that we see here and there, indicate a much more complicated picture.

Regional museums sometimes publish the memoirs of local citizens, which contain nuggets of information. Natural history museums, like the Great Valley Natural History Museum in Lodi, California, will offer much that the restoration gardener needs. Historical societies often have good collections and knowledgeable local volunteers, who may have known the personages and sites you are interested in. Local libraries may have special collections on local history. I once spent an afternoon looking through the collections in a back room at the visitor center at Anza-Borrego State Park. All I had to do was ask.

Artists from an earlier day can give us pictures of how the land was. Our local museum once sponsored an exhibit of early paintings of our area. When the curators gave a talk to the general public, most of the audience had questions and comments about changes in vegetation conveyed by the paintings. Changes in the land rather than painting styles became the subject of the talk.

Recently, the museum sponsored two shows side by side, one showing historic paintings of our lagoon, another paintings of the same subject by contemporary artists. For information on how the land and waters change, stick to the traditionalists. The modern paintings revealed more about the artist's individual vision than about the lagoon.

Look for information on the local tribes that still inhabit or used to inhabit your area. *News from Native California,* published by Heyday Books, is an indispensable source of such information for Californians. Autobiographies of Native Americans are gifts to us, full of information about local plants. For example, the autobiography of Delfino Cuero, a Kumeyaay Indian, includes specific information on native agriculture and uses of fire in the San Diego area.

California has an impressive number of botanic gardens that are either totally focused on native plants or that have significant native plant sections, ranging from the university-sponsored to the grounds of private estates, like El Alisal. Santa Barbara Botanic Garden includes a home demonstration garden, where California pipevine crawls up the fireplace and pots of blooming monkeyflowers grace the deck. An ancient aqueduct flows through the garden. Rancho Santa Ana Botanic Garden is an enormous resource for southern California gardens, with classes, tours, and symposia at its immaculately maintained eighty-acre site. Some universities, colleges, and junior colleges have horticulture or landscape architecture departments that maintain native demonstration gardens. A list of botanic gardens, demonstration gardens, and arboretums with native components is offered in the Resources section at the end of this book.

Volunteers plant and maintain the Nipomo Native Garden on the Nipomo Mesa in San Luis Obispo County. Designed by David Fross, it shows local gardeners a rich palette for their gardens, including the rare and endangered *Ceanothus impressus* var. *nipomensis, Quercus agrifolia, Leptodactylon, Arctostaphylos rudis, Salvia mellifera, Cercocarpus betuloides, Rhamnus californica, Ribes speciosum, Salvia spathacea, Elymus condensatus,* and *Heteromeles arbutifolia.*

Working with Professionals

In building the Resources section of this book, I put a notice in each newsletter of the various chapters of the California Native Plant Society requesting information on native plant gardeners, both professional and amateur. I received a large number of responses in both categories. A surprising number of home gardeners sent in wonderful descriptions of their native plant gardens and their motivations for creating them. Some included plant lists and detailed histories. If, like those gardeners, you want to do everything yourself, I hope this book will help, but professionals can be useful in a range of capacities.

You may want to avail yourself of the help of specialists, for guidance or for the entire job. You may want to buy plants from nurseries or to buy seed and grow your own. Or to collect seed and grow your own, or to collect seed and have someone else grow it. A mix of levels of involvement is possible.

You can do your own research and put your own ideas into practice, or you can hire a consultant, preferably as local as possible, to speed up the process of self-education. Some chapters of CNPS provide lists of landscapers who work with native plants.

Professionals can provide guidance in procedures and plant lists, while you do the actual work. You can hire a designer who supervises a planting crew, after which you do the maintenance. You can hire a designer with a crew for installation who also return for maintenance, while you wander out to pluck a lily blossom and fall asleep in the bunchgrass prairie. Or you can assemble a crew of workers that you direct in planting what you have grown or bought. Or combinations of the above.

Some of our customers hire us to do major plantings. When we are done, they chip away at the project themselves for a while, until they feel financially ready to commission major work again. Sometimes I bring the plants and put them in their proper places, and the client does the actual planting. In all cases, return visits are critical, to evaluate aftercare and note any problems.

The response to my request for the names of landscapers who use native plants indicated that many use native plants as often as they can, as often as clients will let them. In another, smaller category are those who will only take clients who want native plants exclusively. They have not infrequently made financial sacrifices to maintain this position. The professionals are out there, waiting and hoping for the opportunity to do this kind of work.

Working with Nurseries

The conventional nursery in California grows or sells plants from China, Europe, England, and ever more plants from Mediterranean climates such as those found in parts of Australia and Chile. They usually do not offer many plants from California, except for a few regulars, like cultivars of flannel bush, ceanothus, and manzanita. The reasons are many: lack of demand from the public, lack of availability, the idea that natives don't look good in containers (which is sometimes true and sometimes not). It probably is true that, deep-rooted as many California native plants are, or desirous of summer drought, they don't look good in containers very long, although there are many exceptions. The average nursery doesn't want to deal with exceptions. In general, nurseries incline toward mass-produced plants, with predictable results.

The shining exceptions are few but noteworthy. In Resources you will find a list of nurseries that make a concerted effort to carry a good selection of native plants. There are also a few nurseries that carry only natives. Many claim that they would like to carry more natives if the public demanded them. Designers and landscape architects say that they can't come up with plans that include native plants if they can't find the native plants. Nurseries say that they can't carry native plants if nobody will buy them. An impasse is created, which could be broken by the back-yard restoration gardener.

Making requests for specific native species is one way. Contracting with nurseries that grow plants to supply your back-yard project is another, whether they supply the seed or you do. In these situations, there is again room for varying levels of involvement. You may want them to grow the grasses for your prairie restoration from seed that you have collected or from seed they obtain. Growing for specific projects, with a guaranteed buyer, is called "contract growing." Some nurseries only grow and sell on this basis, usually for large-scale restoration projects. More might be willing to work this way with the back-yard restorationist, particularly when it represents a definite sale.

We have a client with 150 acres of blue oak woodlands at the eastern edge of the Central Valley. He began to notice that many native bunchgrasses could still be found there. Discussing techniques and timing, he was able to make several seed collections, which we grew as plugs. He then planted and maintained them.

Another client began his project with intentions of doing a lot of the work himself, but as we worked with him, it became clear that his desire to be involved was greater than the amount of free time he had. Consequently, we took on more of the process, while leaving manageable amounts of maintenance for him. Freed from some of the work, he found time to pull French broom in the open space adjoining his property. Attending plant sales with his young daughters was a particular enjoyment, so we left the finding of rare plants to him. Plant sales, sponsored by CNPS chapters or by botanic gardens, are a major way for aficionados of native plants to stock their gardens.

I often make on-site seed collections when I arrive for the original consultation, or point out what the client could be collecting and when. For local jobs, we are continually collecting and growing our local plants. And we are no longer the only ones. In my town now, there are four of us growing native plants in back-yard nurseries. Some of us are growing mainly for our own design jobs but are delighted to sell to our neighbors as well. A great way to influence your neighbors' choice of plants is to make local natives available to them from your own back-yard nursery.

Literary Ecology

If you are a reader of fiction, you might enjoy delving into the works of those rare writers for whom landscape figures prominently. Novelists, like painters, can be excellent at addressing some of our landscape questions. Descriptions can't be taken as literal truth but nonetheless depict a certain truth. Anthologists like Lawrence Clark Powell, who assembled *California Classics,* help us seek out the early writings about our locale.

A casual list for Californians might include Jessamyn West, *South of the Angels;* Janet Lewis, *Against a Darkening Sky;* John Steinbeck, *East of Eden;* Joaquin Miller, *Life Amongst the Modocs;* Gertrude Atherton, *The Californians;* Mary Austin, *Land of Little Rain*; and Jaime d'Angulo, *Indians in*

Overalls. Gerald Haslam (*That Constant Coyote: California Stories*) and James D. Houston anthologized writings from the Central Valley in *California Heartland. Silverado Squatters,* by Robert Louis Stevenson, gives a detailed, delicious picture of the montane vegetation of Napa County, California.

For Maine gardeners, Sarah Orne Jewett's *The Country of the Pointed Firs* is redolent with the flavor of island dwellers living close to the land and sea. Dorothy Canfield Fisher's Vermont novels and short stories, particularly *The Deepening Stream,* and her wonderful children's book, *Understood Betsy,* are replete with tidbits for the literary ecologist. In the former work, the hero falls in love because of the way a woman watches a sugar maple leaf drift, then land in her hair.

The midwestern gardener might search out the nature writings of the well-known Indiana fiction writer Gene Stratton Porter (*A Girl of the Limberlost, Freckles*). Her description of the significance of farmyard landscaping in the essay "Songs of the Fields," written in the early part of the century, is illuminating and predictive.

Thomas Hardy's English landscape novels, in which setting is critical, have perhaps no equivalent yet either in California or in the rest of the United States. In Hardy's *The Return of the Native,* which is replete with ecological insights, Egdon heath figures almost as a character. The scene set by Hardy presents a grasp of the change of landscapes through time, as well as a strong sense of the impacts of human activity. We learn that gorse, *Ulex europaea,* also called furze, was an important fuel source in the mid 1800s, providing the basis for a whole industry of furze cutters. Gorse is a pest plant of concern in California, growing in the chaparral and coastal scrub as it does in the heath in England, where human use may keep it in bounds.

In Helen Hunt Jackson's *Ramona,* the landscape of California is a constant presence. Many passages attest to Jackson's appreciation of it.

> The billowy hills on either side the valley were covered with verdure and bloom,— myriads of low blossoming plants, so close to the earth that their tints lapped and overlapped on each other, and on the green of the grass, as feathers in fine plumage overlap each other and blend into a changeful color.
>
> The countless curves, hollows, and crests of the coast-hills in Southern California heighten these chameleon effects of the spring verdure; they are

like nothing in nature except the glitter of a brilliant lizard in the sun or the iridescent sheen of a peacock's neck.

Jackson knew more about the ecology of wild mustard than many longtime Californians know today. I think of her when I am not infrequently asked by customers for seeds of wild mustard. One wanted to plant mustard as a "soil-purifier." When asked why her soil needed purifying, she said, "I don't know. It sounded like a good idea."

For entertainingly presented information on current land use practices and issues in the San Joaquin Valley, try the botanically correct murder mysteries written by Rebecca Rothenberg, San Gabriel Mountains CNPS chapter president. The plants, peoples, and landscapes of southern California are given equal time in this enjoyable series. Even Munz's *A California Flora* plays a significant role.

Or visit the South Peninsula in 1898, the time of Gertrude Atherton's heroine Magdalena, in *The Californians,* when Menlo Park was entirely owned by fifteen or twenty wealthy families from San Francisco. Her writings helped me to understand the sharp demarcations between intact oak woodlands around the homes of the wealthy in this area and the entirely different plantings that mark the land sold off from the estates and developed in tracts. One might conclude from the correspondence between expensive property and oaks that the best way to raise one's property values is to plant oak trees, or preserve existing ones.

A year from the following June, and two days after her arrival in Menlo Park, Magdalena went into the middle woods. The great oaks were dusty already, their brilliant greens were dimming; but the depths of the woods were full of the warm shimmer of summer, of the mysterious noises produced by creatures never seen by the very heat itself.

Magdalena left the driveway and pushed in among the brush. Poison oak did not affect her; and she separated the beautiful creeper fearlessly until she reached a spot where she was as sure of being alone and unseen as if she had entered the bowels of the earth. She sat down on the warm dry ground and looked about her for a moment, glad in the sense of absolute freedom. Above the fragrant brush of many greens rose the old twisted oaks, a light breeze rustling their brittle leaves, their arms lifted eagerly to the warm yellow bath from above. Nearby was a high pile of leaves and branches, the home of a wood-rat.

Lucky Magdalena, to be unafraid of poison oak. Did her immunity last? We'll never know, but when I drive the crowded streets of Menlo Park, I imagine the great oak woods that once were there. When I collect acorns from street trees, spilling their abundance on driveways and sidewalks and cars, I remember Magdalena's woods.

PART V

Restoration and Community

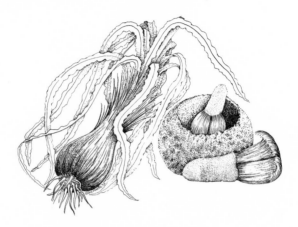

CHAPTER THIRTEEN

In My Town

While it appears that most birds escaped with their lives from the forested ridges, a great many probably died in the coastal scrub southwest of the crest [in the Vision fire of 1995]. Here Wrentits, Bewick's Wrens, California Quail, and Nuttall's White-crowned Sparrows hold year-round territories to which some would cling until time ran out. Some of these sparrows and wrentits are so sessile-by-nature that they have never strayed more than 200 yards from the spot where they were born.   *Rich Stallcup, 1995*

The attachment by northern California Indians to location is excessive. They may indeed be driven off, but they cannot be persuaded to go voluntarily.   *George Gibbs, 1883*

Love of one another is linked to love of place.
Paul Shepard, 1967

I live in a town that is well known for its desire to remain obscure. About 2,000 people reside here, with perhaps 1,998 different utopian visions. The other two people just don't care.

We have permaculturists, horticulturists, organic farmers, fisherpersons, lawyers, dancers, songwriters and singers, musicians, carpenters, surfers, actors, writers, teachers, ornithologists, painters, massage therapists, poets, personal chefs, and journalists. We have lots of tree surgeons; because of misplanted trees, the sound of chain saws is usually heard upon the land. Nearly everyone is at least a little bit disappointed that their particular vision of utopia has not, as yet, prevailed.

The other night, discussing a local issue at a dinner party, I asked, "Do

Part-opening illustration: Soaproot bulb, with soaproot brush and mortar. Drawing by Ane Carla Rovetta.

you think there's anything that everybody in this town could agree about?" We came up with possibilities, but couldn't agree on an answer.

Our local paper, in which everybody in town is a reporter, allowed to print anything they want as long as the article is signed, provides a forum for personal opinion. The value of this venue cannot be overestimated. When griping to a friend about some local issue, one is often told, "Put it in the paper." Yet it takes a certain amount of courage to be published in this organ. Here I tentatively submitted my first discourse on habitat destruction by gardeners.

We have a few relatively intact samples of coastal prairie and coastal scrub here and there in the town. One of the best is adjacent to the parking lot for one of our beaches. It is public land, and except for the increasing threat of Cape ivy and iceplant, it is visually powerful enough to inspire many garden plantings. When I saw that somebody had planted crocosmia, a stubbornly spreading garden plant, in the middle of a stand of *Fritillaria affinis,* the rare chocolate lily, I submitted an article listing the wonderful native plants in bloom in that area and suggesting that this gardener's efforts might be better spent removing the Scotch broom where it was beginning to encroach. Although this article was so tactful that it probably took years off my life, I was wary going downtown for a while.

Not long afterward, a local gardener approached me in front of the grocery store. "Do you really think the earth cares what covers it?" she asked. "Maybe not," I answered, "but the birds, insects, and animals probably do." Then I went into the library to complain to the sympathetic librarian about this latest discouraging event. Although at the time I was disheartened, our little parking lot conversation eventually sparked a whole shift in focus for this open-minded landscaper, who has now involved some of our grade school children in a deep study of coastal scrub, including a performance for the town.

A psychological principle, that it is more painful to be in disagreement with people with whom one has expectations of accord than with declared enemies, is well demonstrated in this town. For some years, I have enjoyed the seedlings of coast live oaks turning up here and there in the garden. Recently, I have noticed seedlings of another oak as well, the Chiapas oak, a fast-growing species from Mexico. Turns out that my neighbor across the street, a retired botanist, has a collection of tropical plants of which he is proud. That some are spreading outside the bounds of his yard does not concern him. He described our neighborhood as so degraded already that protection was irrelevant.

When I told him what we were doing in the yard across the street, he said, "If you limited your garden to local plants, you would only have coyote bush." This inaccurate statement, from a professional botanist, was surprising, but the implicit attitude is a link in the chain of concepts, professional goals, and academic structures that implicitly devalue home.

Valuing Home

When I say that I have traveled to the Carrizo Plains in San Luis Obispo County, to the Warner Mountains of northeastern California, or along the trail to our own spectacular waterfall, no one is as interested as when I say I'm going to El Salvador, Tibet, or Nepal. More people in my town collect *traje* from Guatemala than baskets woven of our own plants by our own indigenes. More people eat Mexican food or Thai food than acorn mush, chia seed cookies, or lemonade from the lemonade bush. More people study the Mayan sacred text *Popul Vuh* or the *Tibetan Book of the Dead* than the stories collected by Alfred Kroeber and J. P. Harrington from native Californians.

My garden has become a place where I investigate and proclaim the value of home. Sometimes the visual beauty of the plants that surround me suffices; at other times, I fall deeper into thought about the ways that humans have used them, and feel gratitude for how they support us, with firewood, fruit, flowers, door knob handles, and shade. Soaproot reminds me of the native Californian who scrupulously used every last bit of the bulb to wash his jet black hair. The seeds of blue wildrye remind me of the hospitable offerings, baskets of roasted, ground bunchgrass seed, made by the coast Miwok to Sir Francis Drake and his men. The sweet bloom of ceanothus reminds me that a decoction of its twigs and leaves was used by the Yurok for baby washing.

The plants of this place are my key, opening the way to the secrets of soil and water, change and stability, and enduring human use. California hazel grows here and there throughout my garden. A nut-bearing shrub with great ornamental potential, it can be pruned to the gardener's taste. Its nuts, should the squirrels and birds spare you some, are easy to like. Sometimes its spare beauty in late winter, male catkins dangling pale chartreuse, buds like beads strung along angular twigs, is enough in itself. At other times, it reminds me of a story told by Lucy Young, a story not sweet like the nuts, but bitter.

Lucy Young of the Wailaki tribe died in 1948 at one hundred years of age. Ten years earlier, Edith Van Allen Murphey, a seed collector and friend of Lucy's, wrote that she was "so patterned toward giving succor, so conscious of need of nurture in famine times past that she processed medicine plants and prepared acorn meal even after she was blinded by cataracts."

As a young girl, Lucy was repeatedly stolen from her mother and sold to white settlers as a slave. Five times she managed to escape and find her mother, who would then flee with her daughters, hiding where soldiers and homesteaders wouldn't find them. Once, their mother hid them deep in thickets of sword fern in the redwoods of Mendocino County. All night long Lucy heard the faint tapping sound of her mother peeling hazelnuts. I too have fed a hungry daughter with those sweet nuts, although in happier circumstances. When I harvest California hazelnuts, or when I sow them, I sometimes think of a mother in desperate flight, bereft of social structures that protect, still able to feed her children from the fruits of *Corylus cornuta*.

When I see native clovers, a too-rare event, I think of the numerous California Indian stories that begin, "She went out to gather clover." This springtime activity, mentioned frequently, is so diverting that our heroine often "forgot to watch for bear." Various disasters ensued.

Listening to Trees

When I was in my twenties, I read a book called *What the Trees Said*. The author, Steven Diamond, has returned to the farmhouse from the snowy woods. He tells his friends, gathered round the woodstove, "The trees talked to me."

His friends respond, "What did they say?"

At the time, it charmed me that his friends didn't question the existence of this intra-species communication, only the nature of the exchange. Now, I wish he had been more specific. In my town, we have a need to hear what the trees say, and not only to hear it, but to agree on what it is that they have said. As I have indicated elsewhere, my town has many eucalyptus groves. An opportunity to remove some of these trees sparked off one of those painful, illuminating debates my town so amply supplies.

A firm that cuts down eucalyptus trees and ships them to Japan for pulpwood is leveling eucalyptus groves all over coastal California. This company doesn't kill the stumps or replant or chip the slash, but they do remove these massive trees, giving us a chance at restoration. Not surprisingly, their methods reflect their desire to make a profit. When they offered to come here, a variety of reactions ensued.

The first town meeting at which this issue was discussed was packed with those wishing to save these and all other eucalyptus groves, calling them "cathedrals," and "sacred groves." Except for a mild interjection from the fire department, indicating that the groves were fire hazards, one might have concluded there was unanimity in my town. A series of letters in the local paper soon laid that thought to rest.

In the pro-eucalyptus camp, descriptions of the beauties of eucalyptus were accompanied by pleas not to add to global warming by cutting eucalyptus groves. Some equated destruction of the groves with the clear-cutting of old-growth forest. Others were repelled by the idea of shipping our eucalyptus, a local resource, to Japan. If they could use it, so could we. A poem was submitted expressing the thought that it is good to ask the trees their opinion. Kokopelli, the Anasazi hunchback flute player, was also cited as being against eucalyptus removal.

The issue widened to include the entire native versus non-native plants debate, including my favorite, the argument that we're not native here either. The pro-eucalyptus camp and the anti-eucalyptus camp both put nature on their side. How can we "know" what is harmful for the land or what the land wants? Can we base decisions on casual or anecdotal observations? We cling, those of us who care for such things, to what we think we understand about the nonhuman world. Who really has nature on their side? At one meeting, someone jestingly suggested that we hire a theologian to decide the issue of whether or not the roadside eucalyptus actually qualified, as some were saying, as a "cathedral."

I considered staying out of the fray (or moving), but I couldn't resist for long, and soon I was sending my own letters to the newspaper. I tried to skirt the question of the sacredness of the eucalyptus groves, instead asking for a tipping of the balance, saying, "It is not so much the presence of eucalyptus that bothers me, as the absence of much else." An informal assessment of biomass in our town indicates that the native element constitutes an increasingly minor percentage. The plants of coastal scrub and forest, creekside and grassland are distinguished by their absence.

I can appreciate the appeal of the colors of eucalyptus bark or of the movement of their leaves to those who see the landscape as a painting rather than a reservoir of relationships, developed over thousands of years and flourishing when Europeans arrived. But I can no longer separate the aesthetic experience from the list of relationships these trees disrupt, including the disappearance of the saw-whet owls, overhunted by raptors now given new, nontraditional nesting sites in eucalyptus groves.

Our birds, which may seem to be benefiting from eucalyptus nectar, have beaks that are not adapted to using eucalyptus flowers. In some cases, the tarry residue from eucalyptus blooms glues beaks shut, resulting in death. In Australia, where the relationship has been a long one, nectar-seeking birds have beaks appropriately shaped for eucalyptus nectar extraction.

To those whose historical view does not travel back before European presence, one-hundred-year-old eucalyptus trees represent continuity and permanence, a sense of history. To others, they are a disheartening symbol of the lack of respect for this land that characterized the land use practices and attitudes of some early Californians. A friend was inspired by the debate to spend a day in the California Room at the Civic Center library. Looking at the sequence of events in the history of our town, he concluded that the eucalyptus were planted on denuded land, land that had been previously pillaged and plundered. Those who had benefited from the pillaging and plundering were ready for more quick profits, to which end they planted the now "sacred" eucalyptus trees.

As a result of the process of our debates, we began to imagine a way in which *Eucalyptus globulus* might serve as a resource to take the pressure off our native forests. The original planters of the groves intended these trees for lumber, but they proved difficult to season. Now there is hope that different seasoning procedures may make these trees usable. Eucalyptus flooring is regularly being milled and installed. A tiny market in peeled, seasoned eucalyptus poles is beginning; we built a shade-house out of eucalyptus poles and also used them in the formation of a new fence. I have a beautiful box made by a local craftsperson, the lid of which is a slab of golden, intricately figured eucalyptus. An enterprising back-yard restorationist has invented a new tool for removing French and Scotch broom. The handles of this ingenious back-saving device, which need to be sturdy, will be made from eucalyptus.

My image of eucalyptus has involved groves inexorably spreading, and tree owners unable to pay the cost of removal or management. With eucalyptus a valued resource, that situation could shift. Although some eucalyptus will be removed from the controversial grove, it will be in a careful, considered manner. At first, I unequivocally wanted the eucalyptus gone, no matter how. My town slowed me down.

Societal brakes that used to be in place no longer exist in most communities. Ways of making decisions, ways painstakingly cognizant of all the decision-makers, once prevailed. Every technology has its negative side, which needs to be evaluated and weighed. This is where our restoration gardens come in, where visions meet a continual reality check, facts and pet theories colliding.

Diversity of opinion, at once tedious and illuminating, like much of life, forces slowness in my town. Therefore, I salute it. Maybe it's okay for this kind of change to proceed at a desert tortoise's pace; we've had enough unconsidered landscape events. Resistance to change is okay too, requiring that we refine, deepen, and broaden our thinking.

Forced to slow down, we learn to hear the rustlings, the sounds that movement makes. Like fire flowing at a walker's measured pace through a Sierran woods. Like creatures in the coyote bush, quick and slow, or sycamore leaves in an inland town on a hot summer day when the wind goes through.

As with using different regimes so that different native grasses may flourish, we can try different solutions to problems, to minimize damage. Just as multiple survival strategies are employed in the nonhuman realms, so multiple ways to grow wildflowers, maintain our roads, make decisions about growth, wash clothes, and earn livings may flourish together.

My town loves ceremonies. I imagine one in which fragrant plant essences, our local incense, are burned: one part California sagebrush, one part bay leaf, one part oak leaf, one part mugwort, one part yerba buena, one part monkeyflower, paintbrush, vanilla grass. And half a part, maybe, of eucalyptus.

Quiet Fire

Attachment to early memories of plants resulted in cuttings and seedlings traveling many times across this country. The eagerness to symbolize home with familiar plants may prevent us from taking a good hard look at where we are, so that we can best figure out how to live there. If we smother the local smells, sights, and gods, how can we be nourished and empowered by them? The good ideas that they embody about living in this place will be unnoticed and gradually lost.

Like the Paleo-Indians before the end of the Ice Age, we have acted as pioneers here, interacting with land on the basis of our existing knowledge rather than on the basis of the potential of the new environment. Now we may begin to adapt ourselves more closely to our new home, always with a sense of the potential for damage. Some think that the many-faceted, finely tuned use of the resources of this land by indigenous Californians began after the demise of the megafauna forced them to adopt a more careful way.

The pinyon jay regulates its reproduction to parallel the future abundance of pinyon nuts. Similarly, the Paiutes of Mono Lake predicted food availability two years in advance by evaluating pinyon nut crops, which take two years to mature. They regulated births accordingly. Maybe the Paiutes learned family planning from the jay.

Native peoples knew that the necessity of taking life, whether plant or animal, required care and reciprocity. Ignoring the nutrient cycling that is part of all life was an impossibility. Mitigation, the recognition of harm done with consequent reparation, was a continuous act. Prairies could be burned and hazels pruned, acorns harvested and salmon caught in carefully pre-scribed fashion, ways that worked.

In this town, some of us are so traumatized by the "de-sacralization" of the modern world that we cling with desperation to those objects we have declared sacred, such as eucalyptus trees. Afraid of our powers of devasta-tion, we reject all harvest. Understandably distrusting our capacity for re-straint, we become afraid to enter the gift exchange at all.

The back-yard restoration garden may offer reassurances of our ability to act positively. It may offer reassurances of resilience that, while not deny-ing the critical nature of environmental problems, provide the necessary hope for continuance. It can be a place to practice skills that don't get much play in other arenas, skills that have grown rusty in our human repertoire of ways to be in this world. In the process of accepting the lessons of weeds, ac-quiescing in the growth rates of oaks and the temperaments of madrones, resisting or limiting herbicide use, and honoring the idiosyncratic appear-ance of seedlings, the restoration gardener builds a sense of personal con-nectedness and learns the peace of moving out from the human-centered.

The fires that occur after years of fire suppression burn an accumulation of inflammable materials that provide ladders up to the crowns of trees. When natural or human-set fires ran their course every eight to eighteen years, they regularly reduced this fuel load. Low-intensity fires moved slowly at ground level, unlike crown fires, with their holocaust-like spread. I try to imagine the movement of such a fire, proceeding in a steady, almost leisurely course over the ground. A fire not terrifying but commanding re-spect. A quiet fire.

That's the kind of movement I hope to learn, slowly counting the yards and gardens, every year a few more that in some way, more or less, acknowledge where we are, what land, what skies we inhabit.

We still have many birds in our lagoon, although the sky no longer darkens with their numbers, nor does the sound of their wings make thunder. The erosion of natural values can be a gradual slide. The return may also be gradual. Each back-yard oak is a candle lit, each median planted with native grasses, each new toyon, elderberry, or willow hedge is a testimony to the power of the land, finally getting through. The scale tips back and forth, but overall, like quiet fire, maybe we will prevail. On those days when the spent blossoms of sky-colored ceanothus drop on our breakfast dishes and in our hair and the young oak blooms for the first time, on those days when pleasantness and goodness surround us, it seems that we will.

RESOURCES

Nursery, Bulb, Seed, and Tool Sources

California Flora
P.O. Box 3
Fulton, CA 95439
(707) 528-8813

Cornflower Farms
P.O. Box 896
Elk Grove, CA 95624
(916) 689-1015
(wholesale)

Go Native Nursery
333 Cypress Avenue
Moss Beach, CA 94308
(415) 728-3067

Larner Seeds
P.O. Box 407
235 Grove Rd.
Bolinas, CA 94924
(415) 868-9407
Fax 415-868-9820
Also sells the RootJack for
removing invasive shrubs.

Moon Mountain
P.O. Box 725
Carpinteria, CA 93014

Mostly Natives Nursery
27215 Highway One
Tomales, CA 94971
(707) 878-2009

Native Here Nursery
101 Golf Course Drive
Berkeley, CA 94708
(510) 549-0211

Native Revival
8022 Soquel Drive
Aptos, CA 95003
(408) 684-1811

Native Sons Wholesale Nursery
379 W. El Campo Rd.
Arroyo Grande, CA 93420
(805) 481-5996

Neglected Bulbs
P.O. Box 1128
Berkeley, CA 94701
(510) 524-5149

New Tribe
5517 Riverbanks Road
Grants Pass, OR 97527
(503) 476-9492
Weed Wrench and other products.

North Coast Native Nursery
P.O. Box 744
Petaluma, CA 97953
(707) 769-1213

Pacific Coast Seed
6144 Industrial Way #A
Livermore, CA 94550
(800) 733-3462

Redwood City Seed Co.
P.O. Box 361
Redwood City, CA 94604
415-325-SEED

San Francisco Bay National Wildlife
    Refuge Native Plant Nursery
P.O. Box 524
One Marshlands Road
Newark, CA 94560
(510) 793-0836

Theodore Payne Foundation
10459 Tuxford St.
La Tuna Canyon, CA 91352
(818) 768-1802

Tree of Life Nursery
P.O. Box 736
San Juan Capistrano, CA 92693
(wholesale)

Village Nursery
10994 Donner Pass Road
Truckee, CA 96161
(916) 587-0771

Ya Ka Ama Native Plant Nursery
6215 Eastside Rd.
Forestville, CA 95436
(707) 887-1586

Yerba Buena Nursery
19500 Skyline Blvd.
Woodside, CA 94072
(415) 851-1668

Organizations and Publications

Butterfly Gardener's Quarterly
P.O. Box 30931
Seattle, WA 98103

California Native Grass Association
P.O. Box 566
Dixon, CA 95620

California Native Plant Society
1722 J St., Suite 17
Sacramento, CA 95814

Growing Native Research Newsletter
P.O. Box 489
Berkeley, CA 94701
(510) 232-9865

North American Butterfly Association
4 Delaware Rd.
Morristown, NJ 07960

Planet Drum
P.O. Box 31251
San Francisco, CA 94131
(415) 285-6566

Society for Ecological Restoration
University of Wisconsin-Madison
    Arboretum
1207 Seminole Highway
Madison, WI 53711
(608) 262-9547

*Wildflower: North America's Magazine
of Wild Flora*
Box 335, Postal Station F
Toronto, Ontario
Canada M4Y 2L7
(416) 924-6807

WildGarden Magazine
P.O. Box 10510
Eugene, OR 97401
(541) 465-1383

The Xerxes Society
4828 SE Hawthorne Blvd.
Portland, OR 97215
(503) 232-6639

Botanic Gardens, Arboretums, and Demonstration Gardens with Native Plant Sections

CalPoly Arboretum
Environmental Horticulture
    Department
San Luis Obispo, CA 93407
(805) 756-93407

Charles F. Lummis House
"El Alisal"
200 East Avenue 43
Highland Park
Los Angeles, CA 90031
(213) 222-0546

Larner Seeds
P.O. Box 407
Bolinas, CA 94924
(415) 868-9407

Mendocino Coast Botanic Gardens
18220 No. Highway One
Fort Bragg, CA 95437
(707) 964-4352

Regional Parks Botanic Garden
Tilden Regional Park
Berkeley, CA 94708
(510) 841-8732

San Luis Obispo Botanical Garden
El Chorro Regional Park
Highway One
(between San Luis Obispo
    and Morro Bay)
(805) 546-3501

Strybing Arboretum
9th Avenue and Lincoln Way
San Francisco, CA 94122
(415) 661-1316

University of California Botanical
    Garden
University of California
200 Centennial Drive # 5045
Berkeley, CA 94720
(510) 643-2755

U.C. Santa Cruz Arboretum
University of California
Santa Cruz, CA 95064
(408) 427-2998

Wright Memorial Botanic Garden
1400 Avalon Canyon Road
Avalon, Catalina Island, CA 90704
(310) 510-2288

Yerba Buena Nursery
19500 Skyline Blvd.
Woodside, CA 94062
(650) 851-1668

NOTES

Chapter 1. Gardening at the Seam

p. 3   "I wish so to live" *The Writings of Henry David Thoreau* (Boston: Houghton Mifflin, 1906).

p. 3   "Biodiversity has recently become" W. David Shuford, *Marin County Breeding Bird Atlas* (Bolinas, Calif.: Bushtit Books, 1993).

p. 3   "It's not as if" Mary Austin, *Cactus Thorn: A Novel,* with foreword and afterword by Melody Graulich (rpt. Reno: Univ. of Nevada Press, 1988).

p. 4   "the nickel-and-diming to death" Paul Ehrlich and Ruth Ehrlich, *The Machinery of Nature* (New York: Simon & Schuster, 1986).

p. 9   "When we lose" Robert Michael Pyle, afterword to *Butterfly Gardening: Creating Summer Magic in Your Garden* (San Francisco: Sierra Club Books, 1990).

p. 12   "They educate us and fit us" Henry David Thoreau, "Wild Fruits" (1860), reprinted in *Faith in a Seed,* ed. Bradley P. Dean (Washington, D.C.: Island Press / Shearwater Books, 1993).

p. 12   "After a week or two" Mary Austin, *Earth Horizon* (Boston: Houghton Mifflin, 1932).

p. 15   "An editor of a gardening magazine questions" George Waters, "But Is It Art?" *Pacific Horticulture,* January 1993, pp. 1–2.

Chapter 2. Planning Back-Yard Restoration Gardens

p. 23   "He who owns a veteran bur oak" Aldo Leopold, *A Sand County Almanac, and Sketches Here and There,* illustrated by Charles W.

Schwartz; introduction by Robert Finch (1949; reprinted, New York: Oxford University Press, 1987).

p. 23   "I cannot think of a more tasteless undertaking" Ansel Adams, letter to the editor, *Independent Journal* (San Rafael, Calif.), Feb. 24, 1966.

p. 31   "Food growers, including permaculturists" See Bill Mollison and David Holmgren, *Permaculture 1: A Perennial Agriculture for Human Settlements* (Melbourne, Australia: Transworld Publishers, 1978).

Chapter 3. Design Thoughts, Principles, and Guidelines

p. 35   "These things it must be" Alfred Robinson, *California Garden* 4, no. 7 (1913): 4.

p. 37   "a frequently consulted reference" Bruce M. Pavlik, Pamela C. Muick, Sharon G. Johnson, and Marjorie Popper, *Oaks of California* (Los Olivos, Calif.: Cachuma Press / California Oak Foundation, 1991).

p. 39   "Robert Michael Pyle" *Wintergreen: Rambles in a Ravaged Land* (New York: Charles Scribner's Sons, 1986).

p. 40   "For an Ojai garden" John O. Sawyer and Todd Keeler-Wolf, *A Manual of California Vegetation* (Sacramento, Calif.: California Native Plant Society, 1995).

Chapter 4. In the Changeful Garden

p. 55   "Does anything ever stay the same?" Michael Barbour, Bruce Pavlik, Frank Drysdale, and Susan Lindstrom, *California's Changing Landscapes* (Sacramento, Calif.: California Native Plant Society, 1993).

p. 55   "The next time you howl" Jack Turner, *The Abstract Wild* (Tucson: University of Arizona Press, 1996).

p. 57   "Fire, a major agent" See Harold Biswell, *Prescribed Burning in California Wildlands Vegetation Management* (Berkeley and Los Angeles: University of California Press, 1989).

p. 58   "In larger gardens, the homeowner" Ronald D. Quinn, *Habitat Preferences and Distribution of Mammals in California Chaparral* (Berkeley: Pacific Southwest Research Station, n.d.).

p. 59   "The California Native Plant Society recommends" Mary Ann Matthews, "The Impacts of Ryegrass Seeding on Plant Communities of the Central Coast: A Literature Review" (1986).

p. 60   "Some of the best descriptions" Chris Maser, *The Redesigned Forest* (San Pedro, Calif.: R. & E. Miles, 1988).

p. 62   "Ecologists do not wish" James Luken, *Directing Ecological Succession* (London: Chapman & Hall, 1900).

Chapter 5. Examples of Back-Yard Restoration Gardens

p. 65   "What gorgeous opportunity" Wilhelm Miller, 1913. As quoted by E. J. Wickson in *California Garden Flowers* (Pacific Rural Press, 1914).

p. 65   "The real California garden" Alfred D. Robinson, "The Fitness of Things*," California Garden* 4 (April 1913).

p. 72   "We have precedents for gardens" Kenneth R. Trapp, *The Arts and Crafts Movement in California: Living the Good Life* (New York: Abbeville Press, 1995).

p. 73   "boomer and sticker" Wendell Berry, "The Conservation of Nature and the Preservation of Humanity," in *Another Turn of the Crank* (Washington, D.C.: Counterpoint, 1995).

p. 73   "the sketched pattern of a suggested recovery" Mary Austin, *Land of the Sun* (1927).

Chapter 6. Along the Flower Trail

p. 77   "A humiliating fact" Charles Francis Saunders, *With the Flowers and Trees in California* (New York: McBride, Nast, & Co., 1919).

p. 78   "This and future generations will never see" Nicolus Hanson, *As I Remember* (Willows, Calif.: Author, 1944).

p. 79   "As we passed below the hills" Frank Latta, *Tailholt Tales* (Santa Cruz, Calif.: Bear State Books, 1976).

p. 79   "The Great Central Plain of California" John Muir, "The Bee Pastures," in *Mountains of California* (1894; reprinted, Golden, Colo.: Fulcrum Books, 1988).

p. 80   "In the spring the Indians were always gathering flowers" Anna Gayton, "Yokuts Life," in *Native Californians: A Theoretical Retrospective* (Novato, Calif.: Ballena Press, 1976).

p. 80   "It was a dry April" Mary Austin, *Earth Horizon* (Boston: Houghton Mifflin, 1932).

p. 81   "One of the most insightful writers about native California flora" See, e.g., James Roof, "Growing California's Field Wildflowers," *The Four Seasons* 3, no. 14 (Tilden Botanic Garden, Berkeley, Calif.).

p. 82   "These wild legumes in various shades" E. J. Wickson, *California Garden Flowers* (Pacific Rural Press, 1914).

p. 84   "the most severe losses of plant species" *Conservation and Management of Rare and Endangered Species,* edited by Dr. Thomas Eliot (Sacramento: California Native Plant Society Publications, 1986).

p. 86   "Many customers inquire about . . . glyphosate" See Caroline Cox, *Journal of Pesticide Reform*, P.O. Box 1393, Eugene, OR 97440 (telephone: 541-344-5044).

p. 86   "Although glyphosate is considered among the least harmful" See Louise Lacey, "Glyphosate — Pro and Con," *Growing Native Research Newsletter,* Jan.–Feb. 1998.

p. 98   "The originator of this grim piece of information" Cited in Charles Francis Saunders, *Western Wildflowers and Their Stories* (Garden City, N.Y.: Doubleday, 1938).

p. 100   "the field appears frosted with whipped cream." Mabel Crittenden, *Wildflowers of the West* (Millbrae, Calif.: Celestial Arts, 1975).

p. 101   "Advise your girls well." Thomas C. Blackburn, ed., *December's Child: A Book of Chumash Oral Narratives* (Berkeley and Los Angeles: University of California Press, 1975).

p. 101   "O radiant and golden-hued poppy" Excerpt from Irene H. Musick, "The Native Daughters' Pride" (Crescent City, Calif., 1901).

Chapter 7. The Land Wore a Tufted Mantle

p. 104   "Mr. Sherwood" Joseph Burtt Davy, *Stock Ranges of Northwestern California* (Washington, D.C.: Government Printing Office, 1902).

p. 105   "that each wolf is a little different" Barry Holstun Lopez, *Of Wolves and Men* (New York: Scribner, 1978).

p. 109   "Anthony Joern has hypothesized" In *Grassland Structure and Function: California Annual Grassland,* ed. L. F. Huenneke and H. A. Mooney (Dordrecht and Boston: Kluwer Academic, 1989), p. 117.

p. 110   "Some botanists divide California grasslands" Beecher Crampton, *Grasses in California* (Berkeley and Los Angeles: University of California Press, 1974). Written by one of the elders honored at the California Native Grass Association conference in November 1996.

p. 110   "Along the coast" Henry W. Elliott and John D. Wehausen, "Vegetational Succession on Coastal Rangeland of Point Reyes Peninsula" (paper, Department of Agronomy and Range Science, University of California, Davis, 1972).

p. 112   "An interesting parallel situation" See Richard Manning, *Grassland: The*

History, Biology, Politics, and Promise of the American Prairie (New York: Penguin Books, 1997).

p. 113   "Quite clearly, every horned lizard" Raymond Cowles, *Desert Journal: A Naturalist Reflects on Arid California* (Berkeley and Los Angeles: University of California Press, 1977).

p. 114   "Native Californians lost knowledge" V. K. Chesnut, *Plants Used by the Indians of Mendocino County* (Mendocino County Historical Society, 1902). Chesnut says that *Leymus triticoides,* "squaw grass," was still regularly harvested by Mendocino Indians around the turn of the century.

p. 114   "Native Californians used fire as a semi-agricultural tool." Henry Lewis, "Patterns of Indian Burning in California: Ecology and Ethnohistory," in *Before the Wilderness: Environmental Management by Native Californians,* ed. Kat Anderson and Thomas C. Blackburn (Menlo Park, Calif.: Ballena Press, 1993).

p. 115   "what is now called 'permaculture.'" See, e.g., B. C. Mollison and Reny Mia Slay, *Introduction to Permaculture* (Harare, Zimbabwe: Tutorial Press; Tyalgum, Australia: Tagari Publications, 1992).

p. 117   "restoration grazing" See Dan Daggett, *Beyond the Rangeland Conflict: Toward a West That Works* (Layton, Utah: Gibbs-Smith and the Grand Canyon Trust, 1995).

p. 118   "No one management strategy will favor all natives." Mark Blummler, letter to *Bay Leaf* (newsletter of the East Bay chapter of the California Native Plant Society), 1992. See also Mark A. Blummler, "Some Myths About California Grasslands and Grazers," *Fremontia* 20, no. 3 (1992): 341.

p. 118   "an old scarred battleground" May Theilgaard Watts, *Reading the Landscape: An Adventure in Ecology* (New York: Macmillan, 1957).

Chapter 8. To See All the Colors, to Hear All the Songs

p. 123   "It was more than a year" Helen Hunt Jackson, *Ramona* (Boston: Little, Brown, 1884).

p. 123   "The Bureau of Land Management" Report prepared by the California Exotic Pest Plant Council Biocontrol Committee, Summer 1995.

p. 123   "Unless greater actions are taken" Deputy Secretary of the Interior John Garamendi, Department of the Interior News Release, Sept. 8, 1995.

p. 125   "Unlike our western chaparral" James A. Young, talk at CalEppc conference, Monterey, Calif., Oct. 1995.

p. 127 "Nutritional inferiority" Harold W. Avery, "Nutritional Ecology of Desert Tortoises (*Gopherus agassizii*) Fed Native Versus Exotic Forage" (report, National Biological Service, Riverside Field Station).

p. 129 "Two Australian sisters" See Joan Bradley, *Bush Regeneration: The Practical Way to Eliminate Exotic Plants from Natural Reserves* (Mosman [Sydney], Australia: Mosman Parklands and Ashton Park Association, 1971). See also T. C. Fuller and G. Douglas Barbe, "The Bradley Method; Eliminating Exotic Plants from Natural Reserves," *Fremontia* 13, no. 2 (July 1985).

p. 132 "The famous success story" California Exotic Pest Plant Council Biocontrol Committee, "Biological Control of Invasive Exotic Pest Plant Species," *CalEppc Newsletter*, Summer 1995.

p. 142 "The old-time people always told us" Leslie Marmon Silko, *Yellow Woman and a Beauty of the Spirit: Essays on Native American Life Today* (New York: Simon & Schuster, 1996).

Chapter 9. Wildland Seed Harvest

p. 145 "When my grandmother started out" Mary E. T. Collier and Sylvia Barker Thalman, eds., *Interviews with Tom Smith and Maria Copa: Isabel Kelly's Ethnographic Notes on the Coast Miwok Indians of Marin and Southern Sonoma Counties* (San Rafael, Calif.: Mapom, 1996).

p. 147 "For valley and blue oaks" Walt Koenig, "Acorn Production in California," *Oaks 'n' Folks* (University of California Integrated Hardwood Range Management Program), April 1995.

p. 149 "Bird pines such as the whitebark pine" Ronald M. Lanner, *Made for Each Other: A Symbiosis of Birds and Pines* (New York: Oxford University Press, 1996).

p. 151 "Shaped like a cone" Louise Amelia Knapp Smith Clappe, *The Shirley Letters* (Salt Lake City, Utah: Peregrine Smith, 1983).

p. 151 "Five miles below" John Muir, *The Mountains of California* (1894; reprinted, Golden, Colo.: Fulcrum, 1988).

Chapter 10. Seed Propagation and Planting Techniques

p. 153 "I have great faith" Henry David Thoreau, *Faith in a Seed: The Dispersion of Seeds and Other Late Natural History Writings,* ed. Bradley P. Dean (Washington, D.C.: Island Press, 1993).

p. 154 "After obtaining the seed" Dara Emery, *Seed Propagation of Native Cali-*

fornia Plants (Santa Barbara, Calif.: Santa Barbara Botanic Garden, 1988); Jeanine de Hart, *Propagation Secrets for California Native Plants* (Encinitas, Calif.: Author, 1995).

Chapter 11. Naturalists and Field Trips

p. 171 "Users want and need" James C. Hickman, ed., *The Jepson Manual: Higher Plants of California* (Berkeley and Los Angeles: University of California Press, 1993).

p. 171 "The dark vision" Gene Logsden, *At Nature's Pace* (New York: Pantheon Books, 1994).

p. 173 "To Yosemite-loving Californians" Elizabeth O'Neill, *Mountain Sage: The Life Story of Carl Sharsmith, Yosemite's Famous Ranger/Naturalist* (Groveland, Calif.: Albicaulis Press, 1996).

p. 179 "That afternoon I sat down with a tape" "Bird Songs of California: Selected Bird Songs from the Sierras to the Pacific," produced by Thomas G. Sander (Wilderness Recordings, 1989).

p. 182 "Alaskan biologists" Barry Holstun Lopez, *Of Wolves and Men* (New York: Charles Scribner's Sons, 1978).

p. 183 "data . . . have often been lumped" John Kelly, *The Ardeid* (Newsletter of the Cypress Grove Preserve, Marshall, Calif.), October 1995.

p. 184 "All time spent with butterflies" Robert Michael Pyle, *Handbook for Butterfly Watchers* (Boston: Houghton Mifflin, 1992).

p. 186 "the moth *Utetheisa*" Thomas Eisner, in *The Nature of Nature: New Essays from America's Finest Writers on Nature,* ed. William H. Shore (San Diego: Harcourt Brace, 1994).

p. 187 "Tolowim Woman" Malcolm Margolin, *The Way We Lived: California Indian Stories, Songs and Reminiscences* (Berkeley: Heyday Books, 1981).

p. 190 "The traditional magician" David Abrams, *The Spell of the Sensuous: Perception and Language in a More-Than-Human World* (New York: Pantheon Books, 1996).

Chapter 12. Tools and Tricks of the Trade

p. 192 "To Be of Use" In Marge Piercy, *Circles on the Water* (Garden City, N.Y.: Doubleday, 1973).

p. 195 "Willis Linn Jepson's *A Manual*" James C. Hickman, ed., *The Jepson Manual: Higher Plants of California* (Berkeley and Los Angeles: University of California Press, 1993).

p. 197 "A new resource" John Sawyer and Todd Keeler-Wolf, *A Manual of California Vegetation* (Sacramento: CNPS Press, 1995).

p. 199 "Autobiographies of Native Americans" Delfina Cuero, *Her Autobiography, An Account of Her Last Years, and Her Ethnobotanic Contributions,* by Florence Shipek (Novato, Calif.: Ballena Press, 1991).

p. 202 "early writings about our locale" See Lawrence Powell Clark, *California Classics* (Santa Barbara, Calif.: Capra Press, 1971).

p. 203 "Songs of the Fields" In Gene Stratton Porter, *Coming Through the Swamp: The Nature Writings of Gene Stratton Porter,* ed. Sydney Landon Plum (Salt Lake City: University of Utah Press, 1996).

p. 204 "botanically correct murder mysteries" Rebecca Rothenberg, *The Shy Tulip Murders* (New York: Warner Books, Mysterious Press, 1996), and *The Dandelion Murders* (New York: Warner Books, Mysterious Press, 1994).

Chapter 13. In My Town

p. 209 "While it appears" Rich Stallcup, "Fire in Birdland," *Point Reyes Observatory Quarterly Journal,* no. 105 (Fall 1995).

p. 209 "The attachment by northern California Indians" George Gibbs (1883) quoted by Skee Hamman, Mendocino County Historical Society, MS.

p. 209 "Love of one another" Paul Shepard, *Man in the Landscape: A Historic View of the Esthetics of Nature* (New York: Knopf, 1967).

p. 210 "Our local paper" In *Pig Earth* (New York: Pantheon Books, 1979), John Berger writes: "Every village's portrait of itself is constructed . . . not out of stone, but out of words, spoken and remembered: out of opinions, stories, eye-witness reports, legends, comments and hearsay. And it is a continuous portrait; work on it never stops."

p. 212 "Lucy Young of the Wailaki tribe" Edith Van Allen Murphey (1938) quoted by Skee Hamman, Mendocino County Historical Society, MS. See also Jack Norton, *Genocide in Northwestern California* (San Francisco: Indian Historian Press, 1979).

p. 212 "When I was in my twenties" Steven Diamond, *What the Trees Said: Life on a New Age Farm* (New York: Delacorte Press, 1971).

p. 216 "Like the Paleo-Indians" Joseph L. Chartkoff and Kerry Kona Chartkoff, *The Archaeology of California* (Stanford, Calif.: Stanford University Press, 1984).

p. 216 "The pinyon jay regulates" Ronald M. Lanner, *The Pinyon Pine: A Natural and Cultural History* (Reno: University of Nevada Press, 1981).

RECOMMENDED READING

Abrams, David. *The Spell of the Sensuous: Perception and Language in a More-than-Human World*. New York: Pantheon Books, 1996.

Barbour, Michael, Bruce Pavlik, Frank Drysdale, and Susan Lindstrom. *California's Changing Landscapes*. Sacramento: California Native Plant Society, 1993.

Barbour, Michael, Robert Craig, Frank Drysdale, and Michael Ghiselin. *Coastal Ecology: Bodega Head*. Berkeley and Los Angeles: University of California Press, 1973. A good example of accessible ecological material valuable for the coastal restoration gardener.

Barth, Friedrich G. *Insects and Flowers: The Biology of a Partnership*. Princeton, N.J.: Princeton University Press, 1991.

Beauchamp, R. Mitchel. *A Flora of San Diego County, California*. Santa Barbara, Calif.: Capra Press, 1986.

Best, Catherine, John Thomas Howell, Walter Knight, Ira Knight, and Mary Wells. *A Flora of Sonoma County: Manual of the Flowering Plants and Ferns of Sonoma County, California*. Sacramento: California Native Plant Society, 1996.

Brown, David E., and Neil B. Carmony, eds. *Aldo Leopold's Southwest*. Albuquerque: University of New Mexico Press, 1990.

Bubel, Nancy. *The Seed-Starter's Handbook*. Emmaus, Pa.: Rodale Press, 1978. A useful, detailed, step-by-step guide to seed propagation, focusing on vegetable seeds.

Buchmann, Stephen L., and Gary Paul Nabhan. *The Forgotten Pollinators*. Washington, D.C.: Island Press / Shearwater Books, 1996.

Clark, Lawrence Powell. *California Classics*. Santa Barbara, Calif.: Capra Press, 1971.

Clebsch, Betsy. *A Book of Salvias.* Portland, Ore.: Timber Press, 1997.

Conner, Nancy, and Barbara Stevens. *Where on Earth? A Gardener's Guide to Growers of Specialty Plants in California.* Berkeley, Calif.: Heyday Books, 1997.

Crosby, Alfred W. *Ecological Imperialism: The Biological Expansion of Europe, 900–1900.* Cambridge: Cambridge University Press, 1986.

Daggett, Dan. *Beyond the Rangeland Conflict: Toward a West That Works.* Layton, Utah: Gibbs-Smith and the Grand Canyon Trust, 1995.

Dale, Nancy. *Flowering Plants of the Santa Monica Mountains: Coastal and Chaparral Regions of Southern California.* Santa Barbara, Calif.: Capra Press, 1986.

de Hart, Jeanine. *Propagation Secrets for California Native Plants.* Encinitas, Calif.: Author, 1995. Includes basic techniques and a good list of treatments for several hundred species. Available for $6 from Jeanine de Hart, 237 Seeman Drive, Encinitas, CA 92024.

DeDecker, Mary. *Flora of the Northern Mojave Desert.* Sacramento: California Native Plant Society, 1984.

Dell, Owen E. *How to Open and Operate a Home-Based Landscaping Business.* Old Saybrook, Conn.: Globe Pequot Press, 1994.

Edwards, Steven. "Observations on the Prehistory and Ecology of Grazing in California." *Fremontia* 20, no. 1 (1992).

Ehrlich, Paul, David Dobkin, and Darryl Wheye. *The Birder's Handbook: A Field Guide to the Natural History of North American Birds.* New York: Simon & Schuster, 1988.

Emery, Dara E. *Seed Propagation of Native California Plants.* Santa Barbara, Calif.: Santa Barbara Botanic Garden, 1988. An indispensable reference for growers of native California plants. From a discussion of various seed treatments to specific treatments for over 800 species of native plants, this book summarizes the results of twenty years of experience in growing natives.

Forages: The Science of Grassland Agriculture. Edited by Harold De Mott Hughes. Ames: Iowa State College Press, 1951. Subsequent editions of *Forages* appeared in 1962, 1973, 1985, ed. Maurice E. Heath, Robert F. Barnes, and Darrel S. Metcalfe, and in 1995, ed. Robert F. Barnes, Darrell A. Miller, and C. Jerry Nelson.

Gillett, George, John Howell, and Hans Leschke. *A Flora of Lassen Volcanic National Park, California.* Sacramento: California Native Plant Society, 1995.

Hamann, Skee. "Seed Seeker of the Flowering West." *Horticulture Magazine* 56, no. 3 (March 1978).

Hartmann, Hudson T., and Dale E. Kester. *Plant Propagation: Principles and Practices.* 3d ed. Englewood Cliffs, N.J.: Prentice-Hall, 1975.

Haslam, Gerald, and James D. Houston, eds. *California Heartland*. Santa Barbara, Calif.: Capra Press, 1978.

Hickman, James C., ed. *The Jepson Manual: Higher Plants of California*. Berkeley and Los Angeles: University of California Press, 1993.

Howell, John Thomas. *Marin Flora: Manual of the Flowering Plants and Ferns of Marin County, California*. Berkeley and Los Angeles: University of California Press, 1970.

Jackson, Wes. *Altars of Unhewn Stone; Science and the Earth*. Berkeley, Calif.: Northpoint Press, 1987.

Joern, Anthony, and Kathleen H. Keeler, eds. *The Changing Prairie: North American Grassland*. New York: Oxford University Press, 1995.

Johnson, Hugh. *Principles of Gardening: A Guide to the Art, History, Science and Practice of Gardening*. New York: Simon & Schuster, 1979.

Junak, Steve, Tina Ayers, Randy Scott, Dieter Wilken, and David Young. *A Flora of Santa Cruz Island*. Sacramento: California Native Plant Society and Santa Barbara Botanic Garden, 1995.

Kozloff, Eugene, and Linda Beidleman. *Plants of the San Francisco Bay Region: Mendocino to Monterey*. Pacific Grove, Calif.: Sagen Press, 1994.

Kruckeberg, Arthur. *Gardening with Native Plants of the Pacific Northwest*. Seattle: University of Washington Press, 1997.

Lenz, Lee. *Native Plants for California Gardens*. Claremont, Calif.: Rancho Santa Ana Botanic Garden, 1977.

Lenz, Lee, and John Dourley. *California Native Trees & Shrubs for Garden & Environmental Use in Southern California and Adjacent Areas*. Claremont, Calif.: Rancho Santa Ana Botanic Garden, 1981.

Leopold, A. Starker. *The California Quail*. Berkeley and Los Angeles: University of California Press, 1977.

McClintock, Elizabeth, Paul Reeberg, and Walter Knight. *A Flora of the San Bruno Mountains*. Sacramento: California Native Plant Society, 1990.

Moe, Maynard L., and Ernest Twisselmann. *A Key to Vascular Plant Species of Kern County, California, and a Flora of Kern County, California*. Sacramento: California Native Plant Society, 1995.

Mollison, B. C. *Permaculture: A Practical Guide for a Sustainable Future*. Washington, D.C.: Island Press, 1990.

Mollison, B. C., and Reny Mia Slay. *Introduction to Permaculture*. Illustrated by Andrew Jeeves. Harare, Zimbabwe: Tutorial Press; Tyalgum, Australia: Tagari Publications, 1992.

Mollison, Bill (B. C.), and David Holmgren. *Permaculture 1: A Perennial Agricul-*

tural System for Human Settlements. Melbourne, Australia: Transworld Publishers, 1978.

Murphy, Alexandra. *Graced by Pines: The Ponderosa Pine in the American West*. Missoula, Mont.: Mountain Press Publishing Co., 1994.

Oosting, Henry J. *The Study of Plant Communities, An Introduction to Plant Ecology*. San Francisco: W. H. Freeman, 1956.

Oswald, Vernon, and Lowell Ahart. *Manual of the Vascular Plants of Butte County, California*. Sacramento: California Native Plant Society, 1994.

Perry, Robert. *Landscape Plants for Western Regions*. Claremont, Calif.: Land Design Publishers, 1992.

Porter, Gene Stratton. *Coming Through the Swamp: The Nature Writings of Gene Stratton Porter*. Edited and with introduction by Sydney Landon Plum. Salt Lake City, Utah: University of Utah Press, 1996.

Powell, Jerry A., and Charles L. Hogue. *California Insects*. Berkeley and Los Angeles: University of California Press, 1979.

Rowntree, Lester. *Hardy Californians*. Salt Lake City, Utah: Peregrine Smith, 1980.

Sawyer, John, and Todd Keeler-Wolf. *A Manual of California Vegetation*. Sacramento: California Native Plant Society, 1995.

Schmidt, Marjorie. *Growing California Native Plants*. Berkeley and Los Angeles: University of California Press, 1980. A classic for those interested in growing California natives.

Seed, John, and Joanna Macy. *Thinking Like a Mountain: Towards a Council of All Beings*. Philadelphia: New Society Publishers, 1988.

Sharsmith, Helen K. *Spring Wildflowers of the San Francisco Bay Region*. Berkeley and Los Angeles: University of California Press, 1965.

———. *Flora of the Mount Hamilton Range of California*. Index compiled by Carl W. Sharsmith and Nobi Kurotori. Grass Valley, Calif.: California Native Plant Society, 1982.

Streatfield, David. *California Gardens: Creating a New Eden*. New York: Abbeville Press, 1994.

Sunset Western Garden Book. Menlo Park, Calif.: Lane Publishing Co., 1996.

Thelanger, Carl, ed. *Life on the Edge: A Guide to California's Endangered Natural Resources*. Santa Cruz, Calif.: Biosystems Books / Heyday Books, 1994.

Turner, Jack. *The Abstract Wild*. Tucson: University of Arizona Press, 1996.

United States Forest Service. *Seeds of Woody Plants in the United States*. Agriculture Handbook No. 450. Washington, D.C.: U.S. Government Printing Office, 1974. The most complete document of its kind, including information on morphology, seed formation, and collection and germination for an astounding number of native trees and shrubs. Has been out of print but is being revised and reprinted.

Wagern, Frederick. "Grazers Past and Present." In *Grassland Structure and Function: California Annual Grassland,* ed. L. F. Huenneke and H. A. Mooney, pp. 154–60. Dordrecht and Boston: Kluwer Academic, 1989.

Work, George R. *Work Ranch.* San Miguel, Calif.: Author, 1996. Can be obtained from George R. Work, 75903 Ranchita Canyon Road, San Miguel, CA 93451.

Young, James, and Cheryl Young. *Collecting, Processing and Germinating Seeds of Wildland Plants.* Portland, Ore.: Timber Press, 1986.

———. *Seeds of Woody Plants in North America.* Portland, Ore.: Dioscorides Press, 1992.

INDEX

Calandrinia ciliata (red maids), 11, 56–57, 81, 94, 150

CalEppc (California Exotic Pest Plant Council), 128–29, 140

California Academy of Sciences, 192

California Classics (Powell), 202

A California Flora (Munz), 196, 204

California Heartland (Houston), 203

California Indian Basketweavers Association, 47

California landscape: art's depiction of, 198–99; exotics' invasion of, 25–26; fictional works on, 202–5; horticultural appeal of, 142–43; native grassland's share of, 107; restorationist's inspiration from, 37–38; sand dunes of, 63; summer dormancy of, 53–54, 92; wildflowers of, in the past, 78–81

California Native Grass Association, 108

California Native Plant Society (CNPS), 174, 177, 197; chapter activities of, 193; *Fremontia* (journal of), 117, 193; on Italian ryegrass, 59; plant community focus of, 200; wildflower shows of, 99, 102–3, 176

The Californians (Atherton), 202, 204–5

The California Quail (Leopold), 52

Calla lily, 124, 134

Calochortus (Mariposa lily, star-tulip), 94, 120, 165–66
   tolmiei (pussy ears), 17, 107

Calycanthus occidentalis (spicebush), 70

Camissonia boothii, 127

Capeweed *(Arctotheca calendula)*, 27, 29–30, 58, 124, 129, 139

Carpobotrus edulis (iceplant), 17, 25, 58, 63, 124, 139

Carrizo Plains (Central California), 68, 99

Ceanothus (ceanothus), 25, 41, 211; with bunchgrass, 105; cultivars, 167–68, 201; drainage for, 117, 160; as host plant, 136–37; pruning of, 58; seed food of, 150
   'Concha,' plate 9
   gloriosus var. *porrectus*, 167

gloriosus var. *porrectus* 'Mt. Vision,' 167–68

impressus var. *nipomensis*, 37, 199

thyrsiflorus 'Snow Flurry,' plate 9

Cedar, 71, plate 10
   deodar, 66

Central California coast: planting season on, 161–62; scrub plant varieties of, 3–5

Central Valley, 68–69, 109

Cercocarpus (mountain mahogany), 66
   betuloides, 197, 199

Chamise, 25, 40, 197

Cheatgrass *(Bromus tectorum)*, 112, 124

Checkerbloom *(Sidalcea malvaeflora)*, 6, 11, 69, 94, 120, 142, plate 15

Cherry, holly-leaf *(Prunus illicifolia)*, 58, 66

Chia *(Salvia columbaria)*, 97–98, 150

Chiapas oak, 210–11

Chinese houses *(Collinsia heterophylla)*, 94

Chlorogalum pomeridianum (soaproot), 47, 211

Choinumne Yokut, 79–80

Choke-cherry, western *(Prunus virginiana* var. *demissa)*, 33

Cholla, jumping, 72

Clapper sticks, 13–14

Clarkia *(Clarkia)*, 15, 18, 82, 89, 91, 95; seeds of, 148, 150
   farewell-to-spring *(amoena)*, 93, 94, plate 6
   Monterey, 94
   mountain garland *(unguiculata)*, 96

Clark's nutcracker, 149

Clay soil, 89, 117

Claytonia
   perfoliata (miner's/Indian lettuce), 10, 11, 15, 23, 45, 52, 66, 95, 150
   sibirica (peppermint candy flower), 10, 11, 95, 137

Clematis, 46

Clover *(Trifolium)*, 11, 120
   native *(wormskioldii)*, 161–62, 212
   subclover *(subterraneum)*, 15

CNPS. *See* California Native Plant Society

Great Central Plain, 79

Great Plains, 112

Great Valley Natural History Museum (Lodi), 198

Greenhouses, 156

Greenway (El Cerrito), 195

Grindelia (gumplant), 45, 70, 93, 162, 188, 189

    stricta, 93, 162, 189

Growing Native Research Newsletter, 127

Gumplant *(Grindelia),* 45, 70, 93, 162, 188, 189

Gutierrezia sarothrae (broom snakeweed), 188

Habitat structure: for birds, 50–51, 141; coyote bush as, 6; native bunchgrass as, 113–14; non-natives' impact on, 126–27, 141; old-growth forests as, 140

Hairgrass *(Deschampsia),* 6, 95, 113, 116, 121, plate 8

Handbook for Butterfly Watchers (Pyle), 184

Hanson, Nicolus, 78

Hardy, Thomas, 203

Harrington, J.P., 101, 211

Haslam, Gerald, 203

Hastings Reservation (Univ. of California), 147

Hawks, 141

Hazel, 15, 31, 41, 44, 53

    California, 9, 13, 18, 25, 55, 212

Hazelnut *(Corylus cornuta),* 212

Hemizonia (tarplant), 6, 150

Herbicides: to control weeds, 86–87, 133; to prepare soil, 121–22

Heteromeles arbutifolia (toyon), 15, 23, 33, 40, 58, 66, 105, 199

Heuchera, 36

Hierochloe occidentale (vanilla grass), 110

Hilum, defined, 148

Honeysuckle, hairy *(Lonicera hispidula),* 15, 33

Hopi, 11–12

Host plants, 15; of aphid-eating mite, 16; and egg-laying needs, 186–87;

of Lange's metalmark, 187–88; and nectaring needs, 184, 186, 189; of pipevine swallowtail, 8–9

Houston, James D., 203

Howell, John Thomas, 194, 197

How to Have a Green Thumb Without an Aching Back (Stout), 26

Huckleberry *(Vaccinium ovatum),* 10, 25, 31, 71, plates 10, 20

Hudson, Grace Carpenter, 81

Hula hoes, 87

Humboldt County, 61, 110

Hummingbird, 16; rufous, 15

Hydrogen peroxide soak, 158

Hypericum perforatum (Klamath weed), 126, 133

Iceplant *(Carpobrotus edulis),* 17, 25, 58, 63, 124, 139

Indians in Overalls (d'Angulo), 202–3

Indigenous peoples. *See* Native Californians

Insects: aphid-eating mite, 16; as biological controls, 130, 133; parasitized relationships of, 180; syrphid fly, 97; Tachina fly, 5–6; *Utetheisa* moth, 186. *See also* Bees; Butterflies

Iris *(Iris),* 94, 117

    Douglas *(douglasiana),* 45, 104, 105, 120, 150, plate 11

Irrigation: amount of, for new plants, 164; drip method, 163; hand method, 163–64; to remove weeds, 86; of wildflower seeds, 91–92

Isenberg, Gerda, 9, 191

Islay seeds *(Prunus illicifolia),* 150

Ithuriel's spear *(Triteleia laxa),* 105

Ivy, 58

    Algerian, 139

    Cape, 17, 27, 124, 126, 133–34, 139, 141

    English, 17, 92, 139

Jackson, Helen Hunt, 123, 128, 203–4

Jackson, Wes, 10

purple bush/shrub *(propinquus)*, 43, 57, 69, 157, 181

sky *(nanus)*, 10–11, 57, 82, 99

varied *(variicolor)*, 69

Lupinus (lupine), 8, 23, 41, 56–57, 142

arboreus, 181

chamissonis, 63, 149

nanus, 10–11, 99

propinquus, 43, 181

succulentus, 90

McKay, Mabel, 7

Madia (tarweed), 6, 81

Madrone *(Arbutus menziesii)*, 15, 24

Mahonia aquifolium (Oregon grape), 31

A Manual of California Vegetation (Sawyer and Keeler-Wolf), 40, 197

A Manual of the Flowering Plants of California (Jepson), 195

Manzanita *(Arctostaphylos)*, 25, 36, 58, 66, 71, 117; cultivars, 167, 201

bigberry *(glauca)*, 39–40

woollyleaf, 197

Maple, 157

vine, 46

Margolin, Malcolm, 187

Marin Flora (Howell), 194, 197

Maser, Chris, 60, 61

Mattole River (Humboldt County), 110

Mayfield, Jeff, 78–80

Meadow foam *(Limnanthes)*, 11, 45, 84, 91, 97, 99

Point Reyes, 95, plate 8

Melica imperfecta (Coast Range melic), 116

Mendocino, 40

Merritt College, 193

Mesquite, 72

Microtus californicus (California meadow vole), 113–14, 183–84

Milkmaid *(Dentaria californica)*, 19

Miller, Joaquin, 202

Miller, Wilhelm, 65

Millet, in birdseed, 51

Mission blue butterfly, 187

Mission Oaks project (Santa Barbara County), 71

Mist-netting, of birds, 182

Mite, aphid-eating, 16

Mitigation: by developers, 28–29; by gardeners, 29–30; by native Californians, 216–17. *See also* Restoration

Miwok, 47, 211

Mohave Desert, 113

Monarch butterfly, 140

Monkeyflower *(Mimulus)*, 16, 36, 55, 148, 199

creek *(guttatus)*, 45, 70

sticky *(aurantiacus)*, 69

Montbretia, 124

Moth: gypsy, 139; *Utethesia,* and poisonous plants, 186

Mountain beaver, 6

Mountain mahogany *(Cercocarpus)*, 66

birchleaf *(betuloides)*, 197, 199

Mountains of California (Muir), 151

Mountain spiraea *(Spiraea densiflora)*, 70

Mount Tamalpais, 110, 135

Mount Vision fire (1995), 167–68

Mowing, to control weeds, 122, 130–31

Muhlenbergia rigens (basketgrass/deergrass), 14, 71, 116, 120

Muir, John, 68, 79, 151

Mulch: v. amendment, 159–60; for native seedlings, 90; from native species, 161; from redwood litter, 67; to smother weeds, 132; weed seeds in, 26

Mule's ear *(Wyethia angustifolia)*, 16, 66, 107, 150, 161–62

Munz, Philip A., 196, 204

Murphey, Edith Van Allen, 212

Museums, as information sources, 198–99

Musical instruments, from plants, 13–14

Myrtle, Pacific wax *(Myrica californica)*, 9–10, 25, 42, 55, 105

Naked ladies, 124, 134

Nassella (=Stipa), 110, 120

cernua (nodding stipa), 119, 120

214; predictability of, 41–42; on public lands, 123–24, 128; to stabilize dunes, 63, 139. *See also* Non-native annual grasses

North American Butterfly Association, 174, 184

Novels, featuring landscape, 202–5

Nurseries: contract growing by, 201; list of, 219–20; native plants from, 201, 202; non-native plants from, 124

Oak (*Quercus*), 24, 31, 32, 42, 53, 112, 144, 162
  black (*kelloggii*), 37, 147
  blue (*douglasii*), 37, 139, 147
  canyon live (*chrysolepis*), 37, 147
  Chiapas, 210–11
  coast live (*agrifolia*), 25, 26–27, 30, 37, 71, 147, 149, 199, plate 15
  Engelman (*engelmanii*), 37
  huckleberry (*vaccinifolia*), 70
  valley (*lobata*), 30, 37, 68, 147

Oakland Museum, 99

Oaks of California, 37

Oatgrass, 110, 150
  California (*Danthonia californica*), 48, 104, 105, 121, 122
  European (*Avena fatua*), 104

O'Brien, Bart, 53, 167

Ocotillo (*Fouquieria splendens*), 72

Of Wolves and Men (Lopez), 105

Ojai, 40

Old-growth forests, 60–61, 140

Oleander, 25

Ornithologists. *See* Birders

Oryzopsis hymenoides. See Ricegrass, Indian

Owens Valley, wildflowers of, 80–81

Owl: great horned, 126–27; saw-whet, 127, 214

Owl's clover (*Castilleja exserta* sp. *exserta*), 68, 89, 96, plate 1

Paintbrush, Indian (*Castilleja*), 16, 39, 45, 104, 105

Paintings, landscape changes in, 198–99

Paiutes, 217

Paleo-Indians, 216

Palomarin whistle, 7

Palos Verdes blue butterfly, 187

Pampas grass, 27, 124, 128, 129, 138

Paper bags, for seed ripening, 148

Pappus, defined, 149

Paradejeania rutillioides (Tachina fly), 5–6

Parker, Julia, 146

Parsnip, cow, 10, 16

Passion flower vine, 17, 124

Payne, Theodore, 73

Penstemon (*Penstemon*), 29, 36, 94
  blue bedder (*heterophyllus* var. *purdyi*), 45, 46

Peppermint candy flower (*Claytonia sibirica*), 10, 11, 95, 137

Pepperweed, 124

Perry, Robert, 73

Perturbation, 57–58. *See also* Fire; Pruning

Peterson, Ray, 51, 174, 190

Phacelia (*Phacelia*)
  Bolander's, 45
  tansy-leaf (*tanacetifolia*), 11, 45, 91, 93, 97

Phlox, mountain, 96

Piazzoni, Gottardo, 37

Pine (*Pinus*), 17, 157
  bishop (*muricata*), 25
  Monterey (*radiata*), 31, 49, 139
  whitebark (*albicaulis*), 149

Pink
  Indian (*Silene californica*), 94, 120, 161–62
  sea (*Armeria maritima*), 69, 94

Pinole (seed food), 150

Pipevine, California, 199

Pipevine swallowtail (*Battus philenor*), 8–9, 187

Plantain, 16–17, 62, 94, 120
  coast (*Plantago subnuda*), 45, 57, 70

Planting season: in California, 163; on California coast, 161–62; for native bulb seeds, 165; for wildflowers, 88–89

Plastic bag treatment, of seeds, 157

Steinbeck, John, 202
Stevenson, Robert Louis, 203
Stewart, Bob, 177–79, 190–91
Stipa. See *Nassella*
Stout, Ruth, 26
Strawberry *(Fragaria)*
 California woodland *(californica)*, 10
 coast *(chiloensis)*, 36
Strybing Arboretum (San Francisco), 195
Subclover *(Trifolium subterraneum)*, 15
Sugar beets, 97
Sugar bush *(Rhus ovata)*, 157
Sulfuric acid, and water, 153
Sunol Regional Park (East Bay), 99
Sunset (magazine), 111–12
Sutter Buttes (Sacramento Valley), 99
Swainson's thrushes, 49
Sword fern *(Polystichum munitum)*, 25, 49,
 59, 66
Symphoricarpos alba (snowberry), 71–72
Syrphid fly, 97

Table Mountain (Central California), 99
Tachina fly *(Paradejeania rutillioides)*, 5–6
Tamarisk, 124, 140
Tanoak *(Lithocarpus densiflora)*, 64
Tarplant *(Hemizonia)*, 6, 150
Tarweed *(Madia)*, 6, 81, 104, 150
The Tarweed Gatherer (Hudson), 81
Taxonomy, 176–77; manuals, 195–97
Temblor Range (San Luis Obispo County),
 100
That Constant Coyote: California Stories
 (Haslam), 203
Thimbleberry *(Rubus parviflorus)*, 10
Thistle, yellow star, 130–31, 140–41, 182
Thomas, John Hunter, 197
Thoreau, Henry David, 3, 12
Tick bush. *See* Coyote bush
Tidy-tips *(Layia)*, 8, 99, plate 1; bloom pe-
 riod of, 93; in British gardens, 82; with
 bunchgrass, 68; in coastal prairie, 95;
 cuttings of, 96; with goldfields and pop-
 pies, 94; seed food of, 150; sowed in pots,
 91

Tilden Park Botanic Garden (Berkeley),
 81, 99, 156
"Tolowim Woman and Butterfly Man"
 (Maidu story), 187
Tortoises, 125, 127
Toyon *(Heteromeles arbutifolia)*, 15, 23, 33,
 40, 58, 66, 105, 199
Traditional gardens, 35–36
Transects, 62
Transplanting: of bulb seedlings, 165–66;
 fertilizer for, 159, 164–65; in the field,
 159; mulch used in, 159–61; of plant
 seedlings, 158–59; and pruning care,
 162; season for, 161–62; and watering
 methods, 163–64
Trifolium (clover), 11, 120
 subterraneum, 15
 wormskioldii, 161–62
Triteleia laxa (Ithuriel's spear), 105
Tule elk reserve (Point Reyes), 112
Turner, Jack, 55
Twinberry *(Lonicera involucrata)*, 58

Ulex europaea (gorse/furze), 203
Understood Betsy (Fisher), 203
University of California Berkeley, Botani-
 cal Garden, 99
Utetheisa (moth), 186

Vacaville Museum, 196
Vancouveria planipetala (redwood sorrel),
 67, 95
Vernal pools, 180
Vetch, crown, 26
Vinca, 124, 126
Viola
 pedunculata (Johnny-jump-up), 82–83,
 99
 sempervirens (redwood violet), 67
Vitis californica (wild grape), 31
Vole *(Microtus californicus)*, 113–14, 183–84

Walker Ridge (Colusa County), 99
Wallflower, coast *(Erysimum concinnum)*,
 45, 57, 69

Designer: Barbara Jellow

Compositor: BookMatters

Text: 11/16 Granjon

Display: Granjon

Printer and Binder: Edwards Brothers, Inc.

Library of Congress Cataloging-in-Publication Data

Lowry, Judith Larner, 1945 –
    Gardening with a wild heart : restoring California's native landscapes at
home / Judith Larner Lowry.
        p.   cm.
    Includes bibliographic references (p.   ) and index.
    ISBN 978-0-520-25174-8 (pbk. : alk. paper)
    1. Native plant gardening—California.   2. Native plants for
cultivation—California.   3. Landscape gardening—California.
    SB439.24.C2L68   1999
    635.9'51794 — dc21
                                                        98-16177